THE BEDFORD SERIES IN HISTORY AND CULTURE

The Black Death

The Great Mortality of 1348–1350

A BRIEF HISTORY WITH DOCUMENTS

Related Titles in
THE BEDFORD SERIES IN HISTORY AND CULTURE
Advisory Editors: Lynn Hunt, *University of California, Los Angeles*
David W. Blight, *Yale University*
Bonnie G. Smith, *Rutgers University*
Natalie Zemon Davis, *Princeton University*
Ernest R. May, *Harvard University*

THE BEDFORD SERIES IN HISTORY AND CULTURE

The Black Death

The Great Mortality of 1348–1350

A BRIEF HISTORY WITH DOCUMENTS

John Aberth

Castleton State College

BEDFORD/ST. MARTIN'S   Boston   ♦   New York

For Bedford/St. Martin's

Executive Editor for History: Mary V. Dougherty
Director of Development for History: Jane Knetzger
Developmental Editor: Dale Anderson
Editorial Assistant: Shannon Hunt
Senior Production Supervisor: Dennis J. Conroy
Senior Marketing Manager: Jenna Bookin Barry
Project Management: Books By Design, Inc.
Text Design: Claire Seng-Niemoeller
Indexer: Books By Design, Inc.
Cover Design: Donna Lee Dennison
Cover Art: Apocalypse Tapestry, Angers. © Caroline Rose/Centre des Monuments
    Nationaux
Composition: Stratford Publishing Services, Inc.
Printing and Binding: RR Donnelley & Sons Company

President: Joan E. Feinberg
Editorial Director: Denise B. Wydra
Director of Marketing: Karen Melton Soeltz
Director of Editing, Design, and Production: Marcia Cohen
Manager, Publishing Services: Emily Berleth

Library of Congress Control Number: 2004107769

Manufactured in the United States of America.

7   6   5   4   3
s   r   q   p   o

For information, write: Bedford/St. Martin's, 75 Arlington Street, Boston, MA 02116
(617-399-4000)

ISBN-10: 0-312-40087-X (paperback)
          1-4039-6802-0 (hardcover)
ISBN-13: 978-0-312-40087-3 (paperback)
          978-1-4039-6802-9 (hardcover)

Distributed outside North America by Palgrave Macmillan.

Acknowledgments

Acknowledgments and copyrights are continued at the back of the book on page 190,
which constitutes an extension of the copyright page.

Foreword

The Bedford Series in History and Culture is designed so that readers can study the past as historians do.

The historian's first task is finding the evidence. Documents, letters, memoirs, interviews, pictures, movies, novels, or poems can provide facts and clues. Then the historian questions and compares the sources. There is more to do than in a courtroom, for hearsay evidence is welcome, and the historian is usually looking for answers beyond act and motive. Different views of an event may be as important as a single verdict. How a story is told may yield as much information as what it says.

Along the way the historian seeks help from other historians and perhaps from specialists in other disciplines. Finally, it is time to write, to decide on an interpretation and how to arrange the evidence for readers.

Each book in this series contains an important historical document or group of documents, each document a witness from the past and open to interpretation in different ways. The documents are combined with some element of historical narrative—an introduction or a biographical essay, for example—that provides students with an analysis of the primary source material and important background information about the world in which it was produced.

Each book in the series focuses on a specific topic within a specific historical period. Each provides a basis for lively thought and discussion about several aspects of the topic and the historian's role. Each is short enough (and inexpensive enough) to be a reasonable one-week assignment in a college course. Whether as classroom or personal reading, each book in the series provides firsthand experience of the challenge—and fun—of discovering, recreating, and interpreting the past.

Lynn Hunt
David W. Blight
Bonnie G. Smith
Natalie Zemon Davis
Ernest R. May

Preface

Toward the end of the year 1347, a disease that was to become known as the Black Death was carried by trading vessels to the major ports in Sicily, Italy, and southern France. The disease probably originated in Central Asia, in the heart of the Mongol Empire, and spread westward along overland trade routes to the Crimea region on the north coast of the Black Sea, where it perhaps made its first contact with European (mostly Italian) merchants. But for most Europeans, their first experience of the plague's terror came in 1348, when the disease spread through Italy, France, Spain, and the Balkans, and invaded Switzerland, Austria, England, and perhaps Denmark. In the eastern Mediterranean, the plague seems to have pursued a similar course, first coming to Egypt, which had the greatest port in the Middle East, toward the end of the year 1347, and then spreading northward to Palestine and Syria by the spring and summer of 1348. Thereafter, in 1349 and 1350, the plague came to all of Germany and eastern Europe, to the Low Countries, all of the British Isles, and all of Scandinavia. While the silence of the records indicates that it skipped over Poland and Bohemia, the plague finally arrived in Russia (probably by way of Sweden) in 1352. Overall, the Black Death killed up to 50 percent of the inhabitants of Europe in a little over two years and returned, with considerably lower mortality, in later outbreaks.

The plague of 1348–50, and its many recurrences in the second half of the fourteenth century and throughout the fifteenth century, is considered by most historians to be the defining event of the late Middle Ages, one that brought in its train a whole host of seismic impacts upon society and culture. This collection of primary sources will allow students to understand and appreciate the myriad and wide-ranging effects that the Black Death had upon Europe and Southwest Asia. Among the issues addressed are the medical, social, economic, religious, psychological, and artistic repercussions of the plague. A great effort has been made to expand the scope of coverage beyond the usual focus on England to include not only more of Europe but also sources from the Muslim and Byzantine worlds as well, and to give attention to subjects, such as the artistic impact of the Black Death, that receive scant notice elsewhere. These issues are important because they played a crucial role in the transition from the medieval to the early modern eras.

To keep the book brief, sources are restricted to those that concern the first outbreak of the Black Death in 1348–50; no attempt is made here to chronicle the many plagues that followed throughout the rest of the fourteenth and the fifteenth centuries. The exception is chapter 7 on artistic responses to the plague, examples of which cannot be found any earlier than the latter period. The chapters are arranged topically, beginning with chapter 1 on "Geographical Origins," followed by chapter 2, "Symptoms and Transmission." These set the stage for how the Black Death first arrived in the West and the initial impressions it made. Subsequent chapters trace the varied impacts of the disease: chapter 3 is devoted to "Medical Responses"; chapter 4 covers the "Societal and Economic Impact"; chapter 5 explores "Religious Mentalities"; chapter 6, "The Psyche of Hysteria," concerns the flagellant movement and Jewish pogroms provoked by the plague; and chapter 7 examines "The Artistic Response." Since the exact chronology of medieval documents is often hard to pin down, sources are arranged within each chapter as thematic necessity dictates. Some authors, such as Giovanni Boccaccio, touched upon several themes when writing about the plague and therefore may appear more than once across chapters or across subtopics within chapters. The topical arrangement of these authors and their works makes it easier for students to discern themes and trends across boundaries of space, culture, and time.

To facilitate students' understanding and interpretation of each selection, the general and chapter introductions outline the medieval context within which the sources were created, as well as modern historiographical concerns. Such background material includes the historical significance and impact of the Black Death, how contemporaries viewed and debated the event, the circumstances of and approaches to their recording of it, how interpretation of the plague has changed over time, and what the current scholarly consensus—if there is one—may be on its various aspects. The headnotes preceding each selection give more specific context concerning the author and date of composition, and gloss notes explain unfamiliar terms or concepts in the documents. The volume closes with a chronology of important events concerning the Black Death, questions for consideration, and a selected bibliography arranged by chapter topic for further reading.

A NOTE ABOUT THE TEXT AND TRANSLATIONS

The majority of the documents in this collection were written in Latin, the universal learned language of western Europe during the Middle Ages. However, by the late medieval period, vernacular languages were coming into vogue, and these survive in a growing number of sources. Thus, a number of other languages are also represented: Italian, German, French, Spanish, and English, as well as Greek and Arabic used in the eastern Mediterranean and one selection in Hebrew. I have done all translations from the most authoritative texts available, except for documents in medieval Italian, German, Greek, Arabic, and Hebrew, for which I have relied on printed translations or the work of colleagues.

ACKNOWLEDGMENTS

Translation of this number and variety of sources would not be possible without substantial help. For translations of Italian and German sources, I have availed myself of the services of Aubry Threlkeld and Thomas Huber of Middlebury College; I am also grateful to Walid Saleh, formerly of Middlebury College, for assistance with the Arabic source of Ibn al-Khatīb, although I am fully responsible for this translation. Samuel Cohn of the University of Glasgow kindly provided me with the Latin testament of Libertus of Monte Feche, along with his English translation. I also have benefited from the constructive comments of several reviewers of the manuscript, including Richard Gyug of Fordham University; Erin Jordan of the University of Northern Colorado; Timothy Kircher of Guilford College; and Carol Quillen of Rice University. In addition, I must thank the interlibrary loan departments of the University of Vermont and of Middlebury College for their assiduous and timely response to my many requests for documents. The students in my Black Death and Inquisition classes have helped me realize which sources are most useful and interesting for a study of this topic. Dale Anderson and Patricia Rossi have been insightful, supportive, and enthusiastic editors. Above all, I must thank my wife, Laura Hamilton, for putting up so long with a man obsessed with so morbid a subject.

John Aberth

Contents

xi

Illustrations

The Black Death

The Great Mortality of 1348–1350

A BRIEF HISTORY WITH DOCUMENTS

PART ONE

Introduction: The Black Death in History

[handwritten annotation: Major explaination that people had for the Plague - Religion (makes sense considering how much church influence @ the time)]

It so happened that in the month of October in the year of our Lord 1347, around the first of that month, twelve Genoese galleys, fleeing our Lord's wrath which came down upon them for their misdeeds, put in at the port of the city of Messina. They brought with them a plague that they carried down to the very marrow of their bones, so that if anyone so much as spoke to them, he was infected with a mortal sickness which brought on an immediate death that he could in no way avoid.[1]

[handwritten annotation in left margin: It would actually spread as far as North America too]

Such is how the Black Death first arrived on the shores of Europe, according to the Sicilian chronicler Michele da Piazza. Within the next two to three years, the epidemic became a pandemic as it spread throughout nearly the entire continent and its islands and wiped out as much as half of its population. Although modern students and historians refer to this pandemic as the Black Death, the men and women who experienced the disease never called it by this name. Instead, medieval accounts speak of the "pestilence," the "plague" (from the Latin word *plaga,* meaning "a blow" or "an affliction"), or the "great mortality." The term "Black Death" was first coined in the sixteenth century and popularized in the nineteenth. Even so, Black Death is now the standard designation for this event, the so-called second pandemic of a disease that afflicted first the Mediterranean region between 541 and 750 CE, and struck a third time in China and India between 1894 and 1930.

[handwritten annotation: There were 3 plague's? All bubonic or different?]

1

THE BLACK DEATH AS HISTORICAL EVENT

The Black Death is a watershed event in history because of the timing, geography, and extent of its appearance. The disease struck at a time when Europe had not known an outbreak of plague since the first pandemic many centuries earlier. Although a "Great Famine" struck northern Europe between 1315 and 1322, nothing prepared Europeans for the horrendous onslaught of the Black Death. One should never discount the initial shock that the disease caused throughout Europe between 1348 and 1350. One chronicler, Agnolo di Tura of Siena (Document 17), reported that "So many have died that everyone believes it is the end of the world." And the Black Death returned, albeit with considerably less virulence, almost once a decade throughout the second half of the fourteenth and at least the first half of the fifteenth centuries. The plague and other diseases kept Europe's population stagnant or even slightly in decline until the dawn of the early modern period.

The great mortality of 1348 was also wide ranging in its geographical incidence. It affected every country and region in Europe, with the probable exception of Poland and Bohemia, whose relative isolation from mercantile contacts may have spared them. The Black Death was therefore a shared experience among medieval Europeans, producing a remarkably similar set of responses. Some European chroniclers were fully aware that they were part of a worldwide phenomenon, which embraced both neighboring regions and lands as far away as India and China. The plague probably began as an *endemic,* that is, a locally confined disease that, once established, is perpetually present in a given area. Such endemics seem to have existed in the Himalayan foothills and the Eurasian steppes, where, it is theorized, the plague bacillus could survive indefinitely in the warm burrows of the native marmot rodents (see chapter 2). It then became *pandemic*—a widespread disease—when flea, rodent, or human populations spread the disease far afield through faster, more efficient trade or communication networks. The establishment of the far-flung Mongol Empire by the second half of the thirteenth century linked Asia to Europe in an overland network of mounted armies, postal carriers, and caravans. Once transmitted from its endemic centers in the East, the plague easily made its way across Europe through well-established trade links (see chapter 1).

Finally, the Black Death was unusually potent in the human mortality it caused. Previously, the prevailing view among modern scholars was that the disease carried off roughly a third of Europe's inhabitants during its first and most devastating outbreak, from 1348 to 1350. New research suggests that this estimate must be revised upwards to an *average* mortality rate of at least 50 percent.[2] English episcopal registers, which record deaths among the parish clergy within a bishop's diocese and are among the most accurate of medieval documents available, yield a mean mortality rate of 45 percent. Manorial records, which also survive from England and which register the deaths of a lord's tenants, all point to death rates between 40 and 70 percent. Although fewer records survive on the continent than in England, a variety of documents, including parish registers, tax assessments, household census returns, scribal records, and episcopal registers from France, Italy, and Spain, record mortalities ranging from 45 to 68 percent. A 50 percent average mortality rate also would be more in line with what medieval chroniclers wrote about the Black Death. Although we must always approach medieval numerical estimates with caution, as they are prone to exaggeration, these estimates nonetheless testify to the perceived severity of the disease. If "the living were hardly able to bury the dead," as many English chroniclers report, then the death rate—regardless of the exact figure—was high enough to create an intolerable burden.

HISTORICAL SIGNIFICANCE
OF THE BLACK DEATH

It is not surprising that modern historians traditionally have viewed the Black Death as playing a pivotal role in late medieval civilization, which resulted in a decline of society and culture. Yet a little more than thirty years ago, a new view emerged in a collection of essays published under the title *The Black Death: A Turning Point in History?* The question mark in the title implies that the Black Death's pivotal role in late medieval society, long assumed, was now being challenged. Arguing on the basis of neo-Malthusian economics, which begins with Thomas Malthus's principle that "the power of population is indefinitely greater than the power in the earth to produce subsistence for man,"[3] the revisionist historians recast the Black Death as a necessary and long-overdue corrective to an overpopulated Europe. In this view, then, the disease was not a sudden and violent eruption but an inevitable consequence of a medieval population that had outgrown its agricultural capacity to feed itself.

Most recently, postrevisionist historians have been swinging the pendulum back, restoring the Black Death as a watershed in late medieval history.[4] Rather than portraying medieval humans as helpless pawns in the grip of economic forces beyond their control, these historians point out that even in the Middle Ages, people had the power to help change their destiny, for good or ill. The people expressed this power, for example, in their decisions to marry and reproduce in response to the mortality created by numerous visitations of the plague. Indeed, some historians now see the Black Death as having had an overall positive impact upon society by forcing Europeans to make technological innovations and changes that helped usher in the modern era. Labor shortages impelled the use of more efficient agricultural techniques and the introduction of better machines of manufacture, such as the printing press. A dearth of men may have created more working opportunities for women, especially in towns, and the "cult of remembrance" that sprang up after the plague may have helped spawn secular patronage of Renaissance art. Declining mortalities from successive plagues as a result of increased immunity may have given physicians the confidence to adopt a more empirical approach to medicine. On the other hand, historians are impressed by the remarkable resilience of late medieval culture and religion in the face of such a catastrophe. The ability of plague survivors to recover and re-invigorate their time-honored customs and beliefs allowed for continuity and a more gradual transition than the artificial dividing lines between the medieval and early modern periods suggest.

As the documents that follow demonstrate, the plague's effects on late medieval society were extremely varied: social, economic, psychological, religious, and artistic. Although the people of the later Middle Ages had relatively primitive medical technologies, they nonetheless possessed a confident outlook that put even an apocalyptic disaster of the magnitude of the Black Death into the perspective of God's secure and benevolent plan for humankind. The English anchoress and mystic, Julian of Norwich, who lived through no fewer than eight national outbreaks of plague, including the one of 1348–49, was yet able to declare that "alle shalle be wele" with the world.[5] Many chroniclers of the plague wrote as if the apocalypse, the end of creation, was at hand, but in medieval eschatology the apocalypse also signified a new beginning. No longer can scholars afford to dismiss the later Middle Ages as simply an era of decline. Rather, Europe's Renaissance, or "rebirth," was forged in the crucible of its terrible yet transcendent ordeal with the Black Death.

STUDYING MEDIEVAL SOURCES

Medieval chroniclers of the Black Death had a growing awareness that they were recording for posterity. One eyewitness, John Clynn, a Franciscan friar from Kilkenny, Ireland, who would himself die as he memorialized the plague's march across his land, writes movingly at the end of his contribution for 1348 and 1349 to the *Annalium Hiberniae Chronicon (Yearly Chronicle of Ireland)*:

> But I, Brother John Clynn, of the order of the Friars Minor of the convent of Kilkenny, have written in this book these notable events which occurred in my time, which I uncovered by my own authority or by a correspondent worthy of belief. And in order that noteworthy deeds may not perish with time and fade from the memory of future generations, I, seeing these many misfortunes and almost the whole world enmeshed in malignity, waiting among the dead for death that yet may come, have set down in writing what I have heard and examined as true. And so that the writing may not perish with the writer, and at the same time the work may not cease with the workman, I bequeath the parchment for continuing the work, if by chance a man, or anyone descended from Adam, should remain behind in the future who can escape this pestilence and continue the work I have begun.[6]

Clynn tells us exactly how he acquired his information and what his motives are in committing it to "parchment." But some early Renaissance writers on the plague went beyond eyewitness testimony and the examination of sources. For Giovanni Boccaccio and Francesco Petrarch (Documents 6, 15, and 16), the Black Death seems to have stirred a newfound realization that the author was a subjective observer of events, rather than the moral certitude that he was recording a history already written by God's salvation plan for the human race, as was typical of most medieval chroniclers. In this sense, the Black Death may have been a turning point in historical writing.[7]

It may be confusing to modern readers that medieval authors gave equal credence to events and explanations with a supernatural or divine origin as to those grounded in what today we would call science. For them, there was no difference between the two. This was especially true with regard to the Black Death, because most medieval authorities assumed that it was ultimately caused by God's will intervening in human affairs as an act of chastisement for humankind's wickedness and sin. Even medical experts, like Gui de Chauliac, physician to the pope, and members of the faculty of medicine at the

University of Paris, when attempting to give "scientific" explanations of the disease, frankly admitted that medicine could not help when the plague came from the will of the Almighty (Documents 9 and 14). Authors like Louis Sanctus (Document 4), who describe the origins of the disease in apocalyptic language, may simply be referencing the Old or New Testament—particularly those sections describing plagues in the book of Exodus or the book of Revelation—to convey the awe-inspiring impact of the disaster. On the other hand, it is entirely possible that they are conveying reports from the East of environmental catastrophes—such as earthquakes, droughts, or floods—which may have actually occurred, precipitating the influx of plague-bearing rodents into areas of human habitation.

These documents make it obvious that medieval people had a completely different outlook on both life and death from our own. Yet there is also much that is similar. Then, as now, parents and children were tormented by the loss of family members and scarred by abandonment in time of crisis. Like present-day AIDS victims, who are willing to experiment with "cocktails" of untested protease inhibitors, medieval patients desperately sought remedies to the plague, including recipes containing chopped-up snakes or ground-up gold and emeralds. And, as in the twentieth century, fourteenth-century Europeans, facing what seemed to be an imminent collapse of their civilization, found convenient scapegoats in the Jews. Understanding medieval people requires an effort to bridge the gulf of time separating us from the past, as well as to re-live their experience in the present. Above all, students of medieval history must learn to read and view records and artifacts through medieval eyes. Only in this way can we begin to comprehend what it was like to experience the Black Death.

NOTES

[1] Michele da Piazza, *Cronaca,* ed. Antonino Giuffrida (Palermo: ILA Palma, 1980), 82.

[2] This evidence is more fully described in John Aberth, *From the Brink of the Apocalypse: Confronting Famine, War, Plague, and Death in the Later Middle Ages* (New York: Routledge, 2000), 122–31.

[3] Thomas Robert Malthus, *First Essay on Population, 1798* (London: Macmillan and Co., 1926), 12.

[4] See David Herlihy, *The Black Death and the Transformation of the West,* ed. Samuel K. Cohn Jr. (Cambridge, Mass.: Harvard University Press, 1997), 39–81; Samuel K.

Cohn Jr., *The Black Death Transformed: Disease and Culture in Early Renaissance Europe* (London and New York: Arnold and Oxford University Press, 2002), 223–52.

[5]Julian of Norwich, *Revelations of Divine Love,* long text, chapter 27.

[6]John Clynn, *Annalium Hiberniae Chronicon (The Annals of Ireland),* ed. Richard Butler (Dublin: Irish Archaeological Society, 1849), 37.

[7]Timothy Kircher, "Anxiety and Freedom in Boccaccio's History of the Plague of 1348," *Letteratura Italiana antica,* 3 (2002): 319–57.

PART TWO

The Documents

1

Geographical Origins

Most chroniclers testify that the Black Death began somewhere in the East. Louis Sanctus (Document 4) seems convinced that the affliction originated in India. Yet the Muslim author Ibn al-Wardī (Document 2) claims that the Black Death spread to India and China from an unspecified point of origin. Moreover, al-Wardī claims that the plague had been present in a mysterious "land of darkness" for fifteen years, which would date it to 1331–32. Which region is al-Wardī referring to? One scholar believes that it is inner Asia or Mongolia (see map on page 12). For nearly a century the Mongols had been the most hated and feared enemy of the Mamluk dynasty that ruled al-Wardī's native Syria.[1] Giovanni Villani (Document 3) confirms that the plague was very virulent among the "Tartars" or Mongols, and another Muslim author, al-Maqrīzī of Cairo, Egypt, reports that in 1341 the plague began "in the land of the Great Khan," or Mongolia. Although al-Maqrīzī was writing in the fifteenth century, he claims that his information came from "the land of the Uzbek [modern Uzbekistan in Central Asia]."[2] Modern epidemiological studies suggest that the plague bacillus (see chapter 2) is endemic in the rodent populations of the central Asian steppes, where it may have become established by the fourteenth century after Mongol armies had brought it there from the Himalayan foothills.[3]

Sanctus's apocalyptic description of the plague's origins in the East was fairly typical of a range of Christian authors who adopted biblical language to announce the disease's advent. A rain of serpents, toads, or "pestilential worms" perhaps reflects a desire to convey the magnitude of the mortality about to sweep Europe. But these accounts could equally well point to real ecological disasters, such as the unseasonable "torrential rains" that al-Maqrīzī says flooded "the land of the Khitai" (people of northern China) at the time the Black Death originated there.[4] These disasters might have forced rodents native to this region

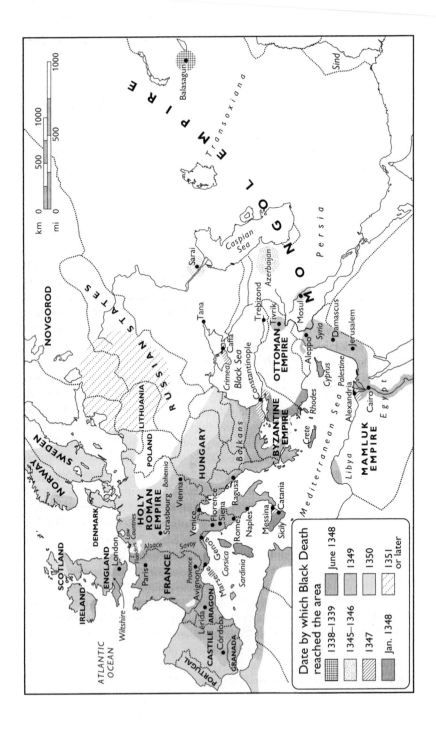

MONGOL EMPIRE

Balasagun

Transoxiana

Sind

km 0 500 1000
mi 0 500 1000

NOVGOROD

RUSSIAN STATES

LITHUANIA

POLAND

Caspian Sea

Sarai

Azerbaijan

Persia

Tana

Trebizond

Tvrik

Mosul

HOLY ROMAN EMPIRE

HUNGARY

Bohemia

Vienna

Strasbourg

Balkans

Crimea

Caffa

Black Sea

Constantinople

OTTOMAN EMPIRE

Aleppo

Syria

Damascus

Jerusalem

BYZANTINE EMPIRE

Rhodes

Cyprus

Palestine

Alexandria

Cairo

Egypt

MAMLUK EMPIRE

NORWAY

SWEDEN

DENMARK

SCOTLAND

IRELAND

ENGLAND

London

Wiltshire

Low Countries

Flanders

Alsace

Paris

FRANCE

Savoy

Provence

Avignon

Marseille

Genoa

Venice

Florence

Siena

Rome

Naples

Ragusa

Messina

Catania

Sicily

Corsica

Sardinia

PORTUGAL

CASTILE

ARAGON

Lerida

Córdoba

GRANADA

ATLANTIC OCEAN

Crete

Mediterranean Sea

Libya

Date by which Black Death reached the area

1338–1339	June 1348	
1345–1346	1349	
1347	1350	
Jan. 1348	1351 or later	

into areas of human habitation, thus allowing bacteria carried by fleas to make the leap from animals to humans.

An elaborate, extensive network of sea and land routes efficiently carried the Black Death throughout Eurasia. The immediate launching point for the plague's arrival in Europe and the Middle East seems to have been the Crimea region of the Black Sea. In the second half of the thirteenth century, Genoa and other Italian cities established their agents at Caffa, Tana, and other cities in the region to facilitate their trade there. Their galleys and sailing vessels loaded up with local products such as grain, alum, slaves, and above all, expensive animal furs, including ermine and marten.

The Italian chronicler Gabriele de Mussis tells a famous story of the first plague contact between Asians and Europeans: A plague-stricken Mongol army called off its siege of Genoese merchants in Caffa (present-day Feodosiya) on the north coast of the Black Sea, but not before the soldiers had "ordered that their cadavers be placed on their catapults and lobbed into the city of Caffa in order that the intolerable stench of those bodies might extinguish everyone [inside]."[5] One wonders, however, whether plague-bearing fleas could survive being catapulted toward new human hosts in this medieval germ warfare.[6] Another possibility is that flea-infested furs first communicated the plague to the Italians. Once on board the confined space of a ship, the fleas hibernating in the cargo could easily make the jump to human passengers. Although the journey from Caffa to Genoa was long—2,200 miles that took from one to three months—these ships still may have carried plague even after the disease had run its course through the rat and human populations on board. Rat fleas can survive up to eighty days without a host, and the bacilli itself can survive up to five weeks in the fleas' feces.[7] Also, the distance and thus the incubation time would have been considerably shorter if the Italians brought the plague back from their colonies and trading posts in the Aegean and the Balkans, rather than all the way from the Black Sea.

By the spring of 1347, plague had arrived at the Byzantine capital of Constantinople, through which all Italian shipping from the Black Sea had to pass (Document 1). The Pisan chronicler Ranieri Sardo claims that two Genoese galleys first brought the plague to Italy from "Romania," the usual medieval term for the Byzantine Empire, and an anonymous Bolognese chronicler testifies that the two galleys passed

---

Opposite: The Path of the Black Death from Central Asia to Europe.

through Constantinople on their way to Messina and Genoa.[8] From Greece, this most deadly export could easily have penetrated Europe through maritime ports along the Mediterranean, particularly in Italy, southern France, and Spain. Thus, Mussis's story may be apocryphal, but it dramatically makes the point that plague followed in the wake of European trade and commerce.

NOTES

[1] Michael W. Dols, *The Black Death in the Middle East* (Princeton, N.J.: Princeton University Press, 1977), 40.

[2] Gaston Wiet, "La Grande Peste Noire en Syrie et en Égypte," *Études d'Orientalisme dédiées à la mémoire de Lévi-Provençal*, 2 vols. (Paris: G.-P. Maisonneuve et Larose, 1962), 1:368.

[3] Wu Lien-Teh, J. W. H. Chun, R. Pollitzer, and C. Y. Wu, *Plague: A Manual for Medical and Public Health Workers* (Shanghai: Weishengshu National Quarantine Service, 1936), 12; Robert Pollitzer, *Plague* (Geneva: World Health Organization, 1954), 13; N. P. Mironov, "The Past Existence of Foci of Plague in the Steppes of Southern Europe," *Journal of Microbiology, Epidemiology and Immunology,* 29 (1958): 1193–98; William H. McNeill, *Plagues and Peoples* (Garden City, N.Y.: Anchor Press/Doubleday, 1976), 111–12, 134, 143–45; Graham Twigg, *The Black Death: A Biological Reappraisal* (New York: Schocken Books, 1985), 44–45.

[4] Wiet, "La Grande Peste Noire," 1:369. Native Chinese annals may support Sanctus's and al-Maqrīzī's testimony, but more work needs to be done on them. See Dols, *Black Death in the Middle East,* 41, n. 16.

[5] A. W. Henschel, "Dokument zur Geschichte des schwarzen Todes," *Archiv für die gesammte Medicin,* 2 (1841): 48.

[6] Vincent Derbes, "De Mussis and the Great Plague of 1348: A Forgotten Episode of Bacteriological Warfare," *Journal of the American Medical Association,* 196 (1966): 59–62.

[7] Twigg, *Black Death,* 7, 51–52.

[8] Ranieri Sardo, *Cronaca di Pisa,* ed. Ottavio Banti (Rome: Fonti per la Storia d'Italia, 99, 1963), 96; *Corpus Chronicorum Bononiensium,* ed. Albano Sorbelli, 2 vols., in *Rerum Italicarum Scriptores,* 18/1 (1910–1938), 2:584.

1

NICEPHORUS GREGORAS
Byzantine History
ca. 1359

An eminent historian and scholar writing in Constantinople, Nicephorus Gregoras provides important testimony to the arrival of the plague in the Greek world. As court librarian to Emperor Andronikos III (1328– 1341), Gregoras undoubtedly had access to some of the best records and sources then available. As the gateway to the Crimea, Constantinople may have played a pivotal role in transmitting the plague to the rest of the Mediterranean basin further south and west. This excerpt is from Gregoras's Historia Byzantina, *or* Byzantine History, *which covers the years 1204 to 1359. Gregoras died in 1360.*

During that time [1347], a serious and pestilential disease invaded humanity. Starting from Scythia [southern Russia] and Maeotis and the mouth of the Tanais [Don River], just as spring began, it lasted for that whole year, passing through and destroying, to be exact, only the continental coast, towns as well as country areas, ours and those that are adjacent to ours, up to Gadera and the columns of Hercules [Straits of Gibraltar].

During the second year [1348] it invaded the Aegean Islands. Then it affected the Rhodians, as well as the Cypriots and those colonizing the other islands. The calamity attacked men as well as women, rich and poor, old and young. To put matters simply, it did not spare those of any age or fortune. Several homes were emptied of all their inhabitants in one day or sometimes in two. No one could help anyone else, not even the neighbors, or the family, or blood relations.

The calamity did not destroy men only, but many animals living with and domesticated by men. I speak of dogs and horses and all the species of birds, even the rats that happened to live within the walls of

Christos S. Bartsocas, "Two Fourteenth-Century Greek Descriptions of the 'Black Death,'" *Journal of the History of Medicine and Allied Sciences,* 21 (1966): 395. Reprinted by permission of Oxford University Press.

the houses. The prominent signs of this disease, signs indicating early death, were tumorous outgrowths at the roots of thighs and arms and simultaneously bleeding ulcerations, which, sometimes the same day, carried the infected rapidly out of this present life, sitting or walking.

2

ABŪ HAFS ᶜUMAR IBN AL-WARDĪ

Essay on the Report of the Pestilence

ca. 1348

Abū Hafs ᶜUmar Ibn al-Wardī was born in northern Palestine between 1290 and 1292. After studying at Muslim schools in Syria, he served as deputy to the qadi, *or religious judge, of Aleppo until 1343, and thereafter devoted himself to writing. His collected works cover a range of topics, including grammar, history, law, mysticism, and the interpretation of dreams. Although plague came to Palestine in May or June 1348, it was not until March 18, 1349, that al-Wardī succumbed to the disease in Aleppo, near his birthplace. His* Risālah al-naba' ᶜan al-waba' *(Essay on the Report of the Pestilence) was therefore written at the height of the epidemic. In addition, al-Wardī was in an ideal geographical position to comment on the plague's transmission from East to West. Scholars think that, like Gabriele de Mussis, he benefited from plague reports he received from his mercantile colleagues. Using a style typical of Arabic scholastic writing, al-Wardī inserts poetic verses into the narrative to aid in memorization of the text.*

God is my security in every adversity. My sufficiency is in God alone. Is not God sufficient protection for His servant? Oh God, pray for our master, Muhammad, and give him peace. Save us for his sake from the attacks of the plague and give us shelter.

Michael W. Dols, "Ibn al-Wardī's *Risālah al-naba' ᶜan al-waba'*, a Translation of a Major Source for the History of the Black Death in the Middle East" in *Near Eastern Numismatics, Iconography, Epigraphy and History: Studies in Honor of George C. Miles,* ed. Dickran K. Kouymjian (Beirut: American University of Beirut, 1974), 447–51.

The plague frightened and killed. It began in the land of darkness. Oh, what a visitor! It has been current for fifteen years. China was not preserved from it nor could the strongest fortress hinder it. The plague afflicted the Indians in India. It weighed upon the Sind.* It seized with its hand and ensnared even the lands of the Uzbeks. How many backs did it break in what is Transoxiana! The plague increased and spread further. It attacked the Persians, extended its steps toward the land of the Khitai,† and gnawed away at the Crimea. It pelted Rūm‡ with live coals and led the outrage to Cyprus and the islands. The plague destroyed mankind in Cairo. Its eye was cast upon Egypt, and behold, the people were wide-awake. It stilled all movement in Alexandria. The plague did its work like a silkworm. It took from the tiraz factory its beauty and did to its workers what fate decreed.§

> Oh Alexandria, this plague is like a lion which extends its arm to you.
> Have patience with the fate of the plague, which leaves of seventy men only seven.

Then, the plague turned to Upper Egypt. It, also, sent forth its storm to Barqa.‖ The plague attacked Gaza, and it shook Ascalon# severely. The plague oppressed Acre. The scourge came to Jerusalem and paid the zakat** [with the souls of men]. It overtook those people who fled to the al-ʿAqsā Mosque, which stands beside the Dome of the Rock.†† If the door of mercy had not been opened, the end of the world would have occurred in a moment. It, then, hastened its pace and attacked the entire maritime plain. The plague trapped Sidon and descended unexpectedly upon Beirut, cunningly. Next, it directed the shooting of its arrows to Damascus. There the plague sat like a king on a throne and swayed with power, killing daily one thousand or more and decimating the population. It destroyed mankind with its pustules. May God the Most High spare Damascus to pursue its own path and extinguish the plague's fires so that they do not come close

---

*The region of the lower Indus river, along the present-day border between northwest India and Pakistan.
†Thought to be northeastern China (Khitai is Cathay, the medieval term for China), or the Jagatai Khanate of Turkestan.
‡The Turkish realm of Anatolia, or modern-day Turkey.
§Tiraz refers to the silk and cloth manufacturing industry in Egypt.
‖A province in present-day Libya.
#Both Gaza and Ascalon were important cities in southwestern Palestine.
**A tax on Muslims.
††The two most holy Muslim sites in Jerusalem.

to her fragrant orchards. ...The plague domesticated itself in Hamā,*
and the banks of the rivers ʿAsi became cold because of the plague's
fever.

> Oh Plague, Hamā is one of the best lands, one of the mightiest
> fortresses.
> Would that you had not breathed her air and poisoned her, kissing
> her and holding her in your embrace.

The plague entered Maʿarrat al-Nuʿmān and said to the city: "You
are safe from me. Hamā is sufficient for your torture. I am satisfied
with that."

> It saw the town of Maʿarrat, like an eye adorned with blackness, but
> its eyebrow decorated with oppression.
> What could the plague do in a country where every day its tyranny
> is a plague?

The plague and its poison spread to Sarmin.† It reviled the Sunni
and the Shi'i.‡ It sharpened its spearheads for the Sunni and advanced
like an army. The plague was spread in the land of the Shi'i with a
ruinous effect. To Antioch the plague gave its share. Then, it left there
quickly with a shyness like a man who has forgotten the memory of
his beloved. Next, it said to Shayzar and to al-Hārim,§ "Do not fear me.
Before I come and after I go, you can easily disregard me because of
your wretchedness. And the ruined places will recover from the time
of the plague." Afterward, the plague humbled ʿAzaz and took from the
people of al-Bābǁ their men of learning. . . . Then, the plague sought
Aleppo, but it did not succeed. By God's mercy the plague was the
lightest oppression. I would not say that plants must grow from their
seeds.

> The pestilence had triumphed and appeared in Aleppo.
> They said: It has made on mankind an attack. I called it a pestilence.

How amazingly does it pursue the people of each house! One of
them spits blood, and everyone in the household is certain of death. It
brings the entire family to their graves after two or three nights.

---

*A town about forty miles south of al-Wardī's birthplace of Maʿarrat.
†A town in northern Syria about midway between Antioch and Maʿarrat.
‡Followers of two rival sects of Islam.
§Both in northern Syria about forty to fifty miles from Aleppo.
ǁBoth towns are about twenty to twenty-six miles from Aleppo.

3

GIOVANNI VILLANI
Chronicle
ca. 1348

The son of a prosperous merchant, Giovanni Villani was one of the leading citizens of Florence in the early 1300s. He was a partner in two important banking houses and held the highest office in the Florentine Republic, the priorate, three times. At the age of twenty, during a pilgrimage to Rome, Villani was inspired to write a history of Florence, in imitation of ancient Latin authors. His Chronicle is invaluable not only as a historical record, but also as an important contribution to the vernacular literature being created by fellow Florentines, Dante, Petrarch, and Boccaccio. Villani died during the Black Death in 1348, while writing the latest installment to his history.

This same pestilence was greater in Pistoia and Prato* than even in Florence with its high death rate. Still greater were the deaths in Bologna and the Romagna and worse at the papal court in Avignon in Provence, and in all of the kingdom of France. But there were uncountable deaths in Turkey and other countries overseas, where the disease lasted longer and did the most harm. God's justice fell harshly among the Tartars [Mongols], so much so that it seemed incredible. It is true, clear, and certain that in the land between the Turks and Chinese, in the country of Parthia, now named the Khanate [of the Mongols, or the Ilkhan Empire], the leader of the Tartars in India began a fire that shot out from the ground. In other words, this flame would come down from the sky and destroy men, animals, houses, trees, rocks and the land. This distended fire burned for more than fifteen days and became quite troublesome. He who did not flee fell victim to its wrath, and it continuously burned every animal and person. The men and women who managed to escape the fires would

*Two other towns in Tuscany near Florence.

Giovanni Villani, *Nuova cronica,* ed. Giuseppe Porta, 3 vols. (Parma: Fondazione Pietro Bembo, 1990–91), 3:486–88. Translated from the Italian by Aubry Threlkeld.

die of the plague. In Tana [Azov] and Trebizond, and in all of the surrounding territories, few remained and the number lost was as high as five men for every one survivor. Most of the land was uninhabited due to the plagues, as well as to the enormous earthquakes and lightning. And according to some letters from trustworthy citizens of our town who were in the area, such as at Sivas [in Anatolia], it rained an immeasurable quantity of vermin,* some as big as eight hands, all black and with tails, some alive and some dead. This frightening scene was made worse by the stench that they emitted, and those who fought against the vermin fell victim to their venom. And in another countryside, in Greece, no one remained alive unless they were female, and even some of them died because of rabies. And a more amazing and almost incredible event came to pass in Arcadia:[†] Men and women and every living animal turned into the likeness of marble statues. The mayors from the surrounding areas stated that this must be a sign to convert to the Christian faith; but they heard from news on the western wind that even Christian lands were troubled with pestilence, so they continued to practice their own religious treachery [Islam].[‡] In the port of Talucco, in [the contado or district of] Lucca, the sea was filled with vermin, better than 10,000 between the seas. Leaving them there, they [Muslims] went from one place to another until they arrived at Lucca, where out of their strong admiration for Christianity, they immediately converted. These pestilences occurred as far away as Turkey and Greece, having come from the area of the rising sun in Mesopotamia, Syria, Chaldea, Cyprus, the islands of Crete and Rhodes, and all of the islands in the Greek Archipelago. And then it happened in Sicily, Sardinia, Corsica, and Elba, and in a similar way on the coastlines and in the rivers of our seas. And of eight Genoese galleys that were stationed in the Black Sea, where many died, only four of them returned, full of the sick and dying. And all those who reached Genoa were nearly dead, and upon their arrival they corrupted the air that they breathed, so much so that whoever offered them refuge would soon die. . . . And this pestilence lasted until _____,[§] and many areas of the city and in the provinces remained desolate.

*Villani seems to refer to the black rats that are thought to have harbored plague-bearing fleas on their bodies; ship-borne specimens may have introduced the Black Death to Europe (see chapter 2).
[†]A territory in Greece on the Peloponnesus, just north of the ancient kingdom of Sparta.
[‡]A very similar tale is told by several other chroniclers.
[§]Here the chronicle is simply left blank.

4

LOUIS SANCTUS

Letter

April 27, 1348

*Louis Sanctus was present at the papal court at Avignon, just up the
Rhone River from the Mediterranean coast of France, when the plague
arrived in the region toward the end of 1347. Originally from present-
day Belgium, Sanctus served as a musician for one of Pope Clement VI's
cardinals, Giovanni Colonna; the cardinal succumbed to the plague on
July 3, 1348. Sanctus was part of an international group of early
Renaissance artists that included Francesco Petrarch, a close friend.
Sanctus's account of the plague comes to us in a missive to his friends at
Bruges, dated April 27, 1348; it was later incorporated into an anonymous Flemish chronicle. Living, as he did, in a Mediterranean city that
also served as the residence of the papacy, Sanctus would have had
access to information from a wide variety of travelers: pilgrims,
courtiers, merchants, and the like.*

In the same year [1347], in the month of September, a great mortality
and pestilence began, as I have seen in a transcript containing the letters of a cantor and canon of St. Donatian [Louis Sanctus] who at that
time was staying at the Roman [papal] court [of Avignon] with his lord
cardinal [Giovanni Colonna]. These letters he had sent to his companions in Bruges for the purpose of giving them news and forebodings:
Namely, that near Greater India in Eastern parts, in a certain province,
terrible events and unheard of tempests overwhelmed that whole
province for three days. On the first day it rained frogs, serpents,
lizards, scorpions, and many venomous beasts of that sort. On the second day thunder was heard, and lightning flashes mixed with hail-
stones of marvelous size fell upon the land, which killed almost all
men, from the greatest to the least. On the third day there fell fire
together with stinking smoke from the heavens, which consumed all

Recueil des chroniques de Flandre, ed. Joseph-Jean de Smet, 4 vols. (Brussels, 1837–65),
3:4–15.

the rest of men and beasts, and burned up all the cities and castles of those parts.

On account of these calamities, that whole province was infected, and it is conjectured that the whole sea-coast and all the neighboring lands were contaminated from that infection through the fetid breath of the wind blowing southwards from the plague regions. And always from day to day more people were infected, and now, by the will of God, it has come to [our] maritime parts in this fashion, as certain men suspect. For on December 31, in the year of our Lord 1348 [1347], three galleys horribly infected and heavily laden with spices and other goods landed at the port of Genoa, after having been forcibly expelled from eastern parts. When the Genoese observed that these [sailors] and other men were suddenly succumbing without remedy, they were expelled from that port with flaming arrows and diverse engines of war, because anyone who dared touch them or have any business dealings with them immediately died.

And thus one of the aforesaid three galleys, after having been driven from port to port, finally put in at Marseille. As before, the sick men did not give any warning of their arrival, so that [the inhabitants of Marseille] themselves were infected and suddenly died. For this reason, therefore, the said galley was expelled by the people of Marseille. In the meantime, having joined up with the other two that it found wandering on the sea, these remaining ships, it is said, are traveling toward the Atlantic Ocean via Spain, and by following [the coast] they will come, if they can, to other regions to the south so that they can unload their wares there. Moreover, these galleys have left behind in the wake of their entire journey so much infection, especially in maritime cities and places—first in Greece, then in Sicily and in Italy, particularly in Tuscany, and subsequently in Marseille, and as a consequence throughout the whole of Languedoc*—that the duration and terror it holds for men can scarcely be believed, let alone described.

---

*Extreme southern France, bordering on northeastern Spain.

2

Symptoms and Transmission

Although we do not know for certain what caused the Black Death, its symptoms most closely resemble those of the modern disease known as plague, which scientists attribute to the bacterium *Yersinia pestis.* Scientists gained a unique opportunity to study the symptoms and transmission of the disease during the third pandemic of 1894 to 1930.

Based on this research and later findings, we know that modern plague appears in three forms, depending on how the bacterium invades the body. The most common form, bubonic plague, is spread through the bite of a flea, whose upper stomach becomes "blocked" by the rapidly multiplying microorganisms and thus constantly feeds and regurgitates bacteria into the bloodstream of its hosts. When its usual animal carriers have died and grown cold, fleas will jump onto the nearest warm body available, including humans. From the time of infection, incubation of the plague bacilli in the human bloodstream can take two days to a week before symptoms appear. The most notable symptom, from which this form of the disease gets its name, is painful swellings of the lymph nodes, known as *buboes,* in the armpits, neck, or groin, depending on where the fleas initially infected the victim. The swellings may be accompanied by high fever, headaches, bleeding just below the skin, vomiting, delirium or stupor, and loss of motor control. Death typically ensues within three to six days after the onset of symptoms. However, approximately 10 to 40 percent of the victims of bubonic plague recover and survive even without medical intervention: A sign of their recovery is that, early in the second week of symptoms, their buboes burst and release their pus. In pneumonic plague, the bacteria are communicated through respiratory fluids, much like communication of the common cold. When it invades the lungs, this form of the disease produces a bloody sputum and typically kills within two to three days in nearly 100 percent of its victims. Septicemic plague, the most mysterious and rare form, seems to spread through a direct invasion, or "poisoning," of the blood, perhaps as the result of tainted medical instruments or the bite of a human flea, *Pulex irritans,* both of which could directly transfer the plague bacteria from the bloodstream of one patient to another. This form of the plague is also universally lethal, and it can apparently kill within hours. The plague is now easily cured by antibiotics, if treated before its advanced stages. Such medicines, of course, were not available in the fourteenth century.

Documents in this chapter provide detailed descriptions of the disease that devastated medieval society from 1348 to 1350. The chroniclers seem to have been writing on the basis of firsthand observation (Document 6) or secondhand expert testimony (Document 7). Louis Sanctus (Document 7) reports that autopsies were conducted on plague victims in Avignon. Certainly, the most clinical medieval diagnosis of plague symptoms is that by a physician, the Spanish Muslim Abū Ja^{c}far Ahmad Ibn Khātima (Document 13). The remarkable consistency—at least in the accounts given here—in the descriptions of symptoms is impressive. Nearly all chroniclers record the omnipresent buboes, or lymphatic swellings, that suggest the bubonic form of the plague. Michele da Piazza (Document 5) even seems to distinguish between the small, primary plague carbuncles or pustules that can appear early at the site of infection (a sign that the patient has a good chance of recovery) and the egg-shaped goiters that typically appear later at the site of the lymph nodes. The chroniclers also note other symptoms, such as fever, headaches, vomiting, petecchiae (skin lesions that appear all over the body and usually portend death), muscular spasms or stiffness, restlessness, delirium, and stupor. In addition, the symptoms described by some authors seem to identify the pneumonic and rare septicemic forms. Bear in mind, however, that the blood spitting that points to the presence of pneumonic plague can also be a secondary symptom of the bubonic form.

For some historians, the description of lymphatic swelling is definitive proof of the existence of bubonic plague (and, similarly, the absence of such a description cause to doubt a plague diagnosis).[1] Others contend that not even lymphatic swelling is conclusive proof, because it can also occur in other diseases (typhus, for example), and because medieval and modern diagnoses differ so markedly. Chroniclers report that medieval victims commonly suffered multiple lymphatic swellings in places other than the groin, as well as pustules and petecchiae, but some claim that these symptoms are rare in the modern experience of plague. In the entire corpus of plague literature from 1347 to 1450, the most noted characteristics of the Black Death are not the buboes and other symptoms, but rather the geographical scope, speedy transmission, and deadly virulence of the disease.[2]

Although a historical diagnosis of plague must depend at least to some extent on the accumulated experience that we have gained of the disease in modern times, when sophisticated techniques of bacteriology have made positive and accurate identifications possible, we cannot posit an exact correspondence between two incidences of a disease so widely separated in time. Even a modern diagnosis of plague may be flawed; the symptoms identified may not necessarily encompass the entire behavior of the disease in all places and at all times. When plague broke out in India in 1896, some of the early findings of the Indian Plague Commission, for example, that plague-bearing fleas were not transported in travelers' clothing and bedding, were contradicted by later reports.[3] Moreover, the British personnel who wrote the first reports on the plague in Bombay in 1896–97 frequently made false diagnoses of plague symptoms.[4] Second, it may be inappropriate to expect medieval chronicles and plague tracts to match the same standards of symptomology as our modern diagnoses. Medieval descriptions of plague may sometimes have masked a "mixture of infection," so we should not allow variations to invalidate an essential agreement in descriptions of plague symptoms, where this occurs.[5] Finally, testing of strains related to *Yersinia pestis* have demonstrated that its DNA can mutate into "hypervirulent" strains that are far more deadly than normal, and other studies have shown that such "atypical" plague bacilli occur regularly in nature. This suggests that searching for a modern-day equivalent to medieval plague may, in the end, be futile and irrelevant. Biomedical researchers from France have recovered *Yersinia* DNA from the dental pulp of fourteenth-century plague victims buried at Montpellier, which may soon allow us to determine whether the plague of our ancestors was the same strain that we know today.[6]

Other objections to identifying the Black Death with plague revolve around the rat-flea nexus that is so crucial to the spread of the bubonic form. Briefly stated, the arguments go something like this: Bubonic plague requires a certain optimum temperature (between 50 and 78 degrees Fahrenheit) within which the rat flea, *Xenopsylla cheopis,* that communicates plague bacteria from rats to humans can be active and reproduce. Yet the climate of some parts of Europe that were afflicted by the disease, such as northern Britain, Scandinavia, and Iceland, would have been too cold, even in summer, to favor flea activity. Further, some regions of the Mediterranean, such as Italy and

Spain, experienced their highest mortalities during the height of summer, when the weather would have been too hot for fleas. Nor can fleas survive for long away from their hosts, and thus their migratory patterns are dependent on their hosts. But the black rat, or *Rattus rattus,* that primarily harbored plague-bearing fleas during the Black Death in Europe is not a migratory animal and did not exist in sufficiently dense populations to spread and sustain a major epidemic. Moreover, medieval chroniclers recorded no disease outbreak among the rat population—an essential precondition for the epidemic spreading to humans, because the fleas must then search for alternative hosts. Although pneumonic plague may explain the contagion and rampant mortality of the disease, it acts too quickly to spread independently of bubonic plague, where it arises as a secondary symptom, and so we come back to our original conundrum. Revisionists seem to propose either accepting the Black Death as plague but denying its high mortality—which is entirely inconsistent with the surviving demographic records—or accepting that this was indeed a catastrophic disease but that it was not plague.[7]

In fact, none of these arguments is itself immune from challenge. A cold climate is no barrier to a flea, as the warm homes and furs of its hosts make perpetually congenial surroundings, and in any case, the winters of 1348 and 1349 were reported to be mild (Document 9). Also, climatologists think that Europe entered a "Little Ice Age" during the fourteenth century, so summers may have been considerably cooler than they are today.[8] Nor can one make precise assertions about medieval climate that would rule out the optimum temperature range of the flea. Even without the necessary concentrations of rats, bubonic plague could have been spread into remote areas, where specialized agriculture made people highly dependent on outside contacts.[9] Rat fleas infected with plague bacilli can survive for long periods without a host, especially by living on grain, a commodity frequently transported along the trade networks of Europe. A number of medieval chroniclers, including Nicephorus Gregoras (Document 1), Giovanni Villani (Document 3), and Fritsche Closener (Document 32) noticed rat mortality in connection with the plague. The concept that a rat epidemic heralded a plague outbreak, as the animals fled to the surface to fall down in a stupor and die, was familiar to contemporaries from the *Canon* of Avicenna.[10] Giovanni Boccaccio (Document 6) and another Florentine chronicler, Marchionne di Coppo Stefani, noticed that the disease was lethal to other animals, such as dogs, cats, pigs, chickens, oxen, donkeys, and sheep, some of whom also carry fleas and thus can trigger epidemics in humans.[11]

Contrary to what most biomedical experts claim, it seems likely that an epidemic of pneumonic plague could erupt and spread independently of the bubonic variety. The chronicler Michele da Piazza (Document 5) testified that victims from Messina with symptoms of pneumonic plague spread their infection to other towns throughout Sicily. Gui de Chauliac, a surgeon who treated himself for the disease (Document 14), diagnosed pneumonic plague before the bubonic form when the disease first came to Avignon in January 1348, and testamentary evidence from nearby Marseille indicates that the largest number of deaths occurred in March of that year.[12] In England, bishops' registers for the southern dioceses of Salisbury, Bath and Wells, Exeter, and Winchester, as well as wills proved in the Court of Hustings in London, record their highest mortalities during the winter and spring months of 1349, again suggesting that pneumonic plague struck before the bubonic variety prevailed in the north during the summer.[13]

Despite their disenchantment with identifying the *Yersinia pestis* plague as the disease of the Black Death, revisionist historians have not proposed credible alternatives.[14] Anthrax, perhaps the most popular candidate, can easily be dismissed on three grounds, if one accepts the contention that the disease was spread in the Middle Ages by eating tainted meat:[15] First, surviving manorial accounts suggest that plenty of fresh meat was available during the Black Death, so people would not have had to eat tainted meat.[16] Second, when people ate tainted meat during the Great Famine of 1315 to 1322, mortality averaged only around 10 percent.[17] Third, some communities, such as Pistoia in Italy, adopted stringent regulations with regard to the handling and supply of meat during the Black Death, but this did not spare them the disease.[18]

So far, no other disease seems to fit the recorded symptoms and mortality patterns of the Black Death better than plague.

NOTES

[1]Ann G. Carmichael, *Plague and the Poor in Renaissance Florence* (Cambridge: Cambridge University Press, 1986), 18–26; idem, "Bubonic Plague: The Black Death," in *Plague, Pox and Pestilence*, ed. Kenneth F. Kiple (London: Weidenfeld and Nicolson, 1997), 60.

[2]Samuel K. Cohn Jr., *The Black Death Transformed: Disease and Culture in Early Renaissance Europe* (London and Oxford: Arnold and Oxford University Press, 2002), 57–139.

³Graham Twigg, *The Black Death: A Biological Reappraisal* (New York: Schocken Books, 1984), 128. David Arnold, *Colonizing the Body: State Medicine and Epidemic Disease in Nineteenth-Century India* (Berkeley and Los Angeles: University of California Press, 1993), 203–5; Cohn, *The Black Death Transformed,* 28.

⁴Rajnarayan Chandavarkar, "Plague Panic and Epidemic Politics in India, 1896–1914," in *Epidemics and Ideas: Essays on the Historical Perception of Pestilence,* ed. Terence Ranger and Paul Slack (Cambridge: Cambridge University Press, 1992), 222.

⁵Carmichael, *Plague and the Poor,* 14–15; Lawrence I. Conrad, Michael Neve, Vivian Nutton, Roy Porter, and Andrew Wear, *Western Medical Tradition: 800 BC to AD 1800* (Cambridge: Cambridge University Press, 1995), 191–92.

⁶Richard E. Lenski, "Evolution of Plague Virulence," and R. Rosqvist, M. Skurnik and H. Wolf-Watz, "Increased Virulence of Yersinia Pseudotuberculosis," *Nature,* 334 (1988): 473–74, 522–25; Michel Drancourt, Gérard Aboudharam, Michel Signoli, Olivier Dutour, and Didier Raoult, "Detection of 400-Year-Old *Yersinia pestis* DNA in Human Dental Pulp: An Approach to the Diagnosis of Ancient Septicemia," *Proceedings of the National Academy of Science,* 95 (1998): 12637–40; idem, "Molecular Identification of 'Suicide PCR' of *Yersinia pestis* as the Agent of the Medieval Black Death," *Proceedings of the National Academy of Science,* 97 (2000): 12800–803. The fact that Drancourt's results have yet to be corroborated does not invalidate them, as Cohn claims. See Cohn, *The Black Death Transformed,* 248, n. 139.

⁷J. F. D. Shrewsbury, *A History of Bubonic Plague in the British Isles* (Cambridge: Cambridge University Press, 1970), 7–53; Twigg, *The Black Death,* 75–146, 200–22; Gunnar Karlsson, "Plague without Rats: The Case of Fifteenth-Century Iceland," *Journal of Medieval History* 22 (1996): 263–84; Cohn, *The Black Death Transformed,* 41–54, 140–87.

⁸H. H. Lamb, *Climate, History and the Modern World,* 2nd ed. (London and New York: Routledge, 1995), 195–207. However, there is some debate about whether the Mediterranean was part of this colder weather pattern. See Cohn, *The Black Death Transformed,* 42.

⁹Ole J. Benedictow, *Plague in the Late Medieval Nordic Countries: Epidemiological Studies* (Oslo: Middelalderforlaget, 1992), 171–92.

¹⁰Avicenna, *Canon Medicinae,* lib. 4, fen. 1, doct. 4.

¹¹Marchionne di Coppo Stefani, *Cronaca Fiorentina,* ed. Niccolò Rodolica, in *Rerum Italicarum Scriptores,* 30/1 (1903): 230.

¹²Francine Michaud, "La Peste, la peure et l'espoir: Le pélerinage jubilaire de Romeux Marsellais en 1350," *Le Moyen Âge,* 3–4 (1998): 408.

¹³Shrewsbury, *A History of Bubonic Plague,* 59–68, 90–93; Cohn, *The Black Death Transformed,* 184.

¹⁴The most recent revisionist historian of the Black Death, Samuel Cohn, is at a loss to find any alternative at all. See Cohn, *The Black Death Transformed,* 247.

¹⁵Norman F. Cantor, *In the Wake of the Plague: The Black Death and the World It Made* (New York: Free Press, 2001), 11–16.

¹⁶D. L. Farmer, "Prices and Wages, 1350–1500," in *The Agrarian History of England and Wales,* vol. 3: 1348–1500, ed. Edward Miller (Cambridge: Cambridge University Press, 1991), 433, 457.

¹⁷John Aberth, *From the Brink of the Apocalypse: Confronting Famine, War, Plague and Death in the Later Middle Ages* (New York: Routledge, 2000), 17–18.

¹⁸A. Chiapelli, "Gli ordinamenti sanitari del comune de Pistoia contro la pestilenza del 1348," *Archivo storico Italiano,* 20 (1887): 12–16.

5

MICHELE DA PIAZZA

Chronicle

1347–1361

A Franciscan friar in the convent of Catania in Sicily, Michele da Piazza records perhaps the first arrival of plague on European soil, in October 1347 at Messina. However, a town rivalry existed between Catania and Messina, which comes through very strongly in Piazza's account, so the chronicler may have awarded Messina the honor of first plague infection out of spite. Here Piazza records the symptoms of bubonic plague, but the size of the swellings seems to vary depending on geographic location: Catania's citizens contract considerably larger buboes than Messina's. Piazza's Chronicle *ends in 1361.*

It so happened that in the month of October in the year of our Lord 1347, around the first of that month, twelve Genoese galleys, fleeing our Lord's wrath which came down upon them for their misdeeds, put in at the port of the city of Messina. They brought with them a plague that they carried down to the very marrow of their bones, so that if anyone so much as spoke to them, he was infected with a mortal sickness which brought on an immediate death that he could in no way avoid. The signs of death which the Genoese and Messinese shared were these: Among those talking together, the breath of infection spread equally among them, until one infected the other so that nearly the entire body succumbed to the woeful disease. From the disease's onslaught and the infectious breath, there arose certain pustules the size of a lentil on the legs or arms. The plague thus infected and penetrated the body so that its victims violently spat out blood and this coughing up of bloody sputum continued incessantly for three days until they expired. And not only did everyone die who spoke with the victims, but also anyone who bought from them, touched them, or had any kind of intercourse with them. . . .

Michele da Piazza, *Cronaca*, ed. Antonino Giuffrida (Palermo: ILA Palma, 1980), 82, 86.

And thus the Messinese spread [the plague] throughout the whole island of Sicily, and when they came to the city of Syracuse, they also in the course of their travels infected the Syracusans, so that the deadly plague indeed killed a diverse and immense number of people. The region of Sciacca and Trapani and the city of Agrigento likewise joined the Messinese as victims of this pestilence, and especially the region of Trapani, which has remained nearly bereft of people. What can we say of the city of Catania, which has been consigned to oblivion? The aforesaid pest appeared in such strength there that not only the pustules, which are called in the vulgar tongue *antrachi* ["burn boil"], but also certain glandular swellings [*glandule*] arose on various members of the body, now on the groin, others on the legs, arms, and on the throat. These were at first the size of hazelnuts, and they appeared along with a chilly stiffness [of the limbs]. And they weakened and assaulted the human body to such an extent that it no longer had the power to stand up, but lay prostrate on the bed burning with a high fever and downcast from a deep depression. Whereupon these glandular swellings grew to the size of a nut, then to the size of a hen or a goose egg and became quite painful, and by putrefying the humors,* they forced the said human body to spit up blood. When the bloody sputum reached the throat from the infected lungs, [this was a sign] that the whole human body was putrefying. After this putrefaction and deficiency of the humors, the victims gave up the ghost. Indeed this disease lasted three days; but by the fourth day at the latest the abovementioned victims had passed from human affairs.

---

*This refers to the medieval medical idea, derived from the ancient Greek physician Hippocrates, that the body was composed of four humors—blood, phlegm, yellow bile, and black bile—that must be kept in balance if the body is to stay healthy.

6

GIOVANNI BOCCACCIO

Introduction to The Decameron

1349–1351

*A leading figure of the early Italian Renaissance, Giovanni Boccaccio
helped create the first vernacular literature in Italian. He was born in or
near Florence, and his father intended him to have a banking career, but
eventually Boccaccio devoted himself to writing literature. Although he
spent the 1330s in Naples at the court of Robert of Anjou, Boccaccio
came back to Florence in 1341 in time to witness the ravages of the
Black Death, which he describes in the introduction to his most famous
work,* The Decameron, *composed between 1349 and 1351. He died at
Certaldo in 1375.*

I say, then, that the sum of thirteen hundred and forty-eight years had
elapsed since the fruitful Incarnation of the Son of God, when the
noble city of Florence, which for its great beauty excels all others in
Italy, was visited by the deadly pestilence. . . . For in the early spring of
the year we have mentioned, the plague began, in a terrifying and
extraordinary manner, to make its disastrous effects apparent. It did
not take the form it had assumed in the East, where if anyone bled
from the nose it was an obvious portent of certain death. On the contrary, its earliest symptom, in men and women alike, was the appearance of certain swellings in the groin or the armpit, some of which
were egg-shaped whilst others were roughly the size of the common
apple. Sometimes the swellings were large, sometimes not so large,
and they were referred to by the populace as *gavòccioli*. From the two
areas already mentioned, this deadly *gavòcciolo* would begin to spread,
and within a short time it would appear at random all over the body.
Later on, the symptoms of the disease changed, and many people
began to find dark blotches and bruises on their arms, thighs, and
other parts of the body, sometimes large and few in number, at other

Giovanni Boccaccio, *The Decameron,* trans. G. H. McWilliam (Harmondsworth, Middle-
sex: Penguin Books, 1972), 50–51.

times tiny and closely spaced. These, to anyone unfortunate enough to contract them, were just as infallible a sign that he would die as the *gavòcciolo* had been earlier, and as indeed it still was.

Against these maladies, it seemed that all the advice of physicians and all the power of medicine were profitless and unavailing. Perhaps the nature of the illness was such that it allowed no remedy: or perhaps those people who were treating the illness (whose numbers had increased enormously because the ranks of the qualified were invaded by people, both men and women, who had never received any training in medicine), being ignorant of its causes, were not prescribing the appropriate cure. At all events, few of those who caught it ever recovered, and in most cases death occurred within three days from the appearance of the symptoms we have described, some people dying more rapidly than others, the majority without any fever or other complications.

But what made this pestilence even more severe was that whenever those suffering from it mixed with people who were still unaffected, it would rush upon these with the speed of a fire racing through dry or oily substances that happened to be placed within its reach. Nor was this the full extent of its evil, for not only did it infect healthy persons who conversed or had any dealings with the sick, making them ill or visiting an equally horrible death upon them, but it also seemed to transfer the sickness to anyone touching the clothes or other objects which had been handled or used by victims.

It is a remarkable story that I have to relate. And were it not for the fact that I am one of many people who saw it with their own eyes, I would scarcely believe it, let alone commit it to paper, even though I had heard it from a person whose word I could trust. The plague I have been describing was of so contagious a nature that very often it visibly did more than simply pass from one person to another. In other words, whenever an animal other than a human being touched anything belonging to a person who had been stricken or exterminated by the disease, it not only caught the sickness, but died from it almost at once. To all of this, as I have just said, my own eyes bore witness on more than one occasion. One day, for instance, the rags of a pauper who had died from the disease were thrown into the street, where they attracted the attention of two pigs. In their wonted fashion, the pigs first of all gave the rags a thorough mauling with their snouts after which they took them between their teeth and shook them against their cheeks. And within a short time they began to writhe as though they had been poisoned, then they both dropped dead to the ground, spreadeagled upon the rags that had brought about their undoing.

7

LOUIS SANCTUS

Letter

April 27, 1348

In the following extract from his letter of April 27, 1348, written from Avignon, Louis Sanctus appears to describe all three forms of the plague: bubonic, pneumonic, and even septicemic. Because Avignon was at the time the seat of the papacy, expert medical attention was available in the city and, by Sanctus's account, autopsies were conducted on plague victims. Sanctus seems to have had access to such expert medical testimony when writing his description of the symptoms of the disease, particularly of the pneumonic variety.

And it is said that the plague is of three types of infection. First, that men feel pain in their lungs, from which there comes a shortness of breath. He who has this malady, or is contaminated by it in any way whatsoever, can in no way escape, but will not live more than two days. Indeed, dissections were carried out by doctors in many Italian cities, and also in Avignon by order and command of the pope, so that the origin of this plague might be known. And many dead bodies were cut up and opened, and it was found that all who die so suddenly have an infection of the lungs and spit up blood. And thus it follows that this plague is indeed most terrible and dangerous to all, namely that it is contagious, because whenever one infected person dies, all who see him during his illness, or visit him, or have dealings with him in any way, or carry him to his grave, straightaway follow him [to their deaths], without any remedy.

There is also another kind of plague, that at present exists alongside the aforesaid [pneumonic plague]: namely that certain apostemes [tumors] suddenly appear on both armpits, from which men die without delay. And there is even a third plague, likewise concurrent with the two mentioned above, but at present it runs its own course: namely

---

Recueil des chroniques de Flandre, ed. Joseph-Jean de Smet, 4 vols. (Brussels, 1837–65), 3:5–16.

that people of both sexes are stricken in the groin, from which they die suddenly. As the aforesaid plague spreads, it has come to pass that the doctor does not visit the sick for fear of this contagion, not even if the patient would give him everything he possessed in this life. Nor does the father visit his son, the mother her daughter, brother his brother, the son his father, the friend his friend, the acquaintance his acquaintance, nor anyone another who may be a blood relation, unless he wishes to suddenly die like him or follow him [to the grave] immediately. And thus an innumerable number of men have died who did their affectionate duty to their relations and who also were known for their piety and charity, but who perchance might have escaped had they not visited them at the time.

8

JOHN VI KANTAKOUZENOS

History

1367–1369

A member of the powerful Kantakouzenos family that owned large estates in Thrace, John VI became emperor of Byzantium in 1341 as the result of a coup in which he claimed to be acting as regent for the legitimate heir to the throne, John V Paleologus. But in 1354, John V, who had attained his majority, forced John VI to abdicate and retire to a monastery. Kantakouzenos used his retirement to write a History *of the Byzantine Empire, which he seems to have composed into its final form between 1367 and 1369. Although some scholars think that Kantakouzenos imitated the literary style of the ancient Greek historian Thucydides in this passage, his detailed observations on the plague appear to be genuine. The plague of Athens of 430–26 BCE (now thought to be typhus fever or smallpox) was a different disease from the Black Death. The emperor had the opportunity to observe this firsthand when his*

Christos S. Bartsocas, "Two Fourteenth Century Greek Descriptions of the 'Black Death,'" *Journal of the History of Medicine and Allied Sciences,* 21 (1966): 396. Reprinted by permission of Oxford University Press.

youngest son, Andronikos, succumbed on the third day after the plague struck Constantinople. John VI himself lived to 1383.

So incurable was the evil, that neither any regularity of life, nor any bodily strength could resist it. Strong and weak bodies were all similarly carried away, and those best cared for died in the same manner as the poor. No other disease of any kind presented itself that year. If someone had a previous illness he always succumbed to this disease and no physician's art was sufficient; neither did the disease take the same course in all persons, but the others, unable to resist, died the same day, a few even within the hour. Those who could resist for two or three days had a very violent fever at first, the disease in such cases attacking the head; they suffered from speechlessness and insensibility to all happenings and then appeared as if sunken into a deep sleep. Then, if from time to time they came to themselves, they wanted to speak but the tongue was hard to move and they uttered inarticulate sounds because the nerves around the occiput [back of the head] were dead; and they died suddenly. In others, the evil attacked not the head, but the lung, and forthwith there was inflammation inside which produced very sharp pains in the chest.

Sputum suffused with blood was brought up and disgusting and stinking breath from within. The throat and tongue, parched from the heat, were black and congested with blood. It made no difference if they drank much or little. Sleeplessness and weakness were established forever.

Abscesses formed on the upper and lower arms, in a few also in the maxillae [jaw], and in others on other parts of the body. In some they were large and in others small. Black blisters appeared. Some people broke out with black spots all over their bodies; in some they were few and very manifest; in others they were obscure and dense. Everyone died the same death from these symptoms. In some people all the symptoms appeared, in others more or fewer of them, and in no small number even one of these was sufficient to provoke death. Those few who were able to escape from among the many who died were no longer possessed by the same evil, but were safe. The disease did not attack twice in order to kill them.

Great abscesses were formed on the legs or the arms, from which, when cut, a large quantity of foul-smelling pus flowed and the disease was differentiated as that which discharged much annoying matter. Even many who were seized by all the symptoms unexpectedly recovered. There was no help from anywhere; if someone brought to another a remedy useful to himself, this became poison to the other patient. Some, by treating others, became infected with the disease. . . . Most terrible was the discouragement. Whenever people felt sick there was no hope left for recovery, but by turning to despair, adding to their prostration and severely aggravating their sickness, they died at once. No words could express the nature of the disease.

3

Medical Responses

Although doctors enjoyed a considerable amount of prestige in medieval urban communities by the fourteenth century, they generally did not fare well at the hands of medieval chroniclers of the Black Death, who accused them of cowardice, impotence, and, above all, greed. Such complaints were not specifically related to the Black Death; rather, doctors were often the butt of satire and objects of scorn in the popular literature of the later Middle Ages. But the Black Death sharpened these complaints. One of the harshest critics was the Florentine chronicler Matteo Villani, who complained that "for this pestilential infirmity [of 1348], doctors from every part of the world had no good remedy or effective cure, neither through natural philosophy, medicine [physic], or the art of astrology. To gain money some went visiting and dispensing their remedies, but these only demonstrated through their patients' death that their art was nonsense and false."[1] In Avignon, however, Louis Sanctus charged doctors with refusing to visit the sick even for large sums (Document 7). Other commentators, such as Boccaccio (Document 6), John VI Kantakouzenos (Document 8), and Agnolo di Tura (Document 17), simply argued that physicians and medicine were powerless in the face of plague, although Boccaccio qualified this with the observation that many quacks had lately entered the profession and that the disease was perhaps incurable or too new to be treated properly. Even the best known doctor of the day, Gui de Chauliac, physician to the pope and a respected surgeon, indicted his own profession during the Black Death (Document 14).

However, like the priests whose behavior was criticized during the plague (chapter 4), many doctors gave their lives in service to the sick. Both Gentile da Foligno (Document 11) and Gui de Chauliac came down with the disease as they were making their rounds, in the former case with fatal results. It is also clear from the documents that doctors were in high demand during this crisis and that people naturally turned to them, as well as to their priests, for succor. Despite the inevitable failure of pre-antibiotic "cures," doctors like Ibn Khātima (Document 13) expressed confidence that bloodletting worked, so some treatments must have coincided with natural recovery. Doctors explained their failures as a consequence of the individual constitution's inability to admit of a cure (which, in any case, was limited to helping the body heal itself). Some medieval medical advice, such as avoiding baths (albeit more permissible in the Muslim world), bleeding patients until they lost consciousness (derived from Galen), and exotic theriacs, or medical compounds, may strike modern readers as completely inappropriate, if not downright harmful. Yet other recommendations, such as fleeing the site of infection, clearing refuse, fumigation, and quarantine were, even from a modern medical standpoint, eminently practical and beneficial. Even if they had no effect whatsoever, drinking wine or burning aromatic woods and herbs at the very least brought some pleasure to people in their last days.

Medical opinion concerning the Black Death was by no means monolithic. Even though the medical faculty at the University of Paris (Document 9) issued what seemed like a canonical pronouncement on the causes of the disease, which they attributed primarily to astrological influences, their explanation was not universally accepted. The Florentine chronicler Matteo Villani rejected the astrological explanation on the grounds that it was sufficient to say that the plague was part of God's inscrutable plan for humankind.[2] A popular scientific writer, Konrad of Megenberg, who was a university-trained cleric but not a professional medical man, argued against both the astrological theory and the widespread notion that the plague was divine retribution for human sin. He preferred a more naturalistic explanation that the plague emanated from within the earth when earthquakes released noxious fumes. This theory was unique to the Black Death, perhaps because it happened to coincide with actual tremors in some parts of Europe.[3] Whereas the medical faculty at Paris preferred to confine itself to traditional miasmatic or atmospheric infection, physicians from the rival medical school at Montpellier, like Alphonso de Córdoba (Document 10) and an anonymous colleague, instead championed theories of human-to-human contagion, revolving around, respectively, the contaminating vehicles of poison and sight.[4] On the issue of how plague arose within the human body, there was also contention. In both his long and short *Consilia* (*Casebooks*) on the plague, Gentile da Foligno argued that once corrupt air entered the body it produced a "poisonous matter" near the heart and lungs. This theory was disputed, however, by a rival at the University of Naples, Giovanni della Penna, who advanced a humoral theory that attributed the disease to over-heated "choleric matter."[5] (Cholera, or yellow bile, was one of the four humors of the body, whose balance was deemed essential for human health. According to this theory, an excess of any one humor caused disease.)

A common impression is that physicians during the Black Death were ineffective because the advice they dispensed in their plague manuals had little to do with reality or the common man.[6] But a close study of these tracts, like those excerpted here, suggests a different interpretation. Physicians attached to the universities were expected to assist their civic communities by responding to epidemic emergencies, and this was particularly true during the crisis of 1348–50. The long *Consilium* of Gentile da Foligno as well as the treatises of the faculty of medicine at the University of Paris and of Jacme d'Agramont (Documents 9 and 12) all state explicitly in their introductions that their works are intended for the wider community, in order to be of "common" or "public utility" and "service."[7] Agramont even wrote in his native language of Catalan and kept theoretical jargon to a minimum to reach a lay audience. Those communities that adopted quarantine and sanitation measures or set up temporary boards of health in order to combat the Black Death—such as Pistoia and Venice in Italy—seem to have done so on the advice and with the guidance of physicians, as Foligno recommends in his short *Consilium* (Document 11). Even though doctors no longer played an advisory role when permanent plague controls were adopted in the fifteenth century, they were nevertheless called upon to diagnose patients for isolation (and perhaps treatment) in plague hospitals and wards.[8] University doctors also modulated their prescriptions to suit the specific needs and circumstances of their patients. The medical faculty at Paris may have prescribed an "amber [smelling] apple" for the king and queen of France, but they also concerned themselves with more humble subjects, for example, advising "that commoners and agricultural laborers, who do not live refined lives, not neglect [to receive] a phlebotomy" either once or twice a day.[9] The long *Consilium* of Gentile da Foligno is famous for providing a recipe containing "potable gold" for wealthy clients who could afford such expensive remedies,[10] but his last short *Consilium* (Document 11) addresses the curative properties of garlic, which he recommended to "ordinary and rustic men, to whom a theriac is not available." Jacme d'Agramont also provided different fumigation recipes depending on social status (Document 12). The dangers, however, of self-help remedies are vividly illustrated by Ibn Khātima's gruesome story of the patient who tried to lance his own plague boil (Document 13). Finally, Alfonso de Córdoba's explanation of human or artificial causes of the Black Death, namely by intentional poisoning, played into a popular psychological need to maintain human control over such an extraordinary disease (Document 10). In a more sinister light, the explanation also provided support and authorization for the pogroms against the Jews that swept parts of Europe between 1348 and 1351 (chapter 6). It demonstrates once again that university physicians were not simply ensconced in their ivory towers, but were very much caught up in the social and psychological forces moving their communities.

NOTES

[1] Matteo Villani, *Cronica,* ed. Giuseppe Porta, 2 vols. (Parma: Fondazione Pietro Bembo, 1995), 1:13.
[2] Timothy Kircher, "Anxiety and Freedom in Boccaccio's History of the Plague of 1348," *Letteratura Italiana antica,* 3 (2002): 329–31.
[3] Partially translated in *The Black Death,* ed. Rosemary Horrox (Manchester: Manchester University Press, 1994), 177–82.
[4] For the tract by the anonymous Montpellier practitioner concerning sight contagion, see the partial translation in *The Black Death,* ed. Horrox, 182–84.
[5] Gentile da Foligno, *Consilium contra Pestilentiam* (Colle di Valdelsa, ca. 1479), fol. 2r; Jon Arrizabalaga, "Facing the Black Death: Perceptions and Reactions of University Medical Practitioners," in *Practical Medicine from Salerno to the Black Death,* ed. L. García-Ballester, R. French, J. Arrizabalaga, and A. Cunningham (Cambridge: Cambridge University Press, 1994), 260–61; Karl Sudhoff, "Pestschriften aus den ersten 150 Jahren nach der Epidemie des 'schwarzen Todes' 1348," *Archiv für Geschichte der Medizin,* 5 (1912): 341–42.
[6] Robert S. Gottfried, *The Black Death: Natural and Human Disaster in Medieval Europe* (New York: Free Press, 1983), 104–17; idem, *Doctors and Medicine in Medieval England, 1340–1530* (Princeton, N.J.: Princeton University Press, 1986), 168–69.
[7] Foligno, *Consilium,* fol. 1r; H. Émile Rébouis, *Étude historique et critique sur la peste* (Paris: A. Picard, 1888), 72; Jacme d'Agramont, "Regiment de preservacio a epidimia o pestilencia e mortaldats," trans. M. L. Duran-Reynals and C.-E. A. Winslow, *Bulletin of the History of Medicine,* 23 (1949): 57.
[8] John Henderson, "The Black Death in Florence: Medical and Communal Responses," in *Death in Towns: Urban Responses to the Dying and the Dead, 100–1600,* ed. Steven Bassett (London and New York: Leicester University Press, 1992), 141–47; Arrizabalaga, "Facing the Black Death," 287; Ann G. Carmichael, *Plague and the Poor in Renaissance Florence* (Cambridge: Cambridge University Press, 1986), 108–21. For the Ordinances of Pistoia, the only ones to survive from 1348, see the translation in *The Black Death,* ed. Horrox, 194–203.
[9] Rébouis, *Étude historique,* 116, 136.
[10] Foligno, *Consilium,* fol. 14v.

9

MEDICAL FACULTY
OF THE UNIVERSITY OF PARIS

Consultation
October 6, 1348 Plague has just broken out

On October 6, 1348, the college of the faculty of medicine at the University of Paris issued a compendium of opinion on the Black Death, apparently in response to a request from the king of France, Philip VI. In addition to relying on their own knowledge and ancient authorities like Aristotle, the faculty consulted "very many knowledgeable men in modern astrology and medicine concerning the causes of the epidemic which has been abroad since 1345." Their pronouncement therefore contained what was considered the most up-to-date scientific information available at the time and quickly became authoritative, as evidenced by its repetition in other plague treatises. The first part of the faculty's treatise addresses the "causes of this pestilence" and is divided into three chapters: one on a "distant" cause "which is up above and in the heavens," a second on a "near" cause "which is lower and on earth," and the third on "prognostications and signs, which are connected to both [above causes]." The second part, devoted to preventions and cures, is omitted because it covers much the same ground as Documents 12 and 13.

Concerning the Universal and Distant Cause.   Therefore we say that the distant and first cause of this pestilence was and is a certain configuration in the heavens. In the year of our Lord 1345, at precisely one hour past noon on the twentieth day of the month of March,* there was a major conjunction [lining up] of three higher planets in Aquarius. Indeed, this conjunction, together with other prior conjunctions and eclipses, being the present cause of the ruinous corruption of the air that is all around us, is a harbinger of mortality and famine

---

*The Paris masters most likely got this date from the *Prognosticatio* of Johannes de Muris, one of the astronomers summoned to the court of Pope Clement VI at Avignon in 1344–45.

H. Émile Rébouis, *Étude historique et critique sur la Peste* (Paris: A. Picard, 1888), 76–92.

and many other things besides, which we will not touch on here because it does not pertain to our subject. Moreover, that this is so is testified by the philosopher, Aristotle, in his book, *Concerning the Causes of the Properties of the Elements.** Around the middle [of the work] he says that mortalities of men and depopulation of kingdoms happen whenever there is a conjunction of two planets, namely Saturn and Jupiter, so that on account of their interaction disasters are magnified threefold to the third power [i.e., nine times], and all this is to be found in [the writings of] ancient philosophers. And Albertus [Magnus] says in his book, *Concerning the Causes of the Properties of the Elements*† (treatise 2, chapter 1), that a conjunction of two planets, namely Mars and Jupiter, brings about a great pestilence in the air, and that this happens especially under a hot and humid sign [i.e., Aquarius], as was the case when the planets lined up [in 1345]. For at that time, Jupiter, being hot and wet, drew up evil vapors from the earth, but Mars, since it is immoderately hot and dry, then ignited the risen vapors, and therefore there were many lightning flashes, sparks, and pestiferous vapors and fires throughout the atmosphere. . . .

Concerning the Particular and Near Cause. Although pestilential sicknesses can arise from a corruption of water and food, as happens in times of famine and poor productivity, nevertheless we are of the opinion that illnesses which proceed from a corruption of the air are more deadly, since this evil is more hurtful than food or drink in that its poison penetrates quickly to the heart and lungs. Moreover, we believe that the present epidemic or plague originated from air that was corrupt in its substance, and not only in its altered properties.‡ For we

*This work was not by Aristotle but was commonly attributed to him. Aristotle was considered the leading authority of the ancient world, and thus was invoked to support all kinds of positions.

†Albertus Magnus wrote commentaries on all of Aristotle's known works, which explains the similarity in the titles by the two authors.

‡The miasmatic theory of disease, that epidemics resulted from a substantial change in the quality of the air, was first advanced by Hippocratic writers and later championed by Galen. The Paris masters seem to define plague as a *result* of the substantial change in air, rather than as the change itself. Jacme d'Agramont, an anonymous Montpellier practitioner, and Gentile da Foligno took an opposite view. For more on this debate, see Jon Arrizabalaga, "Facing the Black Death: Perceptions and Reactions of University Medical Practitioners," in *Practical Medicine from Salerno to the Black Death,* ed. L. Garcia-Ballester, R. French, J. Arrizabalaga, and A. Cunningham (Cambridge: Cambridge University Press, 1994), 242–48.

[handwritten margin left: They are pulling from what they think they know — they trust + what they think they know]

[handwritten top left: 42 is true]

[handwritten margin right: not religious — they understand not everything is religious — so they]

wish it to be understood that air, which is pure and clear by nature, does not putrefy or become corrupt unless it is mixed up with something else, that is, with evil vapors. For many vapors that had been corrupted at the time of the aforesaid conjunctions arose, by virtue of their [nature], from the earth and water, and in the air were spread and multiplied by frequent gusts of thick, wild, and southerly winds, which, on account of the foreign vapors they have brought and are still bringing with them, have corrupted the air in its substance. Thus, the corrupted air, when it is breathed in, necessarily penetrates to the heart and corrupts the substance of the spirit that is in it and putrefies the surrounding moisture, so that the heat that is created goes forth and by its nature corrupts the principle of life, and this is the immediate cause of the current epidemic. What is more, these winds, which have become so prevalent around us, could by their force have brought or carried to us, or perhaps will do so in the future, evil, putrid and poisonous vapors from afar, as, for instance, from swamps, lakes, deep valleys, and, in addition, from dead, unburied or unburned bodies, all of which are deadly. And this could be a cause of the epidemic. And possibly this corruption could have or will come about through other causes, such as rottenness imprisoned in the inner parts of the earth that are released, or already in fact have been released, whenever there are earthquakes. But all of these things which have done and are doing harm, by putrefying the air and water, could have come about through the configurations [of the planets], the aforesaid universal and distant cause.

Concerning Prognostications and Signs. Changes of the seasons are a great source of plagues. For the Ancients, and especially Hippocrates, are agreed that if any of the four seasons was disrupted so that the seasons did not observe their regularity, pestilence and deadly diseases would come to pass in that year. Therefore we speak from experience when we say that for some time now the seasons have not been regular. For the past winter was less cold than it ought to have been, with much rain, and the spring was windy and, at the tail end, rainy. But the summer was late, less hot than it usually is and extremely wet, very unpredictable from day to day and hour to hour, and the skies often cloudy but then clearing up, so that it seemed as if it was about to rain but it never did. Also, the autumn was very rainy and cloudy. Hence for us, this whole year, or most of that time, has been and still is hot and wet, and for that reason the air is pestilential. For air that is hot and wet does not occur during the seasons of the year except in times of pestilence. . . .

Nevertheless, in the judgment of astrologers who base themselves on Ptolemy,* these [plagues] are further reckoned to be likely and possible because there have been seen very many vapor trails and flare-ups, such as a comet and shooting stars. Also, the color of the heavens has customarily appeared yellowish and the sky turned red because of the frequently burnt vapors. In addition, there has been much lightning and frequent flashes, thunder and wind so violent and strong that it has stirred up much of the earth's dust, bringing it from southerly parts. These, especially the powerful earthquakes, quickly make things worse for everyone, leaving behind a legacy of yet more decay, and a multitude of fish, beasts, and other carcasses on the seashore, and also in many places trees covered with dust. And indeed, some confess to have seen a multitude of frogs and snakes, which come forth out of decomposition. All these things seem to come from a great rottenness of the air and land. Moreover, all of the above has been noted before by wise men of worthy memory who made their investigations on the basis of sure experience. . . .

On the other hand, a no small part of the cause of sicknesses is the condition of the patient's body, in that no cause is apt to take effect unless the patient shows a predilection toward it. And it must be particularly emphasized that, although everyone at one time or another incurs the danger of this corrupt air through their necessity to breathe, nevertheless not everyone is made sick by the corruption of the air, but many who are predisposed to it will become [sick]. Truly, those who become sick will not escape, except the very few. Moreover, the bodies that are more susceptible to receive the stamp of this plague are those bodies that are hot and wet, in which decay is more likely. Also [at risk] are: bodies that are full and obstructed with evil humors, in which waste matter is not consumed or expelled as is necessary; that live by a bad regimen, indulging in too much exercise, sex, and bathing; those who are weak and thin and very fearful. Also infants, women, and the young, and those whose bodies are fat and have a ruddy complexion or are choleric are to be on their guard more than others. But those who have bodies that are dry and free of impurities, who govern [their bodies] well and in accordance with a suitable regimen, are more resistant to the pestilence. What is more,

*Claudius Ptolemy (second century CE) was a mathematician and an astronomer in Alexandria.

we should not neglect to mention that an epidemic always proceeds from the divine will, in which case there is no other counsel except that one should humbly turn to God, even though this does not mean forsaking doctors. For the Most High created medicine here on earth, so that, while God alone heals the sick, He allows medicine as a symbol of his humanity. Blessed be the glorious and high God, who never denies His aid but makes plain to those who fear Him a clear diagnosis for being cured.

10

ALFONSO DE CÓRDOBA

Letter and Regimen concerning the Pestilence
ca. 1348 *beginning of plague*

Little is known about Córdoba. Although he obviously came from Spain, an inscription at the end of his treatise, Epistola et Regimen de Pestilentia *(Letter and Regimen concerning the Pestilence), states that it was written at Montpellier in France. No date is given, although it is believed to be either 1348 or 1349. The University of Montpellier was one of the leading medical schools in Europe at the time, and it is clear that Córdoba was connected to it from the way he describes himself at the beginning of his work. Córdoba probably composed his treatise in response to the pronouncement on the plague by the University of Paris in 1348. Rather than positing an astrological or natural cause, like the Paris masters, Córdoba focuses on an artificial or a human one.*

he probably wrote this in 1348

I, Alfonso of Córdoba, master of the liberal and medical arts, have examined with much study the cause and nature of the pestilences which have arisen and begun in the present year of our Lord 1348. The first pestilence was a natural one and its cause was an eclipse of the moon occurring immediately before in the sign of Leo [i.e., July 23–

Karl Sudhoff, "Pestschriften aus den ersten 150 Jahren nach der Epidemie des 'schwarzen Todes' 1348," *Archiv für Geschichte der Medizin,* 3 (1909–10): 224–25.

August 22], accompanied by a powerful conjunction of the unlucky planets. The second was caused by a very strong earthquake which many can recall, and that pestilence was naturally located in regions of Italy and in parts overseas, in the corner of the triangle opposite the house of Europe [i.e., an indefinite region to the East]. But that plague ought to have ceased, and so it has ceased, which it did quickly within the space of a year, and otherwise the strength and vigor of the constellation [of the planets] was not in accordance with how it afterwards spread. And yet today the pestilence is spread throughout all the regions of Christendom.

And there is another cause besides the natural one, and for this reason and out of compassion for the [Christian] faithful who chiefly suffer from it, I have written down this letter and regimen, along with its medicines, so that pious and good people may not be subjected to so many dangers and may know how to prevent the great dangers and evils that especially threaten Christians in this pestilence. Before all else, one must be on one's guard against all food and drink which can be infected and poisoned, especially against non-flowing water, because this can most easily be infected. Experience teaches us that this pestilence does not proceed from some constellation [of the planets] nor as a consequence of any natural infection of the elements, but it proceeds out of a deep-seated malice through the most subtle artifice that can be invented by a profoundly wicked mind.* This is why the wise counsel of doctors does not profit or help those in the grip of this most cruel and pernicious disease. Wherefore the best remedy is this: to flee the plague, because the plague does not follow the fugitive, or to take precautions, inasmuch as possible, against infection of all of life's necessities. . . . [Córdoba proceeds to give some recipes for theriacs and electuaries.] The use of such an electuary may preserve one from the venom and poison.

And the use of pestilential pills is of great value, and may preserve one from infected air, because air can be infected by artifice, as when a certain formula is prepared in a glass amphora [flask]. And when that formula is well fermented, he who wishes to do that evil [i.e., poison others] waits until there comes a strong and steady wind from some part of the world. Then he must go against the wind and place his amphora next to some stones opposite the city or town that he wishes to infect. And after giving this area a wide berth, walking away

*Jacme d'Agramont also mentions this cause: "Another cause from which plague and pestilence may come is from wicked men, children of the devil, who with venoms and diverse poisons corrupt the foodstuffs with evil skill and malevolent industry."

against the wind so that the vapor does not infect him, he should forcefully throw the amphora against the stones, and once the amphora is broken, the vapor spreads and disperses in the air and anyone who comes into contact with that vapor will die as if from pestilential air, and quickly. [Córdoba then gives some more recipes for pestilential pills and recommends fumigating the air with coal fires perfumed by one of the pills.]

11

GENTILE DA FOLIGNO

Short Casebook
1348 beginning.

A physician's son from Foligno, near Perugia in Umbria, Gentile da Foligno was perhaps the most famous and respected doctor in Italy at the time of the Black Death. He studied medicine at the universities of Bologna and Padua. He was a lecturer on medicine at the University of Perugia from 1325 to 1337 and subsequently at Padua until 1345, when he seems to have returned to Perugia. Known for his reliance on practical experience rather than abstract theory when diagnosing or treating diseases, Foligno conducted several public dissections and autopsies, including one at Padua in 1341. He was a prolific writer on a variety of medical topics. His work included commentaries on the entire Canon *of* Avicenna, *and early in 1348 he wrote a long* Consilium contra Pestilentiam *(Casebook against the Pestilence); three shorter* Consilia *are also attributed to him. Although Foligno's authorship of these short* Consilia *is not universally accepted by scholars, they closely reflect his teaching. The following selection is from the third and last short* Consilium, *addressed to the college of physicians of Perugia and written just before his death, when he had acquired more knowledge about the disease. When the plague struck, Foligno, like Chauliac, bravely resolved to perform his duties. He died of the plague on June 18, 1348, apparently*

Karl Sudhoff, "Pestschriften aus den ersten 150 Jahren nach der Epidemie des 'schwarzen Todes' 1348," *Archiv für Geschichte der Medizin,* 5 (1911): 84–86.

*having contracted the disease "from too constant attendance on the sick,"
according to his devoted student, Francesco da Foligno, who attended
him at his deathbed and edited his last* Consilium.

It seems that in times past, there were several wondrous and astounding causes that preceded the pestilence, which now seems to come
from southern and eastern parts to Italy, beginning in the west of the
country. For the famous pestilence of the city of Crannon,* or that
which Thucydides or Galen or Avenzoar wrote about, do not seem
comparable in their evil to [this] pestilence that has chiefly invaded
[Italy].† . . .

Therefore, Gentile da Foligno, together with the venerable college
of the masters of [the University of] Perugia, prescribed with divine
help the following for the preservation and defense against this pestilence:

First, that men should appropriately consume fine food and drink in
measured quantities and of suitable quality, and they ought to understand fine food and drink, to which men in general are accustomed.
But fish is to be avoided, for on no account should men consume it.
Moreover, concerning lettuce, it is advised that if it has been left out in
the cold, men should by no means consume it, but that when its color
comes back, it is safe to eat. Furthermore, from among various foods,
we recommend the eating of good meat, including fowl, chicken, and
starlings. But of beef, [we recommend] gelded cows and lactating
goats and calves, as well as young pork. Also, we recommend bread
carefully prepared and select wines, so that men may live in good
cheer as they give vent to their fear.

Second, that one should make use of purgatives and phlebotomies,‡
and larch fungus with its healing properties is always recommended
as a purgative, in accordance with what doctors have been prescribing, etc.

---

*The location of this city is unknown and the reference to plague here is rather mys-
terious. Avenzoar, or Ibn Zuhr (1090–1162), who was a rival of Avicenna's, also mentions the plague of Crannon.

†This represents a significant change from Gentile's position in his first, long *Consilium*: "This said plague seems to grow ever more frightening, although in its evil [mali-
cie] it is still not so great as that of the city of Crannon which Avenzoar relates in his
Liber Theizir, or which Thucydides or Galen wrote about."

‡Phlebotomy is the medical term for bleeding, a practice meant to restore the balance of bodily humors.

Third, that men should take at least two or three times a week until the end of May [1348] the best theriac* or antidote. And, if the patient is a man, this should be given to him if he is between the ages of fourteen and thirty-one; it can be given to women in the same doses or more if they are between the ages of fourteen and thirty and a half. Moreover, for babies who are in their first year, who should not take these doses, it will suffice to rub their bodily parts, namely the chest, stomach, and nose, with the theriac. Furthermore, the dose should be taken in the morning with pure wine, or with wine diluted with water, but without drinking the usual refreshments. But the theriac ought to have been already aged for one year, and because not all men can obtain a theriac, it is recommended that poor men consume leeks or hyssop and scabiosa [a kind of plant] or scallions, in whatever manner is pleasing to the patient: whether by boiling or liquefying them in wine, or eating them finely chopped, or eating them raw, or drinking wine made from them, or eating them with a little vinegar or wine or with wine only or with water, or drinking their juice. And one can eat only one of the aforementioned things and continue with it, or [eat] one of them in one way and another in a [different] way. Moreover, a dose in any quantity—whether taken once or twice or three times— ought to be sufficient, and these can be useful not only to the poor but also to the rich. But as for the effectiveness of a theriac if it is thus given after the aforesaid month of May, we cannot be the judge.

Fourth, it is recommended that fires be lit in homes and in places where people are living, and that men rest quietly. Also, fires of any kind of fragrant plant should be set up, and the house and city should be cleansed of stenches [i.e., excrement], and because of these stenches, smelling apples and powders, which are described below, are recommended.

Lastly, we will respond to questions posed by the common people, and first among these is whether garlic is effective in this pestilence. And it is recommended that ordinary and rustic men, to whom a theriac is not available, may use this, but that others should not. For its intended use is that it be of some effect against disease, but instead during the plague the heart breaks it down into something else, which happens when it is tainted with water.

---

*A compound of elements used since ancient times and often composed of dozens of ingredients, the most important of which was snakeskin, thought to neutralize the deadly poison inside a sick person. Foligno was a strong advocate of theriac as a cure of plague, because he considered the cause of the disease to be poisonous rather than humoral in nature.

A second question is whether a compound made of Armenian bole,* aloe, myrrh, and saffron be effective in this pestilence, which indeed doctors north of the Alps have prescribed. Our response is that this compound, if prudently made up by doctors in accordance with the conditions of each illness, which may be observed in the patient's members, and even though true [Armenian] bole may not be seen or found in our country, nonetheless if it were to be found and even if it were not genuine, all the same we could accept its use to counteract a certain blocking of the paths of the spirit [i.e., the arteries], which we have found in those men short of breath in the lungs, and because we have found that a tightness of the chest causes harm throughout the body's trunk. But if it should be discovered that the chest is disposed to be tight at certain times, then there is no cause for concern and its use is not recommended.

A third enquiry is whether bitter herbs, vinegar, and verjuice are of any use, and we advise that the vinegar be mixed with wine, provided that the wine is good and the odor is tolerable. But since both will generate heat, it would be safer to use pure vinegar. Moreover, the college recommends that, by the grace of the Lord who is our cure in this, some good men who confer with doctors make regulations for their city, in accordance with [the doctors'] information, so that they safeguard their citizens' well being. All these things, together with many other concerns that we have examined, are elementary to the authors of medical textbooks. But doctors' recommendations, which are treated in these writings above, may be added to or taken away in accordance with what is found to suit the circumstances of each city and locality and individual person. We pray God that He may improve men's health.

*Armenian bole is a form of clay high in iron oxide. Galen prescribed it, and it was well known among medical authorities in the Middle East. It was both taken internally and applied externally as a treatment for the buboe swellings.

12

JACME D'AGRAMONT

Regimen of Protection against Epidemics
April 24, 1348

[handwritten: —when was the first reported outbreak?]

A physician and professor of medicine at the University of Lérida in northeastern Spain, Jacme d'Agramont finished composing his work, Regiment de preservacio a epidimia o pestilencia e mortaldats (Regimen of Protection against Epidemics or Pestilence and Mortality), on April 24, 1348. This makes it the earliest datable plague treatise, and Agramont himself died from the plague shortly afterwards. The Regiment is written in the form of an open letter addressed to the city aldermen and councillors of Lérida, who commissioned the work. It is obviously intended for the general public, as it is written in a vernacular tongue, Catalan, rather than the academic Latin preferred by university scholars. Nonetheless, Agramont is careful to point out in his introduction that his work suggests a regimen of prevention only, a very timely one as rumors of pestilence have come to Lérida from neighboring lands. (The plague was to hit the region in May 1348.) For treatment of the disease, Agramont refers the reader to a trained physician and refuses to provide any "self-help" tips. Only portions of two of the six sections are included here.

[handwritten left margin: I assume the bubonic plague is an airborn disease?]

[handwritten right margin: did all these doctors die because they were infected w/ bodily fluids? or]

Rectification of Air, Putrid and Corrupt in Its Substance. If air is pestilential because of putrefaction and corruption of its substance, one must consider whether its corruption or putrefaction was sent for our deserts in chastisement for our sins, or whether it came through the infection of the earth, or of the water, or of allied things, or whether it came from higher or superior causes such as the influence of conjunctions or appositions of planets. Because if the corruption and putrefaction of the air has come because of our sins, the remedies of the medical art are of little value, for only He who binds can unbind....

Jacme d'Agramont, "Regiment de preservacio a epidimia o pestilencia e mortaldats," trans. M. L. Duran-Reynals and C.- E. A. Winslow, *Bulletin of the History of Medicine,* 23 (1949): 75, 78–85.

But if the putrefaction of the air came from the earth or from the water, in such case one must choose for one's habitat high places and mountains.* But if the putrefaction came through the influence of some conjunction or appositions of the planets, in such case one must choose low places and underground rooms to live in, and also in such cases one must keep windows and embrasures tightly shut.

And one should make fires in the room of good firewood, such as rosemary and myrtle, or of cypress, which one finds in great abundance, or of juniper or Arabic *desticados* [word is unidentified] or of lavender, vulgarly called *espigol.* . . .

[Agramont then gives a special concoction for fumigations by "great lords."] Also one can prepare for the great lords fumigations of a most precious confection which is called *Gallia muscata* [literally, "French musk"], or of another one called "black confection."

But the common folk may use the following regimen. They can make fire in their huts and in their chambers of rosemary and juniper, and make fumigations of incense and myrrh or of other things cheaply to be had such as "cimiama" [cumin] or "herb of thur" [frankincense]. And I will say that the fire alone can effectively rectify air putrid in its substance. I advise that such a regimen be continued as one of the most important and necessary. And again it must be said that it is most beneficial to sprinkle the floor of the room with rose water and vinegar.

Regimen of Exercise.   In such times one must avoid violent exercise because such exercise causes much air which is foul and poisoned to be drawn to the heart. The heart is corrupted and also the blood and its spirits, by air that has the effects spoken of in the fourth article [above].

On Foods and Remedies Which Preserve the Body against Pestilential Maladies.   The regimen of foods and medicines which are to preserve the body from pestilential maladies must be the following: Man should eat and drink as little as possible. Especially, drinking must be temperate and it is advisable that he control his thirst. Also one should

---

*Agramont's hometown of Lérida violated this principle; he describes it as "a town which suffers from many maladies . . . although it is on a height and exposed to winds . . . and open to the rising sun," all of which should have cleansed it of the pestilential air. He resolves this dilemma by claiming that diseases in Lérida are "due not to bad air, but to an excessive regimen of fruits and viands, because of their abundance," an ironic viewpoint given his dietary prescriptions.

still true today. neat.

use in all foods much vinegar, sorrel, juice of oranges and of lemons and other acid things which are most beneficial. Clear fresh wine is better than sweet wine, because wine that contains sweetness putrefies more easily and has great tendency to turn into bile. Also one must avoid in such times birds that feed near stagnant waters, such as water hens, and geese, and ducks and other animals that have naturally humid flesh, such as suckling pigs and lambs. Also, in such times slimy fishes such as lampreys and eels and rapacious fishes, such as dolphin, shark, tunny-fish, and similar fishes should be forbidden. Especially to be avoided, aside from the above-mentioned fishes, are any others when they are rotten and smelling badly. And if perchance one is obliged to partake of them, one should choose whatever is best in the region, such as salmon, sturgeon, mullets, flounder, and haddock and similar fishes, and they should be preserved in vinegar or salt. Fish fried or grilled over the coals is best in such times.

Of fruits in such times, those are better that are rather acid, such as red berries, acid pomegranates, and *taperes en sols* [capers].

Having pointed out what foods are beneficial, and which are objectionable in such times, we must now mention the medicines which preserve our body from pestilential maladies. One should take three times a week in the morning one drachm or three dinars [the weight of three coins] of fine theriac. It is said to be very beneficial, especially if the body is purged in the manner which we will mention in the following chapter.... [Agramont proceeds to give some recipes, including one by Avicenna.]

The Regimen of Sleep. After feeding naturally follows sleeping. I say that for sleeping there should be selected a room according to the principles discussed in the regimen of air.

Regimen of Our Bodies as Regards Purgation and Bleeding. Since few are those that in eating and drinking do not go to excess, for this reason I advise that the body be purged with a light purge, i.e. not too strong to be dangerous.... [Agramont here gives several recipes for purgative syrups.]

However, since many factors will influence the work of the physician, I advise that in this regimen a good and approved physician be consulted. Because a purge cannot be good at all times nor for everybody, just as one shoe can fit but few.

The desired evacuation having taken place, one can shortly after bleed the median vein or some other in order to withdraw blood, 3 or

4 ounces, more or less according to the condition of the person or according to major or minor necessity. And if one asks me in which quarter of the moon it is best to let blood, I say in the third quarter. And also I say that it is better to do it in the middle of this third quarter, provided that the moon in such times is not seen in a sign unfavorable for bloodletting, such as Gemini, Leo, Virgo, Capricorn, and some others.

And in this regimen it is also important that man abstain from carnal intercourse with woman. To go to excess in these matters is at all times of great danger to our body. But, especially in such times, it does signally and notably great harm and damage.

And also I say that in such times habitual bathing is also very dangerous, because the bath opens the pores of the body and through these pores corrupt air enters and has a powerful influence upon our body and on our humors.

Influences on the Soul: Anger, Joy, Fear, Sadness, Anxiety. I declare that in such times gaiety and joyousness are most profitable, unless joyousness is combined with a bad regimen either of food or of dissipation or other things.

But among other influences that must be avoided in such times are especially those of fear and imagination. For from imagination alone, can come any malady. So one will find that some people get into a consumptive state solely by imagination. This influence is of such great force that it will change the form and figure of the infant in the mother's womb.

And to prove the great efficacy and the great power of imagination over our body and our lives, one can quote in proof first the Holy Scripture, where we read in Genesis, chapter 30, that the sheep and goats that Jacob kept, by imagination and by looking at the boughs which were of divers colors put before them by Jacob when they conceived, gave birth to lambs and kids of divers colors and speckled white and black. Another proof of this proposition can be made by the following experiment: When somebody stands on a level board on the flat floor, he can go from one end to the other with nothing to hold on to, so as not to fall off, but when this same board is placed in a high and perilous position, no one would dare to try to pass over the said board. Evidently the difference is due wholly to the imagination. In the first case there is no fear, and in the other there is. Thus, it is evidently very dangerous and perilous in times of pestilence to imagine death and to have fear. No one, therefore, should give up hope or

hypochondria?

despair, because such fear only does great damage and no good what-soever.

For this reason also it is to be recommended that in such times no chimes and bells should toll in case of death, because the sick are sub-ject to evil imaginings when they hear the death bells. . . .

And since in such times maladies and deaths can come from vari-ous causes, since it happens that some die from worms and others from abscesses which invade the heart, and others from other causes, it is advisable that in such times, of those that die suddenly, some should be autopsied and examined diligently by the physicians, so that thousands, and more than thousands could benefit by preventive measures against those things which produce the maladies and deaths discussed.

13

ABŪ JA'FAR AHMAD IBN KHĀTIMA

Description and Remedy for Escaping the Plague
February 1349

A physician and poet from Almería on the coast of southern Spain, at that time part of the Muslim kingdom of Granada, Abū Ja'far Ahmad Ibn Khātima wrote his plague treatise in February 1349. Although grounding himself in earlier theory, such as that of Hippocrates, Galen, and Avenzoar (Ibn Zuhr), particularly with regard to explaining the causes of the plague, Khātima also seems to speak from experience as the result of diagnosing and treating plague patients after the Black Death arrived in Almería on June 1, 1348. His treatise, entitled Tahsīl al-gharad al-qāsid fī tafsīl al-marad al-wāfid *(A Description and Remedy for Escaping the Plague in the Future), is the most detailed of the few medical works in Arabic to have survived from the time of the Black Death. Khātima lived until at least 1369, when he is mentioned by his*

Taha Dinanah, "Die Schrift von Abi G'far Ahmed ibn 'Ali ibn Mohammed ibn 'Ali ibn Hatimah aus Almeriah über die Pest," *Archiv für Geschichte der Medizin*, 19 (1927): 49–78. Translated from the German by Thomas Huber.

friend and fellow physician, Ibn al-Khatīb. The following selection is from primarily the fourth and fifth questions of his treatise.

Infection. It is clear and obvious that it is the nature of the disease to spread and contaminate the surroundings. Both experience and observation confirm this. It has not happened yet that a healthy person came into contact with a sick one without contracting the disease. It is a law which God imposed in this matter. God is the first and foremost maker. With this, we contradict the beliefs maintained by people in error and reject "infection," which Arabs believe in their ignorance of Islam.* We maintain here the proper natural law which holds true for creation. . . .

The best thing we learn from extensive experience is that if someone comes into contact with a diseased person, he immediately is smitten with the same disease, with identical symptoms. If the first diseased person vomited blood, the other one does too. If he is hoarse, the other will be too; if the first had buboes on the glands, the other will have them in the same place; if the first one had a boil, the second will get one too. Also, the second infected person passes on the disease. His family contracts the same kind of disease: If the disease of one family member ends in death, the others will share his fate; if the diseased one can be saved, the others will also live. The disease basically progressed in this way throughout our city, with very few exceptions.

Prevention and Protection. Since the cause of the disease is a change and variation in the nature of the atmosphere, by which the matter of the disease gets to the heart, and since man has to breathe as long as he lives and since he has to breathe in the atmosphere in which he lives, prevention is almost impossible, unless one can find a substitute [way of living]. But as we said, it doesn't suffice that the active agent [of the plague] does its work on its own; there has to be a disposition [in man] to make its work possible. Man needs several things in life, some of them necessary, others are luxuries. He can use them

---

*Obviously, this statement goes against Khātima's own observation and experience of the disease. However, he is obliged to maintain it on Islamic grounds, that a plague can only come from God and represents a martyrdom for Muslim believers. This issue is explored in greater detail in chapter 5.

[margin handwritten note, left: how is the plague transmitted? Plague]

[margin handwritten note, right: airborne? infections? bloodborne? bite infections?]

vicariously, without measure, which makes him irresponsible. Or he can live moderately, as his God-given reason, science and wisdom teach; this is the best protection for any man. . . .

Air. One should always take care to have fresh air by living in houses facing north, by filling them with cold fragrances and aroma of flowers, such as myrtle and oriental poplars, by sprinkling the houses with rose water mixed with vinegar, and also use the same on oneself. Also, anoint your face and hands with the same cool fragrances, frequently smell such things, also sour lemons and limes as well as cooling flowers, such as roses and violets. Also, burn sandal wood, mixed with a little aloe, steeped in rose water. Also, avoid anything which could produce heat, such as rice bran or bran of millet, both of which cause headaches and excite the bodily humors. Also, beware of warm winds, stoves, and everything which produces heat. . . .

Movement and Rest. One should be as quiet as possible. If one needs to move, it should be moderate in order not to strain oneself or cause heavy breathing. The natural heat [of the body] should not be increased so that a person would be forced to breathe more than normal, and thus has to inhale more bad air.

Food and Drink. The best bread is the one you are used to from childhood: wheat of all kinds and barley, if both have been selected with care. It also would not be disadvantageous if bread made from very white, fine flour was replaced by a coarser, black one in order to relax the intestinal channel by thin chymus [food matter]; the opposite is not advisable. . . . [Khātima goes on to list foods he recommends.] The best water is fresh, clear, light running water, or spring water and the like is best. The closer to spring water the better. There's no risk in good barley water, with a little syrup of vinegar and apple syrup, taken in the morning on an empty stomach . . . and all things which calm down the excitement of the blood and cool down the gall, for this appears necessary. Galen recommended big pomegranates: He mentioned that they are of good use against rotting blood; he also recommended the drinking of Armenian clay. . . . [Khātima gives other recipes for medications.]

Sleeping and Waking. The best kind of sleep is normal sleep at night with extension [of the body], which lets the humors ferment, and without contraction, which easily burns up the humors and destroys the life spirit. Sleep should be regulated based on the needs of the individual and the seasons. Day-time napping is not dangerous in the summer. It's advisable to sleep in rooms with a northerly draft in summer; in winter, protected rooms are better.

Elimination and Retention.   There must be regular elimination so that bowel movement remains regular. Retention increases the foul vapors in the body, spoils the life spirit and the bodily fluids, causes lack of appetite and other discomfort. If there's constipation, it should be treated with stewed plums, berries, violet blossoms, tamarind, sugar, and manna, if available. . . . [Khātima lists other remedies.] Cleansing of the stomach by doses of vinegar syrup with warm water or *mel rosarum* [rose petals prepared with honey or sugar] followed by a dose of warm water in which a piece of wet, genuine aloe wood or mastic seeds have been boiled, depending on the character of the person taking the medicine. Vomiting must be avoided, except when it occurs spontaneously and without difficulties for the person who is used to it when compelled. I must stress this aspect, because our people in Andalusia don't throw up so easily. If they were forced, the damage could perhaps be worse than any benefit.

Bleeding.   Here one shouldn't be too fearful or hesitant. It is the best way to maintain one's health during this calamity! . . . But it has to be done, even in the middle of the month when the moon is full or in the second or third hour of the day. If one's powers and age permit, it should be done two or three times [a day], if the person was with a diseased patient or took care of one. Disregard the season, even though normally it has to be observed, but not in this one. The disease changes all seasons into one season, all diseases into one.

I have observed the most wondrous things by bleeding, and I've seen the courage with which people went through it. And I've seen the benefits during the reign of plague. I have seen people who prophylactically gave up to 8 pounds of blood; most people gave about 5. . . .

Intercourse.   If necessary, depending on how one is used to it and on age and strength, this is best to have without force and without disturbing nature, when the seed [semen] flows without exertion, when one feels serene and fresh and no weakness in the limbs follows. Forced intercourse weakens and attacks the life force, especially when it is conducted under duress.

Bathing. When necessary, this is best in a bathing room,* with good and fresh air and lukewarm and agreeable water. The duration should only be as long as the servant is cleansing the body. There shouldn't be any exertion, because this excites the natural [body] heat, which makes the blood boil and, due to circumstances, makes it congregate in one part of the body. After bathing, one should dress in linen clothes, perfumed with a little vinegary rose extract and leaf, but not right away, and gradually. It is safer, though, to do without bathing, even with these precautions. I've seen many dangerous consequences, which could hardly be remedied.

Psychic Aspects. It is most expedient to create joy, serenity, relaxation, and hope. One should attempt to create them with permitted means as often as possible. One should seek out agreeable, dear, and charming company. The best companion is God's own book, of which he [Muhammad] said: "We give many things from the Koran in which healing and grace for believers can be found." Otherwise, read books on history, humor, and romances. Let me warn of disparaging others, especially when it is accompanied by sadness. The latter should be avoided, because it is one of the main causes of the calamity. It strikes intellectuals the hardest, least of all idiots and indolents. Avoid all excitement, all anger and horror, in short, everything which causes emotion.

These are the prescriptions we have for prevention of the disease. They must be followed to the letter without deviation, because major fires start with a small spark. Rely on God; He is the best and most compassionate protector. . . .

Therapy before the Disease Takes Root. . . . Therefore, we found no easier and more successful treatment than bleeding, especially if it is performed immediately when there are signs of the disease, and before the fever takes hold and gruesome symptoms appear. As I've seen myself, I've had miraculous results by bleeding. The sooner it is done, the better chances the treatment has, and that is the main thing with this disease. . . . A fair amount of blood has to be drained, until the

---

*Bathing was much more common in the Muslim world than in the Christian West. Whereas Islam stresses the importance of purification, medieval Christians associated bathing with immorality in general and with houses of prostitution in particular. The medical faculty of the University of Paris, for example, advised people to avoid hot-water baths, except just prior to bleeding when it could help loosen up bad humors and so expel them.

well no wonder the plague is spreading, people are nasty

patient experiences a feeling of faintness, depending on strength and age.* One mustn't wait until the blood has a normal density or color; usually with this disease, it is thickened and black. Its characteristics won't change, even if it were drained completely. Sometimes a thin, greenish liquid comes to the surface, or a grayish mass; that's a very bad sign. If the patient faints before the proper amount is drained, sprinkle his face and extremities with water until he comes back [to consciousness]; then finish the drainage. . . .

A man from Homma Biggana, a village near Almería, came to me and told me that he and some twenty people from the village had fled from there for fear of the plague, which was ravaging the village. He complained about anxiety, depression, arterial cramps, which was his first indication of the disease. I prescribed an immediate bleeding, and twenty-two ounces of blood were drawn. He fully recovered, as if he hadn't had anything. He went on his way, but only a block or two, and then he returned in an identical state as before the bleeding. I felt his pulse, observed him and saw the same symptoms. I ordered another bleeding, and this time eighteen ounces were drawn. This time he was fully free of fever, with only a little weakness, but he was able to walk home. He was rid of his pains and fully healed. I saw him later; he said he was the only one still alive from among those with whom he had fled. It all happened in one week. I don't mention the story of this man as a rare triumph of bloodletting. My experiences in that field are countless. There are countless people, whose number God knows, who were kept alive by this measure. Thus is the might and will of God.

Therapy after the Disease Has Taken Hold. You must realize that the treatment of the disease once it has progressed doesn't make much sense. But since it helps some of those whose case isn't so serious, and for whom God has ordained healing, we must briefly describe our measures which we garnered from experience. . . . [Khātima proceeds to give an explanation of how various symptoms of the disease appear on the body, including the Galenic theory that buboes form at the emunctories, or the drainage points for the body's poisons, i.e. behind the ears for "head materials," the armpits for "heart materials," and the groin for "liver materials."]

*Not all medieval doctors practiced such extreme bloodletting, and Khātima himself advised against extreme bloodletting in the case of those already infected with plague.

[Handwritten margin notes: "what is that?"; "Were these people who were 'immune'?"]

If you ask why treatment shows no results, even when the disease shows these characteristics and symptoms and a prescribed treatment—such as is described by me and outlined by the greatest medical specialists—is done without fail, we have to answer thus. Whenever diseases attack man with a change in the air but without pestilence, the temperament of the heart remains healthy, its natural heat remains intact, and at the most it is disturbed accidentally by the seat of the core of the disease. In this case, the heart takes care of re-establishing order in any way, it distributes the medication to the points where they are needed, and for this reason, treatment is successful and it works. If the disturbance occurs in a time of pestilence, the heart is unable to fulfill its tasks vis-à-vis the other organs because of the corruption of its temperament and the extinguishing of its natural heat. It is unable to distribute medications; indeed, it is even incapable of healing itself. It is small wonder then that the effects of medication don't show and then death reaps the patient in an early or late state of the disease.

However, since treatment was successful in a few cases where God ordained healing, we shall mention what science has worked out, what experience confirms, and whatever proves to be useful. . . .

Buboes.   They can be recognized by palpation, by progressing, piercing pain, or a feeling of pressure in a specific location. They may occur without preceding pain because the symptoms of all kinds of this disease resemble each other. Usually they are accompanied by a freezing sensation of the skin, dull pain in the bones, a heavy feeling in internal organs, spasms in the blood vessels, a fever, but not too high, and there may be other [symptoms]. . . .

Should the patient suffer from a suffocating attack, but neither from repeated, gall-containing vomiting, nor from persistent diarrhea, and if he's not been ill for more than two days, under those circumstances, there are no obstacles to a moderate bleeding, with due consideration for age and strength. The bleeding must occur relative to the painful spot from a suitable blood vessel. It has to be done from the opposite side if the pain is located in the underarm, but on the same side if it is behind the ears or in the groin. Let me warn against extending the bleeding until fainting. Before and after the bleeding, the patient should be administered one potion or another to strengthen the heart and calm the seething of the blood. Two of these potions are: 1) apple syrup, mixed with vinegar syrup and thickened bitteroil juice, or its syrup, or lime syrup; 2) lemon acid, dissolved in rose water with dissolved musk. If these should be beneficial, it is good; if not, there is some relief until death occurs, and it lessens the damage which the nurse suffers from the foul vapors and excrements. Consider this advantage and don't let it slip past! . . . [Khātima gives various recipes for restorative potions to be taken internally, as well as poultices or plasters to be applied externally to the buboes. When the buboes "mature" so that the "blood in them has changed to pus," Khātima advises "to resolve them surgically," or cut them. However, he warns against doing so prematurely.]

A bloodletter told me of a case where an ignorant person, an interloper in his profession, once ordered him to cut into such a boil in the underarm which had just appeared and wasn't ready. As he did this, bright red blood streamed forth, the patient lost consciousness, his heart suffered a collapse and before they left the place the patient had expired. I've also heard of another case where a dissolute man got such a boil in his groin. The pain made him impatient and he took his razor to open it: The blood gushed out and he died immediately.* A reliable informant told me via Christian merchants who had come to Almería that a doctor investigated a buboe on a corpse. His investigation showed that this place is connected by blood vessels to the heart. This report is correct, and research and theory support it. . . .

Spitting Blood.   There is no treatment. Except for one young man, I haven't seen anyone who was cured and lived. It puzzles me still. Right away, on the second day, he brought up blood. Since the blood symptoms were present, I prescribed bloodletting; twenty-four ounces of blood were drawn from his anatomizing blood vessel. Afterwards, he breathed easily, the blood spitting ceased and his general condition improved. During the night, the symptoms returned, including the blood spitting, which this time resembled water in which meat had been. I ordered another bloodletting from the same blood vessel of the other hand; this time, sixteen ounces were drawn and improvement occurred. The blood he brought up got lighter, until it ceased altogether and recovery began. The patient was quite weak. I strengthened him, and in three weeks he had recovered fully and remained healthy and strong. This is a rare occurrence, the only case of this

---

*Evidently, in these cases the patient's artery was severed, a frequent hazard of unskilled bloodletting.

how many died because of blood loss rather than disease?

kind I was able to observe. The usual lack of success is explained by the fact that the blood vessels of the lung shred and tear because of the sharpness and the large amount of blood entering the lungs.

14

GUI DE CHAULIAC

Great Surgery
1363 post plague ',

Gui de Chauliac was one of the leading medical authorities of his day. Physician to three popes, Clement VI (1342–1352), Innocent VI (1352–1362), and Urban V (1362–1370), Chauliac studied medicine at the University of Toulouse and then at Montpellier and Bologna. Around 1363 he wrote what became a widely read medical textbook, Inventarium seu Collectorium in parte Cyrurgicali Medicine *(A Partial Inventory or Collection of Surgical Medicine), often known simply as the* Grande Chirurgie, *or* Great Surgery. *Although Chauliac describes both the plagues of 1348 and 1360–61 in this work, only the former description is included here. Chauliac was in an excellent position to observe the Black Death's symptoms; he himself contracted the bubonic form of the disease during the first outbreak. He died at Lyon in 1368.*

Therefore the said mortality began for us [in Avignon] in the month of January [1348], and lasted seven months. And it took two forms: the first lasted two months, accompanied by continuous fever and a spitting up of blood, and one died within three days. The second lasted the rest of the time, also accompanied by continuous fever and by apostemes [tumors] and antraci [carbuncles] on the external parts, principally under the armpits and in the groin, and one died within

Heinrich Haeser, *Lehrbuch der Geschichte der Medizin und der epidemischen Krankheiten,* 2 vols. (Jena: Mauke, 1853–65), 2:175–76.

[handwritten in left margin: It did reach parts of North America]

five days. And the mortality was so contagious, especially in those who were spitting up blood, that not only did one get it from another by living together, but also by looking at each other,* to the point that people died without servants and were buried without priests. The father did not visit his son, nor the son his father; charity was dead, hope crushed.

And I call the mortality great because it overtook the whole world, or nearly all of it. But it began in the East, and like shooting arrows it passed through us on its way west. And it was so great, that it hardly left a quarter of the human race. And it was unheard of, because we only read of the mortality in the cities of Thrace and Palestine in the *Book of Epidemics*† written in the time of Hippocrates [ca. 460–377 BCE], and of the mortality that afflicted the Roman subjects in the book, *De Epidemia*,‡ in the time of Galen [ca. 129–216 CE], and of the mortality in the city of Rome in the time of [Pope] Gregory [the Great, 590–604 CE]. And none was as great as this one, because those others only attacked a single region, [but] this the whole world. Those others were curable in some way; this in none. For the mortality rendered doctors useless and put them to shame, because they did not dare visit the sick out of fear of being infected. And when they did visit them, they could do little for them and were paid nothing. For all who got sick died, except for a few toward the end, who escaped when their buboes ripened.

Many were uncertain about the cause of this great mortality. In some places, they believed that the Jews had poisoned the world, and so they killed them. In some other areas, that it was a deformity of the poor, and they chased them out; in others, that it was the nobles, and

[handwritten: There was a lot of social blame]

---

*A treatise by an anonymous medical practitioner of Montpellier was devoted to explaining plague contagion by sight. According to this work, written in May 1349, the plague can kill "almost instantly," as "when an aerial spirit leaves the eyes of a sick person and strikes the eyes of a healthy man attending him, especially when he is looking at the sick man in his death throes." Euclid's theory of mirrors generating fire, and the mythical basilisk and Aristotle's Venomous Virgin, both of which can kill on sight, are cited in support of sight contagion.

†This was a collection of case studies probably compiled by a variety of authors who traveled throughout the Greek world. Their main explanation for diseases was bad air, an idea known as the miasmatic theory.

‡This was Galen's commentary on the Hippocratic *Epidemics,* one of many commentaries that he wrote on Hippocrates.

so they [the nobles] hesitated to go out into the world. Finally, it reached the point where guards were posted in cities and towns, and they permitted no one to enter, unless he was well known. And if they found anyone with powders or unguents, they made him swallow them, fearing that these might be poisons.

Regardless of what people might say, the truth was that the cause of this mortality was twofold: one, a universal active cause, the other a particular, passive one.... [Chauliac describes the universal cause as the conjunction of Saturn, Jupiter, and Mars on March 24, 1345.] For [the conjunction] made such an impression upon the air and the other elements that, just as a magnet moves iron, so it changed the thick humors [of the body] into something scorched and venomous, and shepherded them into the interior. And it made apostemes, from which followed continuous fevers and a spitting up of blood in the early stages, when the corrupted blood was strong and disturbed the body's constitution. And afterwards, when the constitution was in remission, it was not so greatly disturbed, and it expelled [the corrupt humors] as well as it could to the external parts, especially to the armpits and the groin. And this caused buboes and other apostemes, so that the exterior apostemes were the effect of interior apostemes. The particular, passive cause was the body's disposition, such as if it was full of evil humors, if it was weak, or bunged up [obstructed]. And for this reason it was the common people, the laborers, and those who lived evil lives who died.

Concerning cures, there was an effort [to find] a preservative before the advent of symptoms and a cure for when symptoms had arrived. For preservation, there was nothing better than to flee the area before it was infected and to purge oneself with pills of aloe and reduce the blood through a phlebotomy, purify the air with a fire, and comfort the heart with a theriac and fruits and sweet-smelling things, to console the humors with Armenian bole, and to halt corruption with sour-tasting things.

For a cure, there are phlebotomies and purgatives [probably vomit-inducing substances or laxatives] and electuaries and syrupy cordials. And the external apostemes were ripened with figs and onions that were cooked and ground up and mixed with leavened bread dough and butter. Afterwards the apostemes would open and they were healed with a treatment for ulcers. The antraci [carbuncles] were ventosed [i.e., a cupping-glass applied], scarified [i.e., cut open], and cauterized.

And I, in order to avoid a bad reputation, did not dare depart [from Avignon], but with a continuous fear I preserved myself as best I could with the aforesaid remedies.* Nonetheless, toward the end of the mortality, I fell into a continuous fever, with an aposteme on the groin, and I was sick for nearly six weeks. And I was in such great danger that all of my friends believed that I would die. And the aposteme ripened and healed, as I have described above, [and] I escaped by God's command.

*Chauliac's decision to stay and tend to the sick in Avignon was not necessarily a choice on his part. According to the medieval biography of Pope Clement VI, Clement "ordered certain doctors and others who ministered to his necessities in life to visit and succor the poor" during the mortality.

4

Societal and Economic Impact

The Black Death severed, at least temporarily, many of the bonds and norms that held medieval society together. Observers movingly describe mass burial scenes (see Figure 1), and the heart-wrenching abandonment of even close family members is described by chronicler after chronicler, including Boccaccio in Florence (Document 16) and Agnolo di Tura in Siena (Document 17). There was a perceived moral laxity in the wake of the Black Death, when a cathartic release of emotions supposedly occurred that swept away a host of social and economic restraints. Any attempts to stem the tide, such as the mandates against concubinage, swearing, and dice-making tried by the city aldermen of Tournai, were short lived.[1]

However, one might argue that such lamentations on the collapse of social mores and customs are literary conventions rather than objective observations of reality. Even before the advent of the Black Death, Jean de Venette and Gilles li Muisis wrote of a social slackening among the inhabitants of Paris and Tournai, respectively.[2] By contrast, a truly unique account of the social effects of the disease is provided by the Italian poet Francesco Petrarch, who mourns the loss of friends and muses on the apparent indifference of an overvengeful God to the travails of humanity during the Black Death (Document 15). Although Petrarch pulls back from the brink of modern atheistic, or even agnostic, despair, his humanistic attempt to approach the disease from an individualistic perspective represents a departure from traditional historical writing. Along with his friend Boccaccio, Petrarch perhaps perceived the need for a new kind of history to chronicle an event on the scale of the Black Death.[3] Petrarch's subjective approach, which challenged the old assumptions, may well be more trustworthy as a social record of the plague than the common denunciations of moral laxity in response to calamity.

Historians have been rather more confident of the difficult economic realities caused by the Black Death. Typically, chroniclers like

Figure 1. Survivors burying the dead in coffins, as mandated by a city ordinance, during the Black Death at Tournai in Flanders in 1349. From a late medieval manuscript copy of the *Chronicle* of Gilles li Muisis. Bibliothèque Royale de Belgique, Brussels, Belgium/Bridgeman Art Library.

Henry Knighton, a canon of Leicester Abbey in England who was writing during the 1390s, testified that the excessive mortality created a shortage of both producers and consumers. The overall effect of this shortage was that wages of agricultural laborers went up and prices of goods went down, resulting in higher living standards for serfs but lower manorial incomes for their lords.[4] But Knighton, like the Muslim chronicler al-Maqrīzī, who recorded a similar set of economic responses in Egypt (Document 19), was writing quite some time after the Black Death had first struck Europe in 1348. His impressions, therefore, may be colored by the cumulative effect of successive plague strikes.

Perhaps better medieval evidence exists in the labor legislation passed during or immediately after the Black Death by the city councils, monarchies, and representative assemblies of Italy, England, France, and Spain (Documents 20 and 21). These documents reveal that wages were indeed rising because of the Black Death, but so were prices, which the English ordinance of 1349 tried to keep "reasonable." English manorial records confirm that prices remained high until the 1370s, which would have negated the buying power of higher wages; peasant laborers, however, may have been compensated in other, "hidden" ways that substantially raised their standards of living, such as increased leisure time and freedom of employment, as suggested by labor laws that complained that peasants were idle.[5] Labor laws specified that lords who granted higher wages were to be punished alongside the serfs who accepted them, which implies that in some cases the new market forces created by the Black Death were so irresistible that only more draconian measures could halt them. But, in fact, the evidence for the enforcement of labor laws, almost exclusively consisting of English court rolls (Document 22), is contradictory. The "hundreds of thousands" of cases of laborers that came before the justices each year may either be evidence of "zealous" enforcement or of rampant evasion.[6] There was thus both a concerted effort by peasants to evade the new laws and an equally determined effort by the English gentry, the dominant presence in the Commons and the local courts, to make the laws stick (provided those being prosecuted were not of their class). Collectively, these labor laws represent a conservative reaction on the part of Europe's ruling elite: a bold attempt to turn back the economic clock to a time before the Black Death.

Europeans' response to the Black Death therefore had almost as great an impact on late medieval society and economy as the devastating mortality of the plague itself. But the long-term social and economic effects of the Black Death are contradictory and extremely complex. Scholars have focused much attention on the plague's impact upon family life throughout the rest of the Middle Ages, with attempts to quantify changes in marriage and fertility rates. Although the mean age at marriage rose in some parts of England in the aftermath of the Black Death, indicating that women deliberately delayed marrying and having children in order to take advantage of new employment opportunities, this measure behaves very differently in other places in Europe, particularly in Mediterranean regions, where it drops, seemingly in response to high mortality.

The Black Death also inaugurated a revolution in the medieval manorial economy. The variety of peasants' experience with labor services and laws created tensions in society that finally erupted in the English Peasants' Revolt of 1381.[7] The death knell of the medieval manorial economy, with a complete transition from serfdom to a rent-paying class, which the English rebels demanded in 1381, finally came to pass in the fifteenth century as the result of repeated plague strikes that kept Europe's population in decline, or at least in stagnation, until 1450. Emancipation, higher wages and living standards, greater land-holdings, and the labor-saving devices that became available as a result of the economic necessities imposed by the Black Death may indeed have dramatically improved the lives of peasant survivors. On the other hand, agricultural laborers in the Muslim lands of Egypt and Syria do not seem to have enjoyed these benefits.[8] It is also important to not forget the very human cost of the new world created by the Black Death. In the words of one economic historian of the plague: "Clearly an age which relies for its prosperity upon large numbers of its members dying at an early age, and suffering the frequent losses of spouses, children, relatives, friends and colleagues, is somewhat less than golden."[9] Especially in an "age of faith," one must measure quality of life in more than just material terms.

NOTES

[1] *Recueil des chroniques de Flandre,* ed. Joseph-Jean de Smet, 4 vols. (Brussels, 1837–65), 2:379–81.

[2] *Chronique Latin de Guillaume de Nangis de 1113 à 1300, avec les continuations de cette chronique,* ed. Hercule Géraud, 2 vols. (Paris: J. Renouard et cie, 1843), 2:185; *Recueil des chroniques de Flandre,* 2:346–47.

[3] Timothy Kircher, "Anxiety and Freedom in Boccaccio's History of the Plague of 1348," *Letteratura Italiana antica,* 3 (2002): 325–57.

[4] Henry Knighton, *Chronicon,* ed. Joseph Rawson Lumby, 2 vols. (Rolls Series, 92, 1889–95), 2:62.

[5] D. L. Farmer, "Crop Yields, Prices, and Wages in Medieval England," *Studies in Medieval and Renaissance History,* n.s. 6 (1983): 117–55; idem, "Prices and Wages, 1350–1500," in *Agrarian History of England and Wales: Vol. 3, 1348–1500,* ed. E. Miller (Cambridge: Cambridge University Press, 1991), 431–525; John Hatchei, "England in the Aftermath of the Black Death," *Past and Present,* 144 (1994): 3–35.

[6] Simon A. C. Penn and Christopher Dyer, "Wages and Earnings in Late Medieval England: Evidence from the Enforcement of the Labour Laws," *Economic History Review,* 2nd ser. 43 (1990): 359; E. B. Fryde, *Peasants and Landlords in Later Medieval England* (New York: St. Martin's Press, 1996), 35.

[7] L. R. Poos, "The Social Context of Statute of Labourers Enforcement," *Law and History Review,* 1 (1983): 27–52; Christopher Dyer, "The Social and Economic Background to the Rural Revolt of 1381," in *The English Rising of 1381,* ed. R. H. Hilton and T. H. Aston (Cambridge: Cambridge University Press, 1984), 9–42.

[8] Michael W. Dols, *The Black Death in the Middle East* (Princeton, N.J.: Princeton University Press, 1977), 281–83.

[9] John Hatcher, *Plague, Population, and the English Economy, 1348–1530* (London: Macmillan, 1977), 73.

15

FRANCESCO PETRARCH

Letters on Familiar Matters

May 1349

One of the giants of early Renaissance Florence, Francesco Petrarch, born in Arezzo in 1304, helped define the emerging spirit of humanism, an intellectual movement that looked back to classical antiquity as the pinnacle of civilization and viewed human endeavors as a fit subject for study. Along with Dante, Villani, and his friend, Boccaccio, Petrarch helped create the first vernacular literature in Italian, although he also wrote extensively in Latin. Yet Petrarch was also firmly rooted in the events of his times, including the Black Death. The following selection is from a letter he wrote from Parma in May 1349 to his friend in Avignon, Louis

Francesco Petrarch, *Epistolae de Rebus Familiaribus et Variae,* ed. Giuseppe Fracassetti, 3 vols. (Florence: Typis Felicis le Monnier, 1859–63), 1:438–40, 442–44.

Sanctus, whom he nicknamed "Socrates." Petrarch laments the effect that the plague is having on human friendship. The letter is part of a collection, Epistolae de Rebus Familiaribus (Letters on Familiar Matters), that he dedicated to Sanctus. Petrarch died in 1374.

If you wish to bemoan the fates of all mortal men, one breast and one tongue will not suffice for you. You have taken on an enormous, miserable, and irksome subject, useless, inexplicable. Tears must be sought from another source: Indeed, they are always springing up out of some recent and unending cause of sorrow, and the two eyes, already worn out, exhausted and dried up, can pour out only a little melancholy moisture. What therefore can you do to forget, except spread the poison, proffered as medicine, to your friends, not being content with your own misery and sickness, in which you keep knowing and wishing that you would fall? . . .

In the year 1348, one that I deplore, we were deprived not only of our friends but of peoples throughout all the world. If anyone escaped, the following year mowed down others, and whatever had been passed over by the storm, is then pursued by a deadly scythe. When will posterity believe this to have been a time in which nearly the whole world—not just this or that part of the earth—is bereft of inhabitants, without there having occurred a conflagration in the heavens or on land, without wars or other visible disasters? When at any time has such a thing been seen or spoken of? Has what happened in these years ever been read about: empty houses, derelict cities, ruined estates, fields strewn with cadavers, a horrible and vast solitude encompassing the whole world? Consult historians, they are silent; ask physicians, they are stupefied; seek the answer from philosophers, they shrug their shoulders, furrow their brows, and with fingers pressed against their lips, bid you be silent. Will posterity believe these things, when we who have seen it can scarcely believe it, thinking it a dream except that we are awake and see these things with our open eyes, and when we know that what we bemoan is absolutely true, as in a city fully lit by the torches of its funerals we head for home, finding our longed-for security in its emptiness? O happy people of the next generation, who will not know these miseries and most probably will reckon our testimony as a fable!

I do not deny that we deserve these misfortunes and even worse; but our forebears deserved them too, and may posterity not deserve them in turn. Therefore why is it, most Just of judges, why is it that the seething rage of Your vengeance has fallen so particularly hard upon our times? Why is it that in times when guilt was not lacking, the lessons of punishment were withheld? While all have sinned alike, we alone bear the lash. We alone, I say; for I hear it affirmed that compared to the number we receive at present, the lashes inflicted upon all men after that most famous ark [of Noah] had borne the remnants of humanity upon the formless sea would have been a delight, a joke, and a respite. Even when it behooves us to wage countless wars against these evils, in the course of which many kinds of remedies are tried, in the end it is not permitted to men to at least die with dignity. For it is a rare solace of death to die well. No remedy is exactly right, and there is no solace. And to the accumulated disaster is added not knowing the causes and origin of the evil. For neither ignorance nor even the plague itself is more hateful than the nonsense and tall tales of certain men, who profess to know everything but in fact know nothing. Nonetheless their mouths, although accustomed to lying, are in the end silent, and although at first impudence had opened them out of habit, at last they are closed by stupidity.

But I return to my inquiry: Whether for those making a long journey it happens that one part of the way is tiring, another easy. For so it is with us that Your forbearance, God, has slackened little by little toward human crimes, and under the heavy burden of Your yoke, the Omnipotent now must set down His provisions, and You, the best traveler, no longer able to support us, throw us onto Your back and in Your anger avert Your eyes of mercy from us. What if we are making atonement not just for our crimes, but also for those of our fathers, whether these be worse I do not know, but certainly they were more pitiable. Or could it be perhaps that certain great truths are to be held suspect, that God does not care for mortal men? But let us drive these foolish thoughts from our minds. If God did not care for us, there would be nothing left to sustain us. For who will provide these necessities for us, if they are not attributed to God, but to nature; what feeling will be left to us, why give ourselves over to the quest for truth? Since Seneca* calls most ungrateful all those who neglect their duties to God, under a different name, are they not denying His due of heavenly majesty by impiously mocking Him? Surely You do care for

---

*Lucius Annaeus Seneca, 4 BCE–65 CE, tutor and advisor to Emperor Nero, was an important writer and leading exponent of the Stoic school of philosophy.

us and our affairs, God. But there is some reason, hidden and un-known to us, why down through all the ages we, who are the most dignified of Your creatures, seem to be the ones most severely pun-ished. Not that Your justice is less because it is concealed, for the depth of Your judgments is inscrutable and inaccessible to human senses. Therefore either we are truly the worst of all beings, which I would like to deny but dare not, or God is reserving us for some future good the more He is exercising and purging us from these present evils, or there is something there that we are altogether un-able to conceive. In any case, whatever the reasons may be and how-ever many are hidden from us, the results are most evident. . . .

Where are our sweet friends now? Where are the beloved faces? Where are the agreeable words, where the soothing and pleasant con-versation? What lightning bolt devoured them? What earthquake over-turned them? What storm submerged them? What abyss swallowed them? Once we were all together, now we are quite alone. We should make new friends, but where or with whom, when the human race is nearly extinct, and it is predicted that the end of the world is soon at hand? We are—why pretend?—truly alone. . . . You see that our great band of friends is reduced in number. And behold, even as we speak we too are drifting apart, and we vanish like shadows. And in the same moment that one hears that the other is gone, he is soon following in his footsteps. . . .

Never does it seem to me to be a sadder occasion than when one inquires with trepidation after a friend. How goes it? How is our friend doing? But as soon as he has heard you say "farewell," he is filled with dread and very quickly his face is wet with tears. And indeed he—I cannot say this without shedding many tears, and I would shed many now when I say this, except that with all the evil events that have hap-pened these eyes have become exhausted and I would rather save all the rest of my tears, if there are any left, for when they are needed—I say that he is suddenly seized by this pestilential disease, which is now ravaging the world, toward evening, after a dinner with friends and that at sundown he goes to bed, after having digested so much from our conversation in the remembrance of our friendship and our exploits together. He passes that night among his last sorrows in a greatly terrified frame of mind. But in the morning he succumbs to a quick death, and as if this misfortune were not enough, within three days, his sons and all his family follow him.

16

GIOVANNI BOCCACCIO

Introduction to The Decameron

1349–1351

*In this selection, Boccaccio describes the social and psychological effects
of the Black Death in Florence, following upon his accounts of the symptoms and transmission of the plague in Document 6. This portion of the
introduction to* The Decameron *is famous for a number of striking
observations that Boccaccio makes about the way his fellow Florentines
responded to the disease: how even close family members changed the
way they related to each other; how human responses fell into one of
three characteristic behaviors—isolation, denial, and moderation; and
how funerals changed as the mortality began to rise.*

Some people were of the opinion that a sober and abstemious mode of
living considerably reduced the risk of infection. They therefore
formed themselves into groups and lived in isolation from everyone
else. Having withdrawn to a comfortable abode where there were no
sick persons, they locked themselves in and settled down to a peace-
able existence, consuming modest quantities of delicate foods and precious wines and avoiding all excesses. They refrained from speaking
to outsiders, refused to receive news of the dead or the sick, and
entertained themselves with music and whatever other amusements
they were able to devise.

Others took the opposite view, and maintained that an infallible way
of warding off this appalling evil was to drink heavily, enjoy life to the
full, go round singing and merrymaking, gratify all of one's cravings
whenever the opportunity offered, and shrug the whole thing off as
one enormous joke. Moreover, they practiced what they preached to
the best of their ability, for they would visit one tavern after another,
drinking all day and night to immoderate excess; or alternatively (and

Giovanni Boccaccio, *The Decameron,* trans. G. H. McWilliam (Harmondsworth, Middle-
sex: Penguin Books, 1972), 52–57.

this was their more frequent custom), they would do their drinking in various private houses, but only in the ones where the conversation was restricted to subjects that were pleasant and entertaining. Such places were easy to find, for people behaved as though their days were numbered, and treated their belongings and their own persons with equal abandon. Hence most houses had become common property, and any passing stranger could make himself at home as naturally as though he were the rightful owner. But for all their riotous manner of living, these people always took good care to avoid any contact with the sick.

In the face of so much affliction and misery, all respect for the laws of God and man had virtually broken down and been extinguished in our city [of Florence]. For like everybody else, those ministers and executors of the laws who were not either dead or ill were left with so few subordinates that they were unable to discharge any of their duties. Hence everyone was free to behave as he pleased.

There were many other people who steered a middle course between the two already mentioned, neither restricting their diet to the same degree as the first group, nor indulging so freely as the second in drinking and other forms of wantonness, but simply doing no more than satisfy their appetite. Instead of incarcerating themselves, these people moved about freely, holding in their hands a posy of flowers or fragrant herbs, or one of a wide range of spices, which they applied at frequent intervals to their nostrils, thinking it an excellent idea to fortify the brain with smells of that particular sort; for the stench of dead bodies, sickness, and medicines seemed to fill and pollute the whole of the atmosphere.

Some people, pursuing what was possibly the safer alternative, callously maintained that there was no better or more efficacious remedy against a plague than to run away from it. Swayed by this argument, and sparing no thought for anyone but themselves, large numbers of men and women abandoned their city, their homes, their relatives, their estates and their belongings, and headed for the countryside, either in Florentine territory or, better still, abroad. It was as though they imagined that the wrath of God would not unleash this plague against men for their iniquities irrespective of where they happened to be, but would only be aroused against those who found themselves within the city walls; or possibly they assumed that the whole of the population would be exterminated and that the city's last hour had come.

Of the people who held these various opinions, not all of them died. Nor, however, did they all survive. On the contrary, many of each different persuasion fell ill here, there, and everywhere, and having themselves, when they were fit and well, set an example to those who were as yet unaffected, they languished away with virtually no one to nurse them. It was not merely a question of one citizen avoiding another, and of people almost invariably neglecting their neighbors and rarely or never visiting their relatives, addressing them only from a distance; this scourge had implanted so great a terror in the hearts of men and women that brothers abandoned brothers, uncles their nephews, sisters their brothers, and in many cases wives deserted their husbands. But even worse, and almost incredible, was the fact that fathers and mothers refused to nurse and assist their own children, as though they did not belong to them.

Hence the countless numbers of people who fell ill, both male and female, were entirely dependent upon either the charity of friends (who were few and far between) or the greed of servants, who remained in short supply despite the attraction of high wages out of all proportion to the services they performed. Furthermore, these latter were men and women of coarse intellect and the majority were unused to such duties, and they did little more than hand things to the invalid when asked to do so and watch over him when he was dying. And in performing this kind of service, they frequently lost their lives as well as their earnings.

As a result of this wholesale desertion of the sick by neighbors, relatives, and friends, and in view of the scarcity of servants, there grew up a practice almost never previously heard of, whereby when a woman fell ill, no matter how gracious or beautiful or gently bred she might be, she raised no objection to being attended by a male servant, whether he was young or not. Nor did she have any scruples about showing him every part of her body as freely as she would have displayed it to a woman, provided that the nature of her infirmity required her to do so; and this explains why those women who recovered were possibly less chaste in the period that followed.

Moreover a great many people died who would perhaps have survived had they received some assistance. And hence, what with the lack of appropriate means for tending the sick, and the virulence of the plague, the number of deaths reported in the city whether by day or night was so enormous that it astonished all who heard tell of it, to say nothing of the people who actually witnessed the carnage. And it was perhaps inevitable that among the citizens who survived there arose certain customs that were quite contrary to established tradition.

It had once been customary, as it is again nowadays, for the women relatives and neighbors of a dead man to assemble in his house in order to mourn in the company of the women who had been closest to him; moreover his kinsfolk would forgather in front of his house along with his neighbors and various other citizens, and there would be a contingent of priests, whose numbers varied according to the quality of the deceased; his body would be taken thence to the church in which he had wanted to be buried, being borne on the shoulders of his peers amidst the funeral pomp of candles and dirges. But as the ferocity of the plague began to mount, this practice all but disappeared entirely and was replaced by different customs. For not only did people die without having many women about them, but a great number departed this life without anyone at all to witness their going. Few indeed were those to whom the lamentations and bitter tears of their relatives were accorded; on the contrary, more often than not bereavement was the signal for laughter and witticisms and general jollification—the art of which the women, having for the most part suppressed their feminine concern for the salvation of the souls of the dead, had learned to perfection. Moreover it was rare for the bodies of the dead to be accompanied by more than ten or twelve neighbors to the church, nor were they borne on the shoulders of worthy and honest citizens, but by a kind of gravedigging fraternity, newly come into being and drawn from the lower orders of society. These people assumed the title of sexton, and demanded a fat fee for their services, which consisted in taking up the coffin and hauling it swiftly away, not to the church specified by the dead man in his will, but usually to the nearest at hand. They would be preceded by a group of four or six clerics, who between them carried one or two candles at most, and sometimes none at all. Nor did the priests go to the trouble of pronouncing solemn and lengthy funeral rites, but, with the aid of these so-called sextons, they hastily lowered the body into the nearest empty grave they could find.

As for the common people and a large proportion of the bourgeoisie, they presented a much more pathetic spectacle, for the majority of them were constrained, either by their poverty or the hope of survival, to remain in their houses. Being confined to their own parts of the city, they fell ill daily in their thousands, and since they had no one to assist them or attend to their needs, they inevitably perished almost without exception. Many dropped dead in the open streets, both by day and by night, whilst a great many others, though dying in their own houses, drew their neighbors' attention to the fact more by the smell of their rotting corpses than by any other means. And what with these, and the others who were dying all over the city, bodies were here, there, and everywhere.

Whenever people died, their neighbors nearly always followed a single, set routine, prompted as much by their fear of being contaminated by the decaying corpse as by any charitable feelings they may have entertained toward the deceased. Either on their own, or with the assistance of bearers whenever these were to be had, they extracted the bodies of the dead from their houses and left them lying outside their front doors, where anyone going about the streets, especially in the early morning, could have observed countless numbers of them. Funeral biers would then be sent for, upon which the dead were taken away, though there were some who, for lack of biers, were carried off on plain boards. It was by no means rare for more than one of these biers to be seen with two or three bodies upon it at a time; on the contrary, many were seen to contain a husband and wife, two or three brothers and sisters, a father and son, or some other pair of close relatives. And times without number it happened that two priests would be on their way to bury someone, holding a cross before them, only to find that bearers carrying three or four additional biers would fall in behind them; so that whereas the priests had thought they had only one burial to attend to, they in fact had six or seven, and sometimes more. Even in these circumstances, however, there were no tears or candles or mourners to honor the dead; in fact, no more respect was accorded to dead people than would nowadays be shown toward dead goats. For it was quite apparent that the one thing which, in normal times, no wise man had ever learned to accept with patient resignation (even though it struck so seldom and unobtrusively), had now been brought home to the feeble-minded as well, but the scale of the calamity caused them to regard it with indifference.

Such was the multitude of corpses (of which further consignments were arriving every day and almost by the hour at each of the churches), that there was not sufficient consecrated ground for them to be buried in, especially if each was to have its own plot in accordance with long-established custom. So when all the graves were full, huge trenches were excavated in the churchyards, into which new arrivals were placed in their hundreds, stowed tier upon tier like ships' cargo, each layer of corpses being covered over with a thin layer of soil till the trench was filled to the top. . . .*

---

*Another Florentine chronicler, Marchionne di Coppo Stefani, compared the layering of dirt and bodies in mass graves to "how one layers lasagna with cheese."

I must mention that, whilst an ill wind was blowing through Florence itself, the surrounding region was no less badly affected. In the fortified towns, conditions were similar to those in the city itself on a minor scale; but in the scattered hamlets and the countryside proper, the poor unfortunate peasants and their families had no physicians or servants whatever to assist them, and collapsed by the wayside, in their fields, and in their cottages at all hours of the day and night, dying more like animals than human beings. Like the townspeople, they too grew apathetic in their ways, disregarded their affairs, and neglected their possessions. Moreover they all behaved as though each day was to be their last, and far from making provision for the future by tilling their lands, tending their flocks, and adding to their previous labors, they tried in every way they could think of to squander the assets already in their possession. Thus it came about that oxen, asses, sheep, goats, pigs, chickens, and even dogs (for all their deep fidelity to man) were driven away and allowed to roam freely through the fields, where the crops lay abandoned and had not even been reaped, let alone gathered in. And after a whole day's feasting, many of these animals, as though possessing the power of reason, would return glutted in the evening to their own quarters, without any shepherd to guide them.

17

AGNOLO DI TURA

Sienese Chronicle

1348–1351

Siena, a town south of Florence in Tuscany, was struck by the Black Death in April or May 1348. The town's chronicler, Agnolo di Tura, describes the devastating effect that the disease had upon his fellow citizens, including his own family. Tura may have worked for the city's financial magistracy and therefore may have had access to official records. However, one should not take his mortality figures at face value, as best esti-

Agnolo di Tura del Grasso, *Cronaca senese*, ed. Alessandro Lisini and Fabio Iacometti, in *Rerum Italicarum Scriptores*, 15/6 (1931–37), 555–56. Translated from the Italian by Aubry Threlkeld.

mates indicate that the city's population shortly before the plague was a little over 52,000, which is precisely the number Tura cites as dying from the Black Death. Di Tura's contribution to his city's history ends in 1351.

The mortality, which was a thing horrible and cruel, began in Siena in the month of May [1348]. I do not know from where came this cruelty or these pitiless ways, which were painful to see and stupefied everyone. There are not words to describe how horrible these events have been and, in fact, whoever can say that they have not lived in utterly horrid conditions can truly consider themselves lucky. The infected die almost immediately. They swell beneath the armpits and in the groin, and fall over while talking. Fathers abandon their sons, wives their husbands, and one brother the other. In the end, everyone escapes and abandons anyone who might be infected. Moreover, it appears that this plague can be communicated through bad breath and even by just seeing one of the infected. In these ways, they die and no one can be found who would want to bury them, not even for money or in the name of friendship. Those who get infected in their own house, they remove them the best way they can and they bury them without the supervision of a priest. No one controls anything and they do not even ring the church bells anymore. Throughout Siena, giant pits are being excavated for the multitudes of the dead and the hundreds that die every night. The bodies are thrown into these mass graves and are covered bit by bit. When those ditches are full, new ditches are dug. So many have died that new pits have to be made every day.

And I, Agnolo di Tura, called the Fat, have buried five of my sons with my own hands. Yet still I do not steal from those who were poorly buried like the dogs that eat them and litter them about the city. There is no one who weeps for any of the dead, for instead everyone awaits their own impending death. So many have died that everyone believes it is the end of the world. Medicine and other cures do not work. In fact, the more medicine people are given the quicker they die. The leaders of the city have elected three citizens that have been given 1,000 florins for the expense of taking care of the homeless and for burying them. These conditions have been so horrible that I do not reflect as often as I used to about the situation. I have thought so much about these events that I cannot tell the stories any longer. This is how the people lived until September [1348], and it would be too much for me to write the whole story. One would find that in this period of time more people died than in twenty years or more. In Siena alone, 36,000 people have died. If you count the elderly and others, the number could be 52,000 in total. In all of the boroughs, the number could be as high as 30,000 more. So it can be seen that in total the death toll may be as high as 80,000. There are only about 10,000 people left in the city and those that live on are hopeless and in utter despair. They leave their homes and other things. Gold, silver, and copper lay scattered about. In the countryside, even more died, so many that farms and agricultural lands are left without people to work them. I cannot write about the cruelties that existed in the countryside: that wolves and other wild beasts eat the improperly buried and other horrors that are too difficult for anyone who would read this account. . . .

The city of Siena appeared uninhabited because almost no one was found there. The pestilence remained and everyone who survived celebrated his or her fate. Of the monks, priests, nuns, women, and others from the secular community, they didn't worry about their expenses or games. Everyone appeared to be rich because they had survived and regained value in life. Now, no one knows how to put their life back in order.

18

JEAN DE VENETTE

Chronicle

ca. 1359–1360

A Carmelite friar, Jean de Venette probably came from humble origins; his hometown lies near Compiègne in northeastern France. He is recorded as prior of the Carmelite convent in Paris from 1339 to 1342 and thereafter was promoted to head of the order's French province, an office he held until his death in 1368 or 1369. In this selection, Venette characterizes French society in the aftermath of the Black Death, dwelling especially on its perceived moral laxity. It seems he wrote this section of his Chronicle *between the fall and spring of 1359–60.*

Chronique Latine de Guillaume de Nangis de 1113 à 1300, avec les continuations de cette chronique, ed. Hercule Géraud, 2 vols. (Paris: J. Renouard et cie, 1843), 2:214–16.

But when the said epidemic, pestilence, and mortality was over, the men and women who remained married each other. Throughout the world wives left behind conceived beyond measure. There was in effect no sterility; but here and there were seen pregnant women.* And many gave birth to twins, and some pushed out three living infants at a time. But what was most astounding was that children born after the mortality, when they began cutting their teeth, commonly had only twenty or twenty-two teeth in their mouth, when before this time children in the normal course of events had thirty-two teeth at a time in their upper and lower jaw.† But I wonder very much what the number of teeth in those born later signifies, unless it is to say that the world and the human race has in some way been renewed by this great mortality of so many men and by their replacement with others and those who survived, so that we are in a new age.

But, oh woe! The world is not changed for the better on account of this renewal of the human race. For men were more greedy and grasping after the plague, since they could possess many more goods than before. They were also more covetous and they liked to stir up strife among themselves through quarrels, disputes, and brawls. Nor was peace restored among kings and lords through this terrible pestilence inflicted by God. On the contrary, the enemies of the king of France and also of the Church were stronger and worse than before: they started wars on sea and land and everywhere gave rise to greater evils. And what was also amazing was that although there was abundance of all things, nevertheless everything was twice as expensive: both utensils as well as victuals, and even merchandise and hired labor, and farm workers and servants.‡ An exception were some estates and houses, which maintained overflowing stores even to this day. Also from that time charity began to grow extremely cold, and wickedness abounded, along with ignorance and sin. For few could be found in homes, villages, and castles who knew or wanted to teach children the rudiments of grammar.

---

*This is directly contradicted by the anonymous author of the *Eulogium Historiarum* (*Eulogy of History*), who says that in England, "the women who survived remained for the most part sterile for many years; if any of them conceived, they nearly always died, along with their fetus, in giving birth."

†This phenomenon is also noted by the English chronicler John of Reading.

‡The French poet Guillaume de Machaut elaborated on this situation in 1349: "For lack of men you saw many a fair and fine heritage lying unploughed. No one could have his fields tilled, his wheat sowed, his vines trimmed without paying triple wages, so many were dead."

19

AHMAD IBN ʿALĪ AL-MAQRĪZĪ

A History of the Ayyubids and Mamluks

15th Century

Ahmad Ibn ʿAlī al-Maqrīzī was born in Cairo, Egypt, in 1364. Following in the footsteps of his father, he pursued a career as an Islamic scholar and administrator until about 1418, when he decided to devote himself to being a full-time historian, perhaps inspired by the example of his friend, Ibn Khaldūn. The following selection concerns the social and economic impact of the Black Death in the Mamluk empire of Egypt and Syria beginning in January 1349; it is taken from one of al-Maqrīzī's many historical works, kitab al-Sulūk li-maʿrifat duwal al-mulūk *(A History of the Ayyubids and Mamluks). Although al-Maqrīzī was writing more than half a century after the first plague outbreak of 1348, his histories are thought to preserve earlier sources now lost. Al-Maqrīzī died in February 1442.*

In January 1349, there appeared new symptoms that consisted of spitting up of blood. The disease caused one to experience an internal fever, followed by an uncontrollable desire to vomit; then one spat up blood and died. The inhabitants of a house were stricken one after the other, and in one night or two, the dwelling became deserted. Each individual lived with this fixed idea that he was going to die in this way. He prepared for himself a good death by distributing alms; he arranged for scenes of reconciliation and his acts of devotion multiplied. . . .

By January 21, Cairo had become an abandoned desert, and one did not see anyone walking along the streets. A man could go from the Port Zuwayla to Bāb al-Nasr* without encountering a living soul. The dead were very numerous, and all the world could think of nothing else. Debris piled up in the streets. People went around with worried

*This was apparently the busiest boulevard in medieval Cairo.

Gaston Wiet, "La Grande Peste Noire en Syrie et en Égypte," *Études d'orientalisme dédiées à la mémoire de Lévi-Provençal,* 2 vols. (Paris: G. -P. Maisonneuve et Larose, 1962), 1:375–80.

faces. Everywhere one heard lamentations, and one could not pass by any house without being overwhelmed by the howling. Cadavers formed a heap on the public highway, funeral processions were so many that they could not file past without bumping into each other, and the dead were transported in some confusion. . . .

One began to have to search for readers of the Koran for funeral ceremonies, and a number of individuals quit their usual occupations in order to recite prayers at the head of funeral processions. In the same way, some people devoted themselves to smearing crypts with plaster; others presented themselves as volunteers to wash the dead or carry them. These latter folk earned substantial salaries. For example, a reader of the Koran took ten *dirhams*.* Also, hardly had he reached the oratory when he slipped away very quickly in order to go officiate at a new [funeral]. Porters demanded 6 *dirhams* at the time they were engaged, and then it was necessary to match it [at the grave]. The gravedigger demanded fifty *dirhams* per grave. Most of the rest of these people died without having taken any profit from their gains. . . . Also families kept their dead on the bare ground, due to the impossibility of having them interred. The inhabitants of a house died by the tens and, since there wasn't a litter ready to hand, one had to carry them away in stages. Moreover, some people appropriated for themselves without scruple the immovable and movable goods and cash of their former owners after their demise. But very few lived long enough to profit thereby, and those who remained alive would have been able to do without. . . .

Family festivities and weddings had no more place [in life]. No one issued an invitation to a feast during the whole time of the epidemic, and one did not hear any concert. The *vizier*† lifted a third of what he was owed from the woman responsible [for collecting] the tax on singers. The call to prayer was canceled in various places, and in the exact same way, those places [where prayer] was most frequent subsisted on a *muezzin*‡ alone. . . .

The men of the [military] troop and the cultivators took a world of trouble to finish their sowing [of fields]. The plague emerged at the end of the season when the fields were becoming green. How many times did one see a laborer, at Gaza, at Ramleh, and along other points

---

dirham: A silver coin used in the Muslim world.
†The chief minister of the caliph, or leader of the Muslim community.
‡*muezzin:* An official of the mosque who called the faithful to prayer from the minaret.

of the Syrian littoral,* guide his plow being pulled by oxen suddenly fall down dead, still holding in his hands his plow, while the oxen stood at their place without a conductor.

It was the same in Egypt: When the harvest time came, there remained only a very small number of *fellahs.*[†] The soldiers and their valets left for the harvest and attempted to hire workers, promising them half of the crop, but they could not find anyone to help them reap it. They loaded the grain on their horses, did the mowing themselves, but, being powerless to carry out the greatest portion of the work, they abandoned this enterprise.

The endowments[‡] passed rapidly from hand to hand as a consequence of the multiplicity of deaths in the army. Such a concession passed from one to the other until the seventh or eighth holder, to fall finally [into the hands] of artisans, such as tailors, shoemakers, or public criers, and these mounted the horse, donned the [military] headdress, and dressed in military tunics.

Actually, no one collected the whole revenue of his endowment, and a number of holders harvested absolutely nothing. During the flooding of the Nile[§] and the time of the sprouting of vegetation, one could procure a laborer only with difficulty: On half the lands only did the harvest reach maturity. Moreover, there was no one to buy the green clover [as feed] and no one sent their horses to graze over the field. This was the ruin of royal properties in the suburbs of Cairo, like Matarieh, Hums, Siryaqus, and Bahtit. In the canton [administrative district] of Nay and Tanan, 1,500 *feddans*[‖] of clover were abandoned where it stood: No one came to buy it, either to pasture their beasts on the place or to gather it into barns and use it as fodder.

The province of Upper Egypt was deserted, in spite of the vast abundance of cultivable terrain. It used to be that, after the land surface was cultivated in the territory of Asyūt,[#] 6,000 individuals were subject to payment of the property tax; now, in the year of the epidemic [1348–49], one could not count on more than 106 contributors.

*The coastal plain of southern Palestine, where the most fertile land was located.

[†]*fellah:* Arabic word for ploughman or tiller, which also denoted the peasantry of Egypt and is the origin of the modern term, *fellahin.*

[‡]Mamluk commanders and elite soldiers, like their Ayyubid predecessors, were paid out of the revenues of land grants, known as *iqtas* (similar to the fiefs in Europe). With the dearth of labor caused by the Black Death, it became far more difficult to extract income from these estates.

[§]This usually took place between September and November of every year.

[‖]A *feddan* is equivalent to 1.038 acres.

[#]Located along the Nile in Upper Egypt, about midway between Cairo and Aswan.

Nevertheless, during this period, the price of wheat did not rise past fifteen *dirhams* per *ardeb*.*

Most of the trades disappeared, for a number of artisans devoted themselves to handling the dead, while the others, no less numerous, occupied themselves in selling off to bidders [the dead's] movable goods and clothing, so well that the price of linen and similar objects fell by a fifth of their real value, at the very least, and still further until one found customers. . . .

Thus the trades disappeared: One could no longer find either a water carrier, or a laundress, or a domestic. The monthly salary of a groom rose from thirty *dirhams* to eighty. A proclamation made in Cairo invited the artisans to take up their old trades, and some of the recalcitrants reformed themselves. Because of the shortage of men and camels, a goatskin of water reached the price of eight *dirhams*, and in order to grind an *ardeb* of wheat, one paid fifteen *dirhams*.

*An *ardeb* is equivalent to 5.62 bushels.

20

CITY COUNCIL OF SIENA

Ordinance

May 1349

Italian city-states were among the first to enact labor legislation in the wake of the Black Death, some as early as 1348. They typically took a two-pronged approach: on the one hand, attempting to restrict laborers' mobility and curb their demands for higher wages; on the other, trying to attract immigrant labor with the promise of attractive conditions. Siena's labor law is included here; the city-states of Venice, Orvieto, and Pisa, as well as Ragusa (modern-day Dubrovnik), across the Adriatic, enacted similar legislation. It is unclear how successful these laws were: Two other labor measures enacted by Siena, dated September 5, 1348, and October 7, 1350, were not renewed. The following ordinance would have been deliberated and voted on by the commune's city council, which was

William M. Bowsky, "The Impact of the Black Death upon Sienese Government and Society," *Speculum,* 39 (1964): 26, n. 145.

composed of 300 permanent and 150 rotating members. The ordinance is dated May 1349.

Item, because laborers of the land and those who have been accustomed to work the land or orchards on the farms of the citizens and *districtuales* [inhabitants] of Siena extort and receive great sums and salaries for the daily labor that they do every day, they have totally destroyed and abandoned the farms and estates of the aforesaid citizens and *districtuales,* which is not without great danger to the aforesaid holders of the farms. The aforesaid wise men [of the city council] provide and ordain that everyone, of whatever condition he may be, who labors and is accustomed to labor with his own hands be bound and ought to pay six gold *florins** every year to the commune of Siena on behalf of the lord, unless the said laborer or cultivator works or cultivates with his own hands and labor eight *staios*† or works eight *staios* of vineyards or orchards in good faith without fraud according to the customs of a good laborer, which at the very least he is bound to render to the said lord. And that everyone who works for hire or wages with oxen or cows or other kinds of plough-teams be bound and ought to pay twelve gold *florins* every year to the commune of Siena on behalf of and in the name of the lord, always with the exception and proviso that the aforesaid laborers with their beasts work, cultivate, and sow twenty *staios* of land, which at the very least they are bound to render to the said lord. And that . . . the *bargello* [exactor] of the commune of Siena be bound and ought to diligently investigate the aforesaid laborers at least every two months, and those whom he finds to have acted against the present provision of laborers . . . should be fined by the said *bargello* in [the amount of] ten Sienese *lira.*‡ And nevertheless he [the *bargello*] is bound to pay the said lord. It is declared that laborers should be understood as comprising those who are fifteen years of age and above, up to the age of seventy. And the aforesaid wise men [of the city council] have decreed and ordained that if, after the approval of the present ordinances, any persons from anywhere else than the city and *contado* [district] of Siena wish to come to work at the

---

*The *florin,* or *fiorino d'oro,* was a gold coin issued by the city of Florence beginning in 1252. It was equivalent to one *libra,* or Italian pound, or three to four English shillings.

†A *staio* was equivalent to about one-third of an acre.

‡One *lira* was equivalent to 0.32 *florin.*

rate of half or more of the said quantity of land, as is stated above [i.e., four *staios* by hand, ten *staios* with beasts], are not bound to contribute anything [i.e., taxes or services] in that community in which they work or live, and they are to hold and ought to hold this said immunity for five years' time after the approval of the present ordinances.

21

THE CÓRTES OF CASTILE

Ordinance

1351

In Spain, the córtes of Castile, a form of government like the English parliament, was convened under the auspices of the crown and comprised prelates, noblemen, country squires, and town merchants or councillors throughout the realm. Scholars dispute the exact role of representative assemblies in Spain's medieval political history: At certain times, for example, during the 1350s and 1360s in the kingdom of Aragon and during the 1380s and 1390s in Castile, the córtes demonstrated impressive consultative, legislative, and financial powers on a par with those of England. But at other times, the córtes met infrequently and was fragmented among regional assemblies along the model of France. The following selection describes labor legislation enacted in response to the Black Death by the córtes convoked by King Pedro I "the Cruel" of Castile (1334–1369) at Valladolid in 1351. The córtes of Aragon passed similar decrees in 1350 (subsequently revoked in 1352). The ordinances of Castile were tailored to each part of the kingdom, suggesting that the plague's impact varied considerably by region. Only the first four ordinances, common to all regions of the kingdom, are included here.

There have been rumors and complaints made to me [Pedro I of Castile] that some persons of my land and of my realms suffer very

Córtes de los antiguos reinos de León y de Castilla, 5 vols. (Madrid: Real Academia de la Historia, 1861–1903), 2:75–77.

great losses because they cannot work their estates to produce bread and wine and other things that maintain men. And this has come about, on the one hand because many men and women wander about idle and do not want to work, and on the other because those who do work demand such great prices and salaries and wages, that those who have estates cannot comply, and for this reason, these estates have become deserted and lack laborers. And also there have been rumors and complaints made to me that those laborers who work and perform other trades [that produce things] for the maintenance of men which they cannot go without, sell things from their trades at their will and for much greater prices than they are worth; and from this situation ensue and arise very great damages to all those who have to buy those things that they need. And I, seeing that this has been to my disservice and great damage and loss in all of my land and seeking and desiring the common welfare of those who live in my realms, deem it good to command that an ordinance be made in each of the regions of my realms concerning these matters, in the manner given here.

First, I deem it good and I command that no man nor woman who is fit and able to work wander about idle through my dominions, neither asking [for things] nor begging, but that all work hard and live by the labor of their hands, except those men and women who become so sick and injured or are of such great age that they cannot do anything and boys and girls of twelve years of age [or younger].

Also, I deem it good and I command that all the laboring men and women and persons who can and ought to earn a living, as is said above, continue to perform the same work on the estates and serve for the salaries and wages at the prices contained below, and the same applies to those who are idle.

Also, I deem it good and I command that all the carpenters and builders and plasterers and servants and workmen and workwomen and day laborers and other workers who are accustomed to hire out their labor go to the public square of each place where they live and have been accustomed to be hired at daybreak of every day, [bringing] with them their implements and their food in a manner such that they can go out of the town or place to perform their labor where they were hired at sunrise, and that they work the whole day. And they are to quit their work at such a time that they return to the town or place where they were hired at sunset. And those who work in the town or place where they were hired are to work from the said time of sunrise, and they are to quit working at sunset.

Also, I deem it good and I command that all the laborers continue to work and employ themselves in the professions that they know and are accustomed to, and that they sell the things that they make in their trades and professions for the prices that are contained and given below. And they are to perform the work of their professions well and faithfully.

22

Wiltshire, England, Assize Roll of Labor Offenders
June 11, 1352

The following selection is from an assize court roll, or record of the jury trial that decided cases on a given date, which took place at Devizes, Wiltshire, before three deputy justices of laborers on June 11, 1352, against offenders from the Kingsbridge hundred. (A hundred was a territorial unit of the shire, roughly equivalent in modern terms to a ward in a county.) It provides an example of the way the English government prosecuted offenders of the Statute of Laborers shortly after it was enacted in February 1351. The statute, following upon an ordinance of 1349, decreed that servants and hired laborers must accept the salaries and wages that they had received in 1346, and on that basis it established set wage rates for each category of worker. Moreover, craftsmen and artisans were to charge the same prices they had charged in 1346. Six hundred forty-two people were prosecuted in the county in 1352 for violating the statute. They were drawn from no less than forty-five different occupations, including both agricultural workers and artisans. The government generally prosecuted agricultural workers for wage violations, and artisans for charging excessive prices. Some offenders practiced more than one trade. Undoubtedly, the profession most represented was brewers or tapsters, who made up 24 percent of the offenders and were overwhelmingly female. Only one man, William Spendlove of Eton, was prosecuted for enticing another into his service with promise of higher wages. The following selection comes from the end of the roll, which provides more

E. M. Thompson, "Offenders against the Statute of Labourers in Wiltshire, AD 1349," *The Wiltshire Archaeological and Natural History Magazine*, 33 (1903–4): 404–7.

detail about the cases, including judgments that were handed down (included here in abridged form).

John Laurok came to Chisledon, a vagabond out of service, and pleaded guilty to leaving the service of William de Stratton of Oxfordshire. He is let out on bail and fined six pence.

William le Coupere [Cooper] of Elcombe, who at another time before the aforesaid justices swore to exercise his trade in accordance with the Statute [of Labourers of 1351], took an extra six pence for his work from various men contrary to his oath. He pleads not guilty and is acquitted by a jury of twelve men.

John Boltash, carter of the parson of Elingdon [Wroughton], pleads guilty to receiving for his livery [upkeep] two bushels of wheat per quarter of grain for ten weeks [of work], whereas he used to be given one bushel of wheat per quarter for eleven weeks. Walter Clement, oxherd of the same parson, pleads guilty to receiving for his livery this year two bushels of wheat per quarter for ten weeks, whereas he used to be given one bushel of wheat per quarter for eleven weeks. Walter Ryche pleads guilty to receiving from the same parson for his livery two bushels of wheat per quarter for twelve weeks, whereas he used to be given no wheat per quarter for twelve weeks. They are let out on bail to appear at the next session. . . .

Edward le Taillour of Wootton Bassett, servant of the prior and convent of Bradenstoke, made an agreement with them to receive his usual diet and salary from Michaelmas [September 29] 1351 until the Michaelmas following but left their service before the feast of St. Nicholas [December 6, 1351] without leave or reasonable cause contrary to the Statute. His arrest is ordered to the bailiff. . . .

Richard the Cobbler of Clack Mount, who at another time swore to exercise his craft in accordance with the Statute, took an extra forty pence from various men for shoes sold by him contrary to the Statute and his oath. Previously, Richard did not appear before the justices because the bailiff answered that he could not be found. Then, when the bailiff tried to arrest him, Richard took flight upon seeing the bailiff and would not halt. Afterwards, Richard was arrested and brought before the justices and additionally charged with contempt of court. Richard pleads innocent but places himself at the mercy of the court and is fined two marks [twenty-six shillings and eight pence]. . . .

Thomas Tonkere of Calne, a fuller, took an extra twelve pence from various men for his trade contrary to the Statute. He does not appear before the justices because the bailiff answers that he cannot be found. He is to be arrested and brought to the next session and is fined in absentia twelve pence. . . .

Edith Paiers, Alice Dounames, Edith Lange, and Isabel Purs of Clyffe Pypard took an extra six pence last autumn from various men for reaping corn into sheaves. They are let out on bail and fined six pence each.

Walter Cook and his wife Agnes, Thomas Averil and his wife Alice, and John London of Thornhill took an extra six pence from various men for reaping corn last autumn contrary to the Statute. They plead guilty and are let out on bail. Cook is fined twelve shillings, while Averil and London are fined twelve pence each.

Thomas, formerly the servant of Ralph de Chusleden, left Ralph's service without reasonable cause before the end of the term agreed upon between them and refused to serve anymore contrary to the Statute. Thomas does not appear before the justices because the bailiff answers that he cannot be found. He is to be arrested and brought to the next session.

John, a shepherd of Walter Halman of Medbourne, took from Walter for his livery two bushels of wheat per quarter of corn for a half-year [of work] instead of two bushels of barley, worth an extra twenty pence. John pleads guilty and is let out on bail and fined two shillings [twenty-four pence].

5

Religious Mentalities

For some European Christians, like Gabriele de Mussis (Document 23), the extraordinary mortality of the Black Death was proof of the righteous judgment of God visited upon a sinful humanity—the clergy, chief among them—which inevitably invited intimations of a coming apocalypse or reign of the Antichrist. But even Mussis, who does not doubt that God's vengeance is just, seems so overwhelmed by the plague that he begins to despair of God's mercy. As we have seen, others, like Petrarch (Document 15), could not understand why humankind deserved such awful punishment and began to question whether God even played a role in their lives. Overall, however, the predominant response seems to have been to seek solace and hope in the prayers and processions led by bishops and the clergy. Christians directed religious appeals to God and to saints especially known for their mercy or power against the plague, such as the Virgin Mary, St. Sebastian, St. Anthony, and St. Roch. Many also resorted to local saint cults, such as the Virgin Agatha of Catania in Sicily (Document 24), or the newly established shrine of St. Thomas Cantilupe in Hereford, England.[1]

A number of documents criticize the priesthood for failing to administer to the needs of parishioners during the Black Death, including hearing confession and giving last rites. Both Michele da Piazza and Jean de Venette contrasted the "cowardly" behavior of priests with the behavior of friars. In some places friars also tended to the needs of the parish and allegedly stayed behind with the sick even though this cost them their lives. One must remember, though, that both these critics were themselves friars. But perhaps the harshest critics of the priesthood were its superiors. In a famous decree issued on January 10, 1349, Bishop Ralph Shrewsbury of Bath and Wells in England granted an unprecedented indulgence to the parishioners of his diocese to confess to a layman, even a woman, on the grounds that "many, we hear, are dying without the sacrament of penance" in parishes decimated by the plague because "priests cannot be found to take on the cares of these places, neither out of devotional zeal nor for payment, or to visit the sick and administer the Church sacraments to them, perhaps because they are infected or have a fear of being infected."[2] The archbishop of Canterbury, Simon Islip, castigated the clergy of his province for abandoning their parishes, blaming such behavior not on fear of contagion, but on the clerics' greed. Priests wanted higher salaries and, particularly, to serve private chapels, or chantries, where a wealthy patron paid to have priests say private masses (Document 25). Islip's desire to regulate the excessive salaries of priests echoes the labor legislation passed by secular governments to rein in an ascendant peasantry (see chapter 4). Islip's successors found that this problem did not diminish with time; the continuing presence of plague made priests' labor just as valuable as the peasants'.

However, one can attempt to exonerate churchmen who faced the onslaught of the Black Death. Mortality of priests serving the parishes of England was high, both in absolute terms and relative to the death rates of other members of society. Approximately 45 percent of the priests in ten dioceses throughout England died during the height of the pestilence in 1349, with mortality in some dioceses, such as Norwich, Exeter, and Winchester, nearing 50 percent.[3] In the diocese of Barcelona in Spain, mortality of the priesthood was even higher, reaching 60 percent in the year between May 1348 and April 1349.[4] This compares favorably with the average mortality of the English peasantry, which, based on surviving manorial and tax records, ranged from 40 to 70 percent.[5] Obviously, priests as well as friars were performing parochial duties and consequently putting their lives at risk during the Black Death. One must also consider that priests who survived the plague expected much lower incomes in offerings and tithes from a flock ravaged by the Black Death and thus of necessity they sought supplemental funds from private masses (Document 26).[6]

Medieval chroniclers asserted that there was a falling off of spiritual fervor among the laity in the wake of the Black Death. Both Bishops John Trillek of Hereford and John Grandisson of Exeter complained of scurrilous plays and obscene gesticulations that were distracting the people's devotion even in years preceding the arrival of plague in 1349.[7] Because some might view these complaints as stereotypical denunciations of one generation by another, wills have formed the basis for a more rigorous and systematic study of the religious mentality of the laity in the post-plague generation. Medieval wills survive in numerous city archives, and some actually seem to have been drawn up as the testators were dying of the plague in 1348–50 (Document 27). Although medieval wills may not be representative of the entire population, scholars have now analyzed a large number of them across a broad temporal and geographical range. The wills that survive from both before and after the Black Death in central Italy and Flanders, for example, seem to point to a new "cult of remembrance" that grew up in the wake of the plague and to the fear of oblivion that the catastrophe may have engendered. Commissions for portraiture of the patron may have anticipated the individualism that characterized the Renaissance.[8]

There were fundamental differences in the way Islam and Christianity responded to the Black Death. Sunni Islam did not so readily draw upon apocalyptic traditions as Christians did when faced with the plague, and Muslims displayed no scapegoating tendencies against the Jews, as was true of European Christians during the Black Death (chapter 6). Muslims, scholars claim, had not developed a theology of original sin that saddled them with a heavy burden of guilt as plague victims, but instead viewed the disease as a natural disaster that God allowed with no reference to human culpability or punishment.[9] Above all, Muslims rejected the concept of contagion, because this posited a cause of the disease outside the direct agency of God. Even the leader of Christendom, Pope Clement VI, bowed to the principle of contagion by fleeing from his plague-stricken seat at Avignon. Parallel stories told by Gilles li Muisis and Ibn Battūta illustrate the contrast well: The Christian chronicler relates how some pilgrims "left in great haste" once they learned in the morning that their host and his whole family were dead; Battūta and his companion, on the other hand, stay to pray over and bury a *faqir,* or Muslim holy man, who died in their company during the night.[10] Whereas Muslims continued to indulge in communal prayers, processions, and funerals even at the height of the plague (Document 28), several Christian communities prohibited these gatherings in order to avoid the effects of contagion.

Medieval Christians had little understanding of the religious views of Muslims toward the plague. Muslims regarded plague as a mercy and martyrdom that held forth the promise of paradise to believers, equivalent to what one might obtain through *jihad,* or holy war. Even as well informed a chronicler as Matteo Villani of Florence displays his ignorance of Islamic culture when he declares: "It commenced with the infidels [Muslims] this cruel inhumanity, that mothers and fathers abandoned their children, and children their fathers and mothers, one brother the other and other relatives, a thing cruel and astonishing, and something very foreign to human nature, detestable to faithful Christians, who yet soon followed the barbaric nations in practicing this same cruelty."[11] Given Islamic taboos against flight from a plague region, the exact opposite was more likely to have been true. Nevertheless, religious proscriptions against contagion do not seem to have interfered with the practice of medicine in the Muslim world, which was authorized by the Koran, and there seems to have been some debate within the Muslim religio-legal community, or *ulama,* concerning Islamic teachings on plague.[12] One brave soul, Ibn al-Khatīb (Document 30), openly subscribed to the idea of contagion on the basis of practical observation, even when his friend and colleague, Ibn Khatīma, took the more prudent approach of doing so only tacitly (Document 13). Khatīb was eventually lynched by a mob, however, for his defiance of such long-held *fatwas,* or religious teachings—proof that Muslims could be just as intolerant as Christians. Disputes between advocates of religion and science also occurred in the Christian community, particularly concerning the causes of the Black Death, as the German writer, Konrad of Megenberg, testifies.[13]

Finally, Ibn al-Wardī argues that Muslims, like Christians, viewed plague as God's punishment for their sins and sought to eliminate it through prayer, even though this view conflicted with the idea that it was a mercy and martyrdom (Document 29). For both religions, of course, God was the ultimate author of the plague; there were Christians as well as Muslims who felt that this terrible calamity was a blessing in disguise that worked for the salvation of true believers. Gabriele de Mussis and Ibn Kathīr tell almost identical stories of how prophecies uttered by holy men could spur renewed religious fervor among a populace threatened with plague (Documents 23 and 28). As always, animosity and lack of understanding between followers of the two religions hides what they have in common.

NOTES

[1] *Registrum Johannis de Trillek, Episcopi Herefordensis, AD 1344–1361,* ed. J. H. Parry (London: Canterbury and York Society, 1912), 147–48.

[2] David Wilkins, *Concilia Magnae Britanniae et Hiberniae,* 4 vols. (London: Sumptibus R. Gosling, 1737), 2:745–46.

[3] John Aberth, *From the Brink of the Apocalypse: Confronting Famine, War, Plague, and Death in the Later Middle Ages* (New York: Routledge, 2000), 125, 272.

[4] Richard Gyug, "The Effects and Extent of the Black Death of 1348: New Evidence for Clerical Mortality in Barcelona," *Mediaeval Studies,* 45 (1983): 391.

[5] Aberth, *From the Brink of the Apocalypse,* 127.

[6]R. N. Swanson, "Standard of Livings: Parochial Revenues in Pre-Reformation England," in *Religious Belief and Ecclesiastical Careers in Late Medieval England,* ed. Christopher Harper-Bill (Woodbridge, Suffolk: Boydell Press, 1991), 151–96.

[7]*Chronique Latine de Guillaume de Nangis de 1113 à 1300, avec les continuations de cette chronique,* ed. Hercule Géraud, 2 vols. (Paris: J. Renouard et cie, 1843), 185; *Recueil des chroniques de Flandre,* ed. Joseph-Jean de Smet, 4 vols. (Brussels: 1837–65), 2:346–47; *Registrum Johannis de Trillek,* 141–42; *The Register of John de Grandisson, Bishop of Exeter, AD 1327–1369,* ed. F. C. Hingeston-Randolph, 3 vols. (London: G. Bell and Sons, 1894–99), 2:723.

[8]Samuel K. Cohn Jr., *The Cult of Remembrance and the Black Death: Six Renaissance Cities in Central Italy* (Baltimore: The Johns Hopkins University Press, 1992); idem, "The Place of the Dead in Flanders and Tuscany: Towards a Comparative History of the Black Death," in *The Place of the Dead: Death and Remembrance in Late Medieval and Early Modern Europe,* ed. B. Gordon and P. Marshall (Cambridge: Cambridge University Press, 2000), 17–43.

[9]Michael W. Dols, "The Comparative Communal Responses to the Black Death," *Viator,* 5 (1974): 284–85; idem, *The Black Death in the Middle East* (Princeton, N.J.: Princeton University Press, 1977), 296–97.

[10]*Recueil des chroniques de Flandre,* 2:280; Ibn Baṭṭūṭa, *Travels, AD 1325–1354,* trans. H. A. R. Gibb, 5 vols. (Cambridge: The Hakluyt Society, 1958–2000), 4:919.

[11]Matteo Villani, *Cronica,* ed. Giuseppe Porta, 2 vols. (Parma: Fondazione Pietro Bembo, 1995), 1:1.

[12]Dols, "Comparative Communal Responses to the Black Death," 277; idem, *The Black Death in the Middle East,* 291.

[13]Karl Sudhoff, "Pestschriften aus den ersten 150 Jahren nach der Epidemie des 'schwarzen Todes' 1348," *Archiv für Geschichte der Medizin,* 11 (1919): 44–47.

23

GABRIELE DE MUSSIS

History of the Plague

1348

*Gabriele de Mussis was a lawyer from Piacenza, a city in Lombardy in northern Italy, who died in 1356. In this selection, which opens his His-*toria de Morbo, *or* History of the Plague, *allegedly composed in 1348, Mussis imagines a dialogue between God and the earth as an explanation for why the Black Death suddenly has arrived on the scene. He then borrows from the book of Revelation to convey the awesome judgment handed down by God upon humanity.*

A. W. Henschel, "Dokument zur Geschichte des schwarzen Todes," *Archiv für gesammte Medizin,* 2 (1841): 45–47, 56–57.

Let all those present and future take this as a perpetual reminder that Almighty God, king of heaven, who is lord of the living and the dead and holds all things in His hand, looked down from on high upon the entire human race and saw it sinking and sliding into all kinds of wickedness, embracing out of sheer persistence numberless crimes and transgressions, and immersing itself to the very core, out of an unfathomable malice, in every type of vice; saw it bereft of any redeeming goodness, not dreading the judgments of God, and that it hastened to perform every kind of evil deed. Unable to bear any longer so many abominations and horrors, He called out to the Earth: "What are you doing, Earth, held captive by gangs of worthless men, defiled by their sordid sins? Are you totally helpless? What are you doing? Why do you not demand vengeance with human blood for their evil deeds? Why do you suffer my enemies and adversaries to live? You ought to have already suffocated my enemies, in fulfillment of a long-standing desire. Prepare yourself to exercise the vengeance of which you are capable."

"And I, the Earth, founded by your Majesty, will open my veins and swallow the numberless criminals in accordance with your commands. I will refuse them their accustomed harvest. I will not produce grain, wine, and oil."* . . .

And after mortals had thus been warned, the quivering spear of the Almighty, in the form of the plague, was sent down to infect the whole human race, aiming its cruel darts everywhere. Indeed, Orion, that cruel star, and the ferocious tail of the dragon, and the angel casting vials of poison into the sea, and the horrible and unseasonable weather of Saturn were all given leave to harm land and sea, men and trees; advancing from east to west with plague-bearing steps, they poured out bowls of poison throughout the various regions of the world, leaving their fiery seals upon the sick.† On account of this, the horrible onslaught of death, running its course throughout the world and threatening ruin, devoured mortal men with a sudden blow, as will be explained below. Wring, wring your hands, people, and call upon the mercy of God. . . .

---

*A reference to Joel 1:10.

†This passage mixes apocalyptic and astrological imagery. Mussis is especially evocative here of chapters 15 and 16 from the book of Revelation, which begin: "And I saw another sign in heaven, great and wonderful: seven angels having the seven last plagues. For in them is filled up the wrath of God. . . . And I heard a great voice out of the temple, saying to the seven angels: 'Go, and pour out the seven vials of the wrath of God upon the earth.'"

Truly, then was a time of bitterness and sorrow, and human endeavor was directed toward serving the Lord. I will tell what happened.
After having a vision, a certain holy person issued a warning: that
people of both sexes in every diocese, city, castle, and region should
gather for three consecutive days in their parish church and with
great devotion and lighted candles in their hands hear the mass of the
Blessed Anastasia, which is usually celebrated on Christmas morning.
And they should humbly implore mercy from the saint, that they might
be delivered from the plague through the merits of the holy mass.
Some people directed their prayers to a blessed martyr. Others humbly
turned to other saints, thinking that they might be able to escape the
plague's deformity. For some of the aforementioned martyrs, as history tells us, were said to have died from a number of blows in the
name of Jesus Christ, and for this reason, many held the opinion that
they could preserve their health against the plague's arrows. And then
in 1350 the most holy Pope Clement [VI] issued out of the apostolic
consistory a general indulgence, which was to last for a year, to all
those who confessed and were truly repentant of their faults and
sins.* As a result, an infinite number of people of both sexes made the
pilgrimage to Rome, visiting with great reverence and devotion the
basilicas of the blessed apostles, Peter and Paul, and of St. John.

*This was the "jubilee" that had been called by the pope once before, in 1300, invit-
ing people to make a pilgrimage to Rome.

24

MICHELE DA PIAZZA

Chronicle

1347–1361

*In this selection, Piazza testifies to the powerful appeal of local religious
shrines, such as those of the blessed Virgin Agatha of Catania and the
blessed Virgin Mary of Santa Maria della Scala, toward which large
numbers of people turned for succor, spiritual and otherwise, during the*

Michele da Piazza, *Cronaca,* ed. Antonino Giuffrida (Palermo: ILA Palma, 1980), 82–87.

plague. Piazza reports that supplications to these shrines were accompanied by incidents of the marvelous, although none of them involved healing. At the same time, Piazza also records the rancorous secular rivalries that existed between the Sicilian towns of Messina and Catania, which evidently persisted even at the height of the plague and from which not even Piazza, a Franciscan friar, could disentangle himself.

Wherefore the Messinese, taking stock of this terrible and monstrous calamity, chose to leave the city rather than stay there to die; and not only did they refuse to enter the city, but even to go near it. They camped out with their families in the open air and in the vineyards outside the city. But some, and they were the majority of the citizens, went to the city of Catania, believing that the Blessed Virgin Agatha of Catania would deliver them from this illness. . . . Indeed, very many Messinese were staying in the city of Catania, where with one voice they implored the lord patriarch through the pious petitions submitted to him, that for the sake of devotion he go personally to Messina, bringing with him with all due honor some of the relics of the Virgin Agatha. "For we believe," they said, "that with the arrival of the relics, the city of Messina will be completely delivered from this sickness." So the patriarch, deeply moved by their prayers, agreed to go personally to Messina with the aforesaid relics. And this was around the end of the month of November in the year of our Lord 1347. The holy Virgin Agatha, seeing through the inward deceit and stratagems of the Messinese—who have always wanted to keep the virgin's relics at Messina and were exploiting the situation for that end—prayed to the Lord to see to it that the whole populace of the city betake themselves to the patriarch, shouting and saying that such a plan in no way pleased them. And wresting the keys away from the churchwarden, they soundly rebuked the patriarch, asserting that he should choose death before agreeing to transfer the relics to Messina. After this scolding, the patriarch could do nothing else but enter the place where the relics were kept in a spirit of great devotion and honor, accompanied by a monastic choir intoning religious chants and holy prayers, and lave [bathe] the holy relics with some pure water; it was this holy water which he arranged to be brought to the city of Messina, when he personally crossed over to there by ship. But oh, what a foolish idea you Messinese had, to think you could steal away the relics of the Blessed Virgin Agatha in this secret manner, under cover of a zealous devotion. Have you forgotten that when the body of the virgin was at Constantinople and desired to go back to her own country, to the city of Catania, she appeared in dreams to Gislebert and Goselin and ordered them to bring her body back to the city of Catania?* Don't you know that if she had wanted to make her home in Messina, she by all means would have allowed this to happen? What more is there to say? Afterwards, the patriarch came to the city of Messina, bringing with him the aforesaid holy water, and he cured many and various sick people by sprinkling and touching them with the water. Therefore the citizens of Messina flocked to the patriarch, rushing to see him with great joy and giving many thanks to him and to God. For demons appeared in the city, having changed themselves into the shape of dogs, and they inflicted much harm on the bodies of the Messinese. Struck numb with terror, no one dared leave their homes. Nevertheless, by the general agreement of all and following the wishes of the archbishop of Messina, the citizens resolved to devoutly process around the city while chanting litanies. And as the whole populace of Messina was entering the city, a black dog carrying a drawn sword in its paw appeared among them; growling, it rushed the crowd and broke silver vessels, lamps, and candelabra that were on the altars, and shattered various other kinds of things. At this sight, everyone all at once fell flat on their faces, half-dead with fear. But after a while the men recovered and got up, and they saw the dog leave the church, but no one dared follow it or approach it.

But the Messinese were terrified by this extraordinary vision, so that they all grew fearful to a marvelous degree. Therefore they decided to all walk barefoot in a priest-led procession to the [shrine of the] blessed Virgin [Mary] of Santa Maria della Scala, six miles away from Messina. When they drew near to the Virgin, everyone all at once became transfixed, and on bended knee with tears in their eyes they called with great devotion upon God and the blessed Virgin for aid. And they entered the church saying devout prayers, while the priests chanted the psalm, *misere nostri Deus* (Lord have mercy), and laid their hands upon the sculpted image of the mother of God, set up there since ancient times. They decided to bring this image back to the city of Messina, because they reckoned that with it they could rid

*This is a rather hypocritical passage, considering that Agatha's body often changed hands. Agatha was a third-century Christian martyr from Catania or Palermo, and her relics were removed to Constantinople during the ninth century when Sicily was conquered by the Muslims. In 1126, Gislebert and Goselin stole them and took them back to Catania.

the city of demonic visions and apparitions, and completely deliver it from this mortality. Accordingly, they chose a suitable priest to honorably carry the image in his arms while riding on his horse. And as they were going back to the city with the aforesaid image, the holy mother of God, when she saw and approached the city, judged it to be loathsome and totally bloodied with sin, so that she turned her back on it and not only refused to enter the city but averted her eyes from it. As a result the earth opened wide, and the horse, upon which the image of the mother of God was being carried, remained fixed and immovable like a rock, unable to go forwards or back. When the people of Messina witnessed this miracle, they gasped with a sharp intake of breath, and weeping copious tears, they prayed to the blessed Virgin to not take new vengeance for their past sins; added to these humble prayers were the sacred entreaties which the holy bride of Christ, the Virgin herself, addressed to the Lord. Whereupon the earth that at first had opened is closed, and the horse moves: but when she came to the city gate, the holy mother of God refused to enter it in any way. Finally, after pious prayers were addressed to her, she entered the great church of the city of Messina, namely the Santa Maria la Nuova. The women of Messina showered the image with silk cloth and precious jewels. But could not the holy mother of God have remained in her church and completely refused to enter the city? Or are we perhaps suggesting that she could be carried away from her station, albeit unwilling? In truth, she could have remained in her original location, because no amount of force could bear her away, she to whom God's power granted all mercy, all might, all goodness. But was this not to terrify the people so that out of fear they might completely purge themselves of their worldly temptations? What more is there to say? The arrival of the image availed nothing; on the contrary, the mortality entrenched itself even further, so that there was nothing else that could be done.

25

SIMON ISLIP, ARCHBISHOP OF CANTERBURY

Effrenata (Unbridled)

May 28, 1350

From August 1348 to August 1349, England saw the passing of three archbishops of Canterbury: the first victim, John Stratford, probably died of old age in August 1348, but John Offord and Thomas Bradwardine died of the plague in May and August 1349, respectively. Simon Islip, who succeeded Bradwardine, endured longer as archbishop, surviving until 1366. The document printed here is from Islip's constitution, Effre-nata (Unbridled), issued on May 28, 1350, to the bishops of the southern province of England. Islip tried to do for the clergy what the ordinance of laborers did for peasant opportunists, that is, to stop parish priests from leaving their churches to work for more lucrative salaries elsewhere, especially in private chapels, or chantries.

The unbridled greed of the human race would, out of its innate malice, grow to the point that charity would be banished from the bounds of the earth, unless its momentum was checked by the power of justice. Well, the [House of] Commons have brought to us their complaint, and experience, that effective teacher, shows us that surviving priests, who are unmindful of the fact that divine intervention spared them from the recent pestilence—not by reason of their own merits—but so that they can carry out the ministry that was committed to them on behalf of God's people and the public welfare, and who do not blush for shame when their insatiable greed provides a wicked and pernicious example for other workers, even among the laity, now have no regard for the care of souls, which is most worthy of attention from the Church's ministers and which can merit glory to the unwilling man who takes it up, even if he should miserably fail in the rest of his duties. But priests are unwilling to take on the care of souls and to bear the burdens of their cures in mutual charity, but rather they

Registrum Simonis de Sudbiria Diocesis Londoniensis, AD 1362–1375, ed. R. C. Fowler, 2 vols. (Canterbury and York Society, 34, 38, 1927–1938), 1:190–92.

wholly abandon these to devote themselves to celebrating anniversary masses and other private services. So that they can more easily revive old extravagances, they are not content with being paid ordinary salaries but demand for their services excessive wages, and thus they win more profit for themselves than curates do, in exchange only for their status and little work. Unless their unreasonable appetite is reduced to equitable levels, the greater number of anniversary masses and the size of their salaries, moderated by no sense of balance, will mean more and more churches, prebends, and chapels throughout our province, and in our diocese as well as yours, left wholly destitute of the services of priests, and what adds to our sorrow, curates, attracted by similar wages, will be easily distracted toward these same private services, completely abandoning their cures. Wishing therefore to rein in the insatiable desire of these priests, on account of the above perils and other losses which could arise if we did not apply appropriate remedies, we require and exhort you, father, in the bowels of Jesus Christ, that, paying heed to the danger to souls and other causes mentioned above, you suitably provide before all else for the good governance of parish churches, prebends, and chapels whose care of souls is in jeopardy and in accordance with their needs, appointing for them the better and more qualified chaplains that can be found in service to anyone other than a parish. And you are to use whatever censures are sanctioned by the Church in order to act against those who do not comply and against their patrons and those who retain their services despite our ordinance and against all those who have the temerity to violate the ordinance, so that chaplains and anyone else performing any kind of religious service anywhere in your diocese may be content with a moderate salary. And if anyone who defies you seeks on that account to have himself transferred to our diocese or to the diocese of a fellow bishop, we will and order you to make his first and last name known to us through your letters, or to the bishop into whose diocese he has transferred, and inform us of what actions you or your officials have taken against him. For we wish to follow up the actions that you or a fellow bishop has taken against those who come into our diocese, and to execute to the full force of the law the censures that have been inflicted upon them. We require and order that this likewise be done and carried out by all our fellow bishops in their dioceses. And so that it may be clear to you what level of salary has been fixed by us, we have ordained for our diocese [of Canterbury] that chaplains of a parish church, prebend, or chapel with a cure of souls be content to be paid a salary of one mark [just over half a pound] beyond what was formerly accustomed to be paid to a priest with the same cure of souls, but otherwise we wish that the salary of stipendiary priests be limited to the going rate that was in force in times past.

26

HAMO HETHE, BISHOP OF ROCHESTER, AND THOMAS DE LISLE, BISHOP OF ELY

Post-Plague Parish Poverty

July 1, 1349, and September 20, 1349

The following two selections from the registers of Hamo Hethe, bishop of Rochester, and Thomas de Lisle, bishop of Ely, illustrate alternative responses to the death of parishioners from the plague, and the attendant falling off of priests' income from their oblations or offerings. Most of a parish priest's income came from the "voluntary" contributions of parishioners, which paid for his services at baptisms, last rites, marriages, confessions, and communions; in addition, parishioners were expected to tithe, or contribute a tenth of their produce, to the church every year. In the second document, the granter of the annual sustenance is John de Oo, who was acting as Thomas de Lisle's vicar-general while the bishop was away on a pilgrimage to Rome. The beneficiaries of the sustenance were two Cambridge priests. The excerpts are dated, respectively, July 1, 1349, and September 20, 1349.

Hamo Hethe, Bishop of Rochester

[July 1, 1349] Several priests and clerics refuse to accept benefices when these are lawfully offered to them, benefices where the curates have been forced to leave,* or even those that are well and truly vacant. Moreover, in some of these benefices the priests are still absent,

---

*The exact term used here is *exilia* or, literally, "exiled." Use of this word suggests that priests have abandoned their parishes out of financial necessity, rather than fear of the plague.

Registrum Hamonis Hethe, Diocesis Roffensis, AD 1319–1352, ed. Charles Johnson, 2 vols. (Canterbury and York Society, 48, 1948), 2:886; Cambridge University Library, Ely Diocesan Records; G/I/1, Register Thomas de Lisle, fol. 27v.

and have been for a long time, on account of the fact that by now it is well known that their incomes have been diminished by the mortality of the parishioners in these places, so that no one can live or support himself on what is left. We have learned that in many places where this has happened, the parish churches have for a long time remained unserved, and the cures [of souls] there are in danger of being almost abandoned, to the grave peril of souls. We, wishing to apply a remedy for this in so far as we are able right now, concede and grant by the tenor of these presents to all and several rectors and vicars already instituted or about to be instituted in our city and diocese, who have been forced to leave their benefices and whose annual income is ten marks [approximately six and a half pounds] or less, that each of them, while his poverty lasts, can licitly celebrate, or cause to be celebrated, by himself or another, one anniversary mass per year, or any number of masses whose total value equals it, on behalf of his parishioners or patrons from anywhere else outside the diocese, so long as the anniversary masses are celebrated in the parish church in which he was instituted. This is to last until we see fit to decree otherwise.

Thomas de Lisle, Bishop of Ely

[September 20, 1349]   A clear, urgent necessity demands that we provide you with pious aid. We are fully informed by your ample accounts and by the testimony of other trustworthy people that a portion is allotted to you in the aforesaid church from the oblations [offerings]—in so far as these are known—of its parishioners, and that the same parishioners have in the meantime suffered for so long from the pestilence, which is well known to be taking hold in this year, so that the oblations accruing from the said church are by no mean sufficient for the necessities of your life, nor can you obtain these elsewhere to allow you to support the burdens incumbent [upon your office]. For this reason you have humbly petitioned us to have an annual sustenance for the necessities of your life for two years. Truly, because it is not seemly for a person of your status in the holy Church of God to beg for life's necessities, such as these consist in your food and clothing, we, by the authority and office of the said father [Bishop Thomas de Lisle], grant that the support be awarded to you, in accordance with what you have requested. Nevertheless, we enjoin through these presents that as soon as you are able to be supported at a suitable level of your necessities through the proceeds and income of your portion, you altogether desist from the collection of this annual [sustenance], which you are strictly bound to do by virtue of the obedience that you have sworn to the said father.

27

LIBERTUS OF MONTE FECHE

Last Will and Testament

September 21, 1348

One of the best windows we have onto the religious mind-set of secular people during the Middle Ages is their wills. The way they allocate their resources reveals their religious priorities, at least when they made their will. We are fortunate to have the will of one man, Libertus of Monte Feche, from Liège in Flanders, who actually dictated the document as he lay dying from his "illness," probably the plague. The will is dated September 21, 1348, and was drawn up at Arezzo, a town south of Florence in Tuscany. Some of the legalistic language has been omitted from this selection.

The noble, wise and prudent man, Libertus, son of Raynerius of Monte Feche from the diocese of Liège, constable [and] knight of the officers of the magnificent and honorable commune, the commune of Florence, by the grace of God of sound mind and intellect but of failing body, wishing at this moment through wisdom to petition to have recorded and ordained in the presence of witnesses [and] in order to avoid any scandal between those who survive over his property, disposes of his goods in the present oral testament in the following manner:

In the first place, if he should die from this illness, he elects to be buried among the Servite friars of St. Mary of the city of Arezzo, within this church. For this place and for these friars, this testator leaves as a legal legacy and wishes to give from his goods five *florins* of a just and legal tender, ordering the aforementioned brothers to be and stay content with the above-stated five florins and not to ask for more of the testator's property.

Item, he leaves . . . for the health of his soul one gold *florin* to the church of the Blessed Anthony, near the city of Arezzo, outside and

---

Archivio Capitolare di Arezzo, Pace Puccii Notario, no. 57, fol. 143r. Translated from the Latin by Samuel Cohn.

near the gate of the Holy Ghost, which is to be used for the beautification of this church. . . .

Item, he leaves . . . the confraternity of the Blessed Virgin Mary of Mercy in the city of Arezzo all the testator's personal armor, with the sole exception of his helmet, which he wishes to give and place in the above-mentioned church of the Servite brothers, above his grave along with his other insignia.

Item, he leaves . . . and wishes to offer each year in perpetuity [to be placed] on the altar of the church of the Blessed Anthony a cross made from old silver called "Turonic"* to be paid for from the harvests and the other rents of a strip of land belonging to the above-mentioned testator, which lies in the curia and district of the village of Monte Feche or from another estate in a place called "Doncio."

Item, he leaves . . . to the church of Saint Anthony of Tragetto twenty-five *florins* to be taken from the value of the above-mentioned strip of land in the place called "Doncio" and for twenty-five *florins* from part of its sale to be used for commissioning a painting of the person of this testator to be placed in this church, and the residual portion is to be for the church's use, as the below-stated Renciardo, his nephew and executor, should see fit.

Item, the testator leaves . . . for the health of his soul and that of his relatives and for the remission of their sins three *florins* . . . to the church of St. Anthony of Tragetto.

Item, he leaves . . . and assigns to Libionus, the below-mentioned son of Lambertus of Monte [Feche], his esteemed and excellent blood relative, four *bennaria*† of land belonging to the testator in a place called "Mensa" in the curia and district and territory of the village of [Monte] Feche, and if this land cannot be acquired,‡ then the testator leaves . . . to this Libionus land of the testator located in a place called "Bustalglia". . . .

Item, this testator leaves . . . to John, his illegitimate son, 200 *florins*. . . .

Item, this testator leaves . . . to Angela, his illegitimate daughter, 80 *florins*. . . .

Item, this testator leaves . . . to Libotus, his illegitimate son, 60 *florins*. . . .

---

*Designating that the metal came from Tours, France.

†*bennarius:* The amount of land ploughed in one boon-work.

‡That is, if the land should be disputed by another relative, so that Libionus cannot inherit it.

Item, this testator leaves ... as above to Nicholas, his illegitimate son, 30 *florins*. ...

Item, this testator leaves ... to Udelecta, another illegitimate daughter, 30 *florins*. ...

Item, this testator leaves ... as above to Marietta, another illegitimate daughter, 30 *florins*. ...

Item, in regard to all other property, movables, real estate, salaries and credits of any sort, he institutes, wants, and demands that Renoardus,* the above-stated nephew, be his universal heir, demanding and ordering that the above Renoardus, his nephew and heir, be held to enact and to initiate and maintain all of the above-stated legacies, ... and this the above-stated testator asserts to be his last will, which he wishes to be valued and held by the right of an oral testament.

*This is Renciardo Jannis, Libertus's nephew and executor, mentioned above.

28

ʿIMĀD AL-DĪN ABŪ 'L-FIDĀ' ISMĀʿĪL B. ʿUMAR IBN KATHĪR

The Beginning and End: On History

ca. 1350–1351

The following selection is by ʿImād al-Dīn Abū 'l-Fidā' Ismāʿīl b. ʿUmar Ibn Kathīr, who was born in Syria in 1300. Ibn Kathīr was in a good position to observe the religious effects of the plague in Damascus; in February 1348, just a few months before the Black Death arrived, he was appointed teacher of the hadith, *or religious traditions relating to Muhammad, at one of the city's religious schools. This excerpt comes from Kathīr's* al-Bidāya wa-ᶜl-nihāya fī'l-tārīkh (The Beginning and End: On History), *at the end of which is a chronicle of Damascus. Ibn Kathīr died in February 1374.*

Gaston Wiet, "La Grande Peste Noire en Syrie et en Égypt," *Études d'Orientalisme dédiées à la mémoire de Lévi-Provençal*, 2 vols. (Paris: G.-P. Maisonneuve et Larose, 1962), 1:381–83.

At Damascus, a reading of the *Traditions* of Bukhārī* took place on June 5 of this year [1348] after the public prayer—with the great magistrates there assisting, in the presence of a very dense crowd—the ceremony continued with a recitation of a section of the Koran, and the people poured out their supplications that the city be spared the plague. Indeed, the population of Damascus had learned that the epidemic extended over the [Syrian] littoral and various points of the province, so that it was predicted and feared that it would become a menace to Damascus, and several inhabitants of the city had already been victims of the disease. On the morning of June 7, the crowd reassembled before the *mihrab*† of the Companions of the Prophet, and it resumed the recitation of the flood of Noah, of which a reading was made 3,363 times, in accordance with the counsel of a man to whom the Prophet had appeared in song and had suggested this prayer.‡ During this month [of June], the mortality increased among the population of Damascus, until it reached a daily average of more than 100 persons. . . .

On Monday, July 21, a proclamation made in the city invited the population to fast for three days; they were further asked to go on the fourth day, a Friday, to the Mosque of the Foot in order to humbly beseech God to take away this plague. Most of the Damascenes fasted, several passed the night in the mosque indulging in acts of devotion, conforming to the ritual of the month of Ramadan.§ On the morning of July 25, the inhabitants threw themselves [into these ceremonies] at every opportunity from "every precipitous passage":‖

---

*Al-Bukhārī was a famous collector of Islamic traditions who lived in the ninth century. The work being read from is undoubtedly al-Bukhārī's *Sahih,* a collection of more than 7,000 traditions on a variety of subjects, including the creation, heaven and hell, and the Prophet Muhammad. According to al-Maqrīzī, the reading took place at the Omayyad Mosque and lasted three days and nights.

†*mihrab:* An arched niche used for prayer, which pointed in the direction of Mecca.

‡More details of this story are given by al-Maqrīzī, according to whom the holy man came "from the mountains of Asia Minor" and first communicated his vision to the great *qadi,* or judge, of Damascus. His instructions were to "read 3,360 times the flood of Noah and ask God to end this plague that afflicts you." Al-Maqrīzī reports that the Damascenes carried out the holy man's instructions "in a perfect spirit of humility and with an intense repentance of their past sins"; they also allegedly sacrificed a "great number" of sheep and cattle, whose meat was distributed to the poor. After this went on for a week, al-Maqrīzī claims, the plague began to "diminish daily" before disappearing from Damascus entirely. This conflicts with Kathīr's testimony.

§One of the five pillars of Islam, fasting during the sacred month of Ramadan is prescribed by the Koran and usually takes place in October and November.

‖This seems to be a quotation from Koran 22:27: "And proclaim the Pilgrimage among men: They will come to thee on foot and [mounted] on every kind of camel, lean on account of journeys through deep and distant mountain highways." The twenty-second *sura,* or chapter, is on pilgrimage, so this is Kathīr's way of saying that the Damascenes embarked on a plague procession.

One saw in this multitude Jews, Christians, Samaritans, old men, old women, young children, poor men, emirs, notables, magistrates, who processed after the morning prayer, not ceasing to chant their prayers until daybreak. That was a memorable ceremony. . . .

On Monday, October 5, after the call to afternoon prayer, a violent storm broke over Damascus and its environs, stirring up a very thick cloud of dust. The atmosphere became yellowish, then black and was totally dark. The population was in a state of anguish for about a quarter of an hour, imploring God, asking His pardon and lamenting all the more that it was afflicted by this cruel mortality. Others imagined that this cataclysm marked the end of their misfortunes, but they did not dwell too much on this. Indeed, the number of cadavers brought to the Omayyad Mosque exceeded the figure of 150, without including the dead in the suburbs, and the non-Muslim dead. Now, in the environs of the capital, the dead were innumerable, a thousand in a few days.

29

ABŪ HAFS ᶜUMAR IBN AL-WARDĪ

Essay on the Report of the Pestilence

ca. 1348

In this selection, Ibn al-Wardī of Aleppo, Syria, provides a classic account of the Muslim religious view of the plague, largely derived from the Koran and the hadith, or traditions ascribed to the prophet Muhammad. As in the previous selection of his (Document 2), al-Wardī inserts poetic verses as a memory aid.

This plague is for the Muslims a martyrdom and a reward, and for the disbelievers a punishment and a rebuke. When the Muslim endures

Michael W. Dols, "Ibn al-Wardī's *Risālah al-naba' ʿan al-waba'*, A Translation of a Major Source for the History of the Black Death in the Middle East" in *Near Eastern Numismatics, Iconography, Epigraphy and History: Studies in Honor of George C. Miles,* ed. Dickran K. Kouymjian (Beirut: American University of Beirut, 1974), 454–55.

misfortune, then patience is his worship. It has been established by
our Prophet, God bless him and give him peace, that the plague-
stricken are martyrs. This noble tradition is true and assures martyrdom. And this secret should be pleasing to the true believer. If
someone says it causes infection and destruction, say: God creates
and recreates. If the liar disputes the matter of infection and tries to
find an explanation, I say that the Prophet, on him be peace, said: who
infected the first? If we acknowledge the plague's devastation of the
people, it is the will of the Chosen Doer. So it happened again and
again.

I take refuge in God from the yoke of the plague. Its high explosion
has burst into all countries and was an examiner of astonishing things.
Its sudden attacks perplex the people. The plague chases the scream-
ing without pity and does not accept a treasure for ransom. Its engine
is far-reaching. The plague enters into the house and swears it will not
leave except with all of its inhabitants: "I have an order from the *qadi*
[religious judge] to arrest all those in the house." Among the benefits
of this order is the removal of one's hopes and the improvement of his
earthly works. It awakens men from their indifference for the provi-
sioning of their final journey.

One man begs another to take care of his children, and one says
goodbye to his neighbors.
A third perfects his works, and another prepares his shroud.
A fifth is reconciled with his enemies, and another treats his friends
with kindness.
One is very generous; another makes friends with those who have
betrayed him.
Another man puts aside his property; one frees his servants.*
One man changes his character while another mends his ways.
For this plague has captured all people and is about to send its
ultimate destruction.
There is no protection today from it other than His mercy, praise be
to God.

Nothing prevented us from running away from the plague except
our devotion to noble tradition. Come then, seek the aid of God Almighty for raising the plague, for He is the best helper. Oh God, we
call You better than anyone did before. We call You to raise from us
the pestilence and plague. We do not take refuge in its removal other
than with You. We do not depend on our good health against the

*Slavery was common in the Muslim world.

plague but on You. We seek Your protection, oh Lord of creation, from the blows of this stick. We ask for Your mercy which is wider than our sins even as they are the number of the sands and pebbles. We plead with You, by the most honored of the advocates, Muhammad, the Prophet of mercy, that You take away from us this distress. Protect us from the evil and the torture and preserve us. For You are our sole support; what a perfect trustee!

30

LISĀN AL-DĪN IBN AL-KHATĪB

A Very Useful Inquiry into the Horrible Sickness

1349–1352

A Muslim scholar and physician, Lisān al-Dīn Ibn al-Khatīb hailed from Loja, a town near Granada, the capital city of an important and tenacious Moorish kingdom in southern Spain. A friend of Ibn Khatīma, Ibn al-Khatīb wrote his own medical account of the plague, entitled Muqniᶜat as-sā'il ᶜan al-marad al-hā'il *(A Very Useful Inquiry into the Horrible Sickness). Since he incorporated Ibn Battūta's famous description of the plague in Southeast Asia, al-Khatīb likely wrote his treatise during his friend's visit to Granada between 1349 and 1352. In this selection, al-Khatīb explains why he rejects the Islamic religious proscription against plague contagion, which was well documented by physicians. His outspokenness against a long-established* hadith, *or religious tradition, backed up by the Shari'a, or Muslim law, was perhaps triggered by the fact that his friend, Khātima, felt compelled to bow to Islamic precept despite empirical observation on the same subject in his own treatise (Document 13). Al-Khatīb's brave defense of contagion may have contributed to his forced exile from Granada in 1371, when proceedings began for his trial for heresy on the basis of his writings. Before the trial could begin, however, a mob broke into his prison at Fez and lynched him in 1374.*

M. J. Müller, "Ibnulkhatīb's Bericht über die Pest," *Sitzungsberichte der Königl. Bayerischen Akademie der Wissenchaften*, 2 (1863): 2–12. Translated from the Arabic with assistance from Walid Saleh.

If it were asked, how do we submit to the th
already the divine law has refuted the notic
answer: The existence of contagion has bee
deduction, the senses, observation, and by
these aforementioned categories are the den
it is not a secret to whoever has looked into t
be aware of it that those who come into con
mostly die, while those who do not come into contact sui vi v.

over, disease occurs in a household or neighborhood because of the
mere presence of a contagious dress or utensil; even a [contaminated]
earring has been known to kill whoever wears it and his whole household. And when it happens in a city, it starts in one house and then
affects the visitors of the house, then the neighbors, the relatives, and
other visitors until it spreads throughout the city. And coastal cities
are free of the disease until it comes from the sea through a visitor
from another city that has the disease, and thus the appearance of the
disease in the safe city coincides with the arrival of this man from the
contagious city. And the safety of those who have gone into isolation is
demonstrated by the example of the ascetic, Ibn Abū Madyan, who
lived in the city of Salé [unidentified]. He believed in contagion, and
so he hoarded food and bricked up the door on his family (and his
family was large!), and the city was obliterated by the plague and not
one soul [except Madyan] was left in that whole town. And reports
were unanimous that isolated places that have no roads to them and
are not frequented by people have escaped unscathed from the
plague. And let me tell you of the miraculous survival in our time of
the Muslim prisoners who were spared in the prison of the city of
Seville, and they were in the thousands. They were not struck by the
bubonic plague, yet it almost obliterated the city. And it has been confirmed that nomads and tent dwellers in Africa and other nomadic
places have escaped unscathed because their air is not enclosed and it
is improbable that it can be corrupted.

And amidst the horrible afflictions that the plague has imposed
upon the people, God has afflicted the people with some learned religious scholars who issue *fatwas** [against fleeing the plague], so that
the quills with which the scholars wrote these *fatwas* were like swords
upon which the Muslims died. . . . Although the intent of the divine

fatwa: A ruling or an opinion based on Islamic law handed down by a qualified legal
scholar.

ent of harm, when a prophetic statement is contradicted
ses and observation, it is incumbent upon us to interpret it
y so that the *hadith* fits reality, even if we claim to subscribe to
teral meaning of the *hadith* and, lest we forget, to the fundamen-
s of the *Shari'a* [Islamic law] that everybody knows about. And the
truth of this matter is that it should be interpreted in accordance with
those who affirm the theory of contagion. Moreover, there are in the
divine law many indications that support the theory of contagion, such
as the statement of Muhammad: "A disease should not visit a healthy
man," or the statement that: "One escapes the fate of God to meet the
fate of God." But this is not the place to go on at length concerning
this matter, because the discussion about whether the divine law
agrees or disagrees with the contagion theory is not the business of
the medical art, but is incidental to it. And in conclusion, to ignore the
proofs for plague contagion is an indecency and an affront to God and
holds cheap the lives of Muslims. And some of the learned holy men
have retracted their *fatwas* for fear of helping people to their deaths.

May God keep us from committing error in word and deed!

6

The Psyche of Hysteria

The flagellant movement and the pogroms against the Jews, although not always uncontrolled, were certainly hysterical—highly emotional—responses to the Black Death. Flagellation, or whipping—performed for a variety of motives including penitential atonement, mortification of the flesh, imitation of Christ, or divine supplication—was not unusual in the Middle Ages. As a punishment for sinful behavior it appears from an early date in Christianity and was included in the first monastic rules from the fourth to the sixth centuries. Self-inflicted flagellation became common in Christian observance during the eleventh and twelfth centuries. In 1260, there arose in Perugia, Italy, a public, collective, processional movement of voluntary flagellants, the forerunner of the movement during the Black Death.[1]

Scapegoating of minority groups seems to be a common failing in times of crisis, and medieval Christian society during the Black Death was no exception. The pogroms from 1348 to 1351 took place within the context of centuries of assaults and "blood libels" directed against the Jews by Christians. Beginning in the eleventh century, Jews were attacked as "Christ killers" who had betrayed Jesus Christ to Pontius Pilate and rejected him as the messiah.[2] Nevertheless, by the fourteenth century there was also a long tradition whereby Church fathers argued for toleration of Jews, because their conversion at the end of time would serve as witness to the final triumph of Christianity.[3] At the same time, the economic position of many Jewish communities in Europe was being steadily undermined. Since the eleventh century, Jews had been ousted from farming and various crafts and trades by Christian regulations and competition. By the middle of the twelfth century they were being stereotyped as money lenders; usury—the lending of money at exorbitant interest rates—was technically off-limits to Christians by canon law and became practically the only profession left open to them.[4] Not even the specific accusation of well poisoning leveled against the Jews in 1348 was unprecedented. In

France and Spain, both Jews and Muslims were implicated in the so-
called "lepers' plot" of 1321, which charged that members of both
groups had induced lepers to poison Christians.[5] It may be no accident
that the first attacks upon the Jews during the Black Death took place
in these same countries.

THE FLAGELLANTS

The flagellant movement, which got its name from the *flagella,* or whips
used in penitential ceremonies, revived in response to the arrival of
the Black Death in 1348 (see Figure 2). The movement seems to have
begun in late 1348 in Austria or Hungary, and progressed from there
to Thuringia and Franconia in central Germany by the spring of 1349,
when scholars think it entered its most radical phase. It came to south
Germany and the Rhineland that summer and continued to the Low
Countries, where it persisted until the autumn of 1349, when Pope
Clement VI and King Philip VI of France determined to suppress it.[6]

Given the prevalent Christian belief that the plague was a righteous
scourge sent down by God in retribution for man's wickedness and sin
(chapter 5), it was perfectly logical for people to want to try to avert or
atone for God's extraordinary wrath by performing an extraordinary
penance. During the movement of 1348 to 1350, flagellation was gov-
erned by numerous rituals and protocols, but some medieval eye-
witnesses, such as Heinrich of Herford (Document 31) and Gilles li
Muisis (Document 33) testify to the exceptional emotion, even hysteria, the ceremonies could arouse in both participants and spectators.

From the very beginning, it seems, opinion was divided about the
flagellants, a point that comes through clearly despite the fact that
nearly all medieval chroniclers, members of the Church establishment whom the flagellants allegedly opposed, were hostile observers.
Some chroniclers hint at unorthodoxy among the flagellants. Herford,
Fritsche Closener, and Muisis (Documents 31, 32, and 33) each point
to various disturbing aspects of the movement, such as millenarian ex-
pectations, resistance to clerical authority, doctrinal error—in particular, concerning the salutary power of the flagellants' extraordinary
penance—and lack of ecclesiastical guidance and authorization, thus
relegating the flagellants to the status of a mere "sect." But whether
this qualifies the movement as heretical is still open to debate. Changes
in the geographic focus of the movement may have brought the flagellants into areas, such as Thuringia, where heresy was already prevalent, but there seems to be no evidence that local heresies actually

Figure 2. Flagellants, from a Fifteenth-Century Chronicle from Constance, Switzerland.

© Bettmann/CORBIS.

influenced the flagellants. One can also attribute opposition to flagellants to the fact that an initially broad-based, disciplined movement, like that described by Hugo of Reutlingen, later developed into unruly mobs. The chronology doesn't always correspond to a "two-phase" theory, however. Some flagellants experienced opposition early in the movement, and some later flagellants, like those in Flanders described by Gilles li Muisis, displayed no less discipline than their predecessors. It is possible, however, that the flagellants were at their most hysterical in the early days, when they anticipated the plague's arrival in their localities, but then grew considerably less anxious later, when the shock of the disease had worn off.[7]

Some medieval chroniclers also charged flagellants with being responsible for pogroms against the Jews. A Benedictine monk and master of theology at the University of Paris, Jean de Fayt, preached a sermon before the pope at Avignon on October 5, 1349, in which he alleged that "everywhere [flagellants] strive to kill Jews, thinking that it pleases God to exterminate them." Fayt went on to elaborate that flagellants rejected traditional Church teaching that urged the preservation of Jews as witnesses to the ultimate triumph of Christianity at the Last Judgment. Fayt also claimed that flagellants accused the Jews of well poisoning, which went against scientific explanations that attributed the cause of the plague to a conjunction of the planets.[8] Pope Clement VI endorsed Fayt's views when he issued a mandate to suppress the flagellants on October 20, 1349.[9] However, neither Fayt nor the pope cite specific evidence of a connection between this movement and the anti-Jewish pogroms.

Some chroniclers provide more concrete examples. Heinrich of Rebdorf alleges that the Jews of Bamberg attacked and killed "14 flagellants or thereabouts, and other citizens who were their defenders."[10] Gilles li Muisis relates how some Jewish astrologers had premonitions "that there would appear men carrying red crosses, and they had no doubt that then their sect would be destroyed." He goes on to tell the story of a rich baptized Jew of Brabant in Flanders, who appealed to Duke John III for protection when the flagellants arrived in town, on the grounds that "since the men who do such things are here, it is certain that I and the whole Jewish sect, wherever we can be found, will be destroyed." Muisis then relates that six hundred Jews of Brabant, including the Christian convert on friendly terms with the duke, were killed on the grounds of well poisoning and other blood libels, but he does not mention that the flagellants played a role in the massacre.[11] A contemporary verse chronicle from Brabant also makes the connection between the flagellants and Jewish pogroms, but allegations of a similar connection at Cologne and Frankfurt receive no such corroboration.[12]

One can imagine that the extreme emotionalism literally whipped up by the flagellants would easily lend itself to other acts of violence. But in many cases, the timing was not quite right. The famous Jewish pogrom at Strasbourg, for instance, which occurred on February 14, 1349, preceded the arrival of the flagellants there that June or July (Documents 32 and 38). One therefore has to examine the documents carefully to decide whether a connection between the flagellants and Jewish pogroms in a given area is even possible.

NOTES

[1]Norman Cohn, *The Pursuit of the Millennium: Revolutionary Messianism in Medieval and Reformation Europe and Its Bearing on Modern Totalitarian Movements,* 2nd ed. (New York: Harper and Brothers, 1961), 125–27; John Henderson, "The Flagellant

Movement and Flagellant Confraternities in Central Italy, 1260–1400," in *Religious Motivation: Biographical and Sociological Problems for the Church Historian,* ed. Derek Baker (Oxford: Basil Blackwell, 1978), 149–51; Gary Dickson, "The Flagellants of 1260 and the Crusades," *Journal of Medieval History,* 15 (1989): 221–45, 251–58.

²On the origins of medieval anti-Judaism/anti-Semitism, see Jeremy Cohen, "The Jews as the Killers of Christ in the Latin Tradition, from Augustine to the Friars," *Traditio,* 39 (1983): 1–27; Gavin Langmuir, *Toward a Definition of Antisemitism* (Berkeley and Los Angeles: University of California Press, 1990), 57–99; idem, *History, Religion, and Antisemitism* (Berkeley and Los Angeles: University of California Press, 1990), 275–305; Kenneth R. Stow, *Alienated Minority: The Jews of Medieval Latin Europe* (Cambridge, Mass.: Harvard University Press, 1992), 6–64.

³Kenneth R. Stow, "Hatred of Jews or Love of the Church," in *Antisemitism Through the Ages,* ed. Shmuel Almog (Oxford: Pergamon Press, 1988), 71–89.

⁴George Caro, *Sozial- und Wirtschaftsgeschichte der Juden,* 2 vols. (Frankfurt, 1920–24), 1:220–23; Stow, *Alienated Minority,* 210–30.

⁵David Nirenberg, *Communities of Violence: Persecution of Minorities in the Middle Ages* (Princeton, N.J.: Princeton University Press, 1996).

⁶Frantisek Graus, *Pest, Geissler, Judenmorde: Das 14 Jahrhundert als Krisenzeit* (Göttingen: Vandenhoek and Ruprecht, 1987), 38–59. For English histories of the 1348–50 flagellant movement, see: Gordon Leff, *Heresy in the Later Middle Ages: The Relation of Heterodoxy to Dissent, c. 1250–c. 1450,* 2 vols. (Manchester: Manchester University Press, 1967), 2:485–93; Norman Cohn, *The Pursuit of the Millennium,* 129–42; Philip Ziegler, *The Black Death* (New York: Harper and Row, 1969), 86–97; Richard Kieckhefer, "Radical Tendencies in the Flagellant Movement of the Mid-Fourteenth Century," *Journal of Medieval and Renaissance Studies,* 4 (1974): 157–76.

⁷Kieckhefer, "Radical Tendencies in the Flagellant Movement," 157–76. For Hugo of Reutlingen's chronicle of the flagellants, see Johannes Nohl, *The Black Death: A Chronicle of the Plague,* trans. C. H. Clarke (New York: Harper and Row, 1969), 243–47.

⁸*Corpus Documentorum Inquisitionis Haereticae Pravitatis Neerlandicae,* ed. Paul Frédéricq, 3 vols. (Ghent: J. Vuylsteke, 1889–1906), 3:36–37.

⁹*The Apostolic See and the Jews,* ed. Shlomo Simonsohn, 8 vols. (Toronto: The Pontifical Institute of Medieval Studies, 1988–91), 1:399–402.

¹⁰*Fontes Rerum Germanicarum: Geschichtsquellen Deutschlands,* ed. Johann Friedrich Boehmer and Alfons Huber, 4 vols. (Stuttgart: J. G. Cotta'scher Verlag, 1843–68), 4:561.

¹¹*Recueil des chroniques de Flandre,* ed. Joseph-Jean de Smet, 4 vols. (Brussels, 1837–65), 2:342–43.

¹²*Corpus Documentorum,* 1:194–95; Kieckhefer, "Radical Tendencies in the Flagellant Movement," 162 and sources cited in nn. 28–31.

31

HEINRICH OF HERFORD

Book of Memorable Matters

ca. 1349–1355

Coming from a town in Westphalia in Germany, Heinrich of Herford was a Dominican friar who died at the convent of Minden on October 9, 1370. Herford betrays his Dominican sympathies in his famous account of the flagellants, whom he regarded as the order's enemies. He also seems to view the flagellants in millennial terms as perhaps heralding the reign of the Antichrist, and appended to his account is an excerpt (not included here) from a tract attributed to Gerhard of Cosvelde, a monk of Westphalia, in which the arrival of the flagellants is elaborately foretold by a conjunction of the planets. Nonetheless, Heinrich does not tell us whether the flagellants themselves saw their movement in millenarian terms. His account is most valuable for its lengthy and detailed description of flagellation processions and ceremonies. Although Heinrich was clearly hostile to the flagellants, he speaks of them from firsthand observation and describes the arguments made by both their defenders and detractors. His chronicle ends in 1355.

In the same year [1349], a race without a head, calling themselves cruciferians [cross-bearers] or flagellants, unexpectedly arose from all parts of Germany, whose numbers and the suddenness of their coming was a source of universal wonder. They were said to be without a head, as if in confirmation of the prophecy,* either because they liter-

---

*This refers to the Cedar of Lebanon prophecy, which had been circulating in Europe since around 1240. The version that was resurrected to fit the Black Death, which redated the prophecy to 1347, seems to have been very popular. The prophecy predicted a series of apocalyptic disasters that, in addition to plague and the "people without a head," would include famine, war, and political and religious upheaval. Thereafter would follow a period of fifteen years during which there would be peace, plenty, conversion of the heathen, and reconquest of Jerusalem and the Holy Land. In the midst of this tranquillity would come news of the Antichrist.

Henricus de Hervordia, *Liber de Rebus Memorabilioribus sive Chronicon,* ed. Augustus Potthast (Göttingen: Dieterich, 1859), 280–82.

ally had no head—that is to say, no one to unite or guide them—or
because they were without the sense of the head—that is to say, they
lacked prudence and were fools, pretending to a kind of piety but wal-
lowing in their stupidity so that, as will be made clear, they tainted
everything. Moreover, they were called cruciferians, either because in
their wanderings a cross was carried before them and they followed it,
or because during their processions they would prostrate themselves
in the shape of a cross, or because the sign of the cross was sewn onto
their clothing. But they were called the flagellants on account of the
flagella [whips] with which they were seen to do penance. Each whip
consisted of a stick from which hung down three cords tied with great
knots on their ends, so that passing through the knots from both sides
in the shape of a cross were two pieces of iron sharpened to a point,
which stuck out of the knots as far as a medium-sized grain of wheat
or less. With these *flagella* they beat and whipped their naked bodies
to the point that the scourged skin swelled up black and blue and
blood flowed down to their lower members and even spattered the
walls nearby. I have seen, when they whipped themselves, how the
iron points became so embedded in the flesh that sometimes one pull,
sometimes two, was not enough to extract them.

Gathering themselves from various nations, or perhaps from the
cities, they wandered the land, through fields and open country without any order, as if this could have occurred to them, following their
cross. But when they came to cities, towns, and large villages and set-
tlements, they marched down the street in procession, with their
hoods or hats pulled down a little to cover their foreheads and with
sad and downcast eyes, singing a religious song that had a pleasant
melody. And so they enter* the church, shut themselves inside and
strip off their clothes, which they entrust to someone's custody. Wearing a many-pleated linen skirt, similar to a woman's undergarment
which in Germany is called a *kedel* [girtle], they cover their bodies
from the navel down, leaving the upper part totally nude. They take up
the whips in their hands. This done, the south door of the church, if
there is one, is opened. The senior flagellant leaves the church first
and prostrates himself upon the ground next to the public walkway on
the eastern side of the door. After him the second flagellant prostrates
himself on the western side, then the third lies next to the first, and
the fourth next to the second, and so on in succession. Some raise

---

*At this point, the verb tense changes to the present, giving the description that fol-
lows a more immediate quality.

their right hand as if they are about to take an oath, some lie on their stomachs, some on their backs, some on their right side or the left, as if to express the nature of their sins, for which they have been doing penance. After this, one of them strikes the first flagellant with a whip, saying: "God grants you remission of all your sins, arise!" And he gets up. Then he does the same to the second and so on through the order of each of the others. When they are all standing and processing two by two in good order and in unison, two of them in the middle of the procession start to sing in a high voice a religious song with a pleasant melody, singing through one verse out of the whole song. And then the whole procession recapitulates that verse, while the two singers proceed to the second verse. And after they are finished, the procession once again sings through the same verse and so on until the end of the song. Moreover, whenever in the course of their psalmody they come to a part of the song where the passion of Christ is mentioned, all together they suddenly throw themselves to the ground from a high incline [i.e., bending over, so that they fall on their faces] wherever they happen to be and on whatever is lying there, either on the earth, or on mud, or thorns, or thistles, or nettles or stones. They do not fall down in stages on their knees, or by supporting themselves in any other way, but they drop like logs, flat upon their belly and face with their arms outstretched, so that they lie there in the shape of a cross, and in this posture they pray. One would need a heart of stone to be able to watch this without tears. At a sign given by one of them, they get up and sing through their song while in procession, as before. And most often they sing the said song in its entirety three times, and each time they fall thrice to the ground, as is described above. And then when they arrive back at the door of the church, through which they had come out, they go back into the church, put on their clothes, take off their linen skirts, and process out of the church. They ask for nothing from anyone, neither food nor lodging, but offerings* are freely made to them and they accept many of these with gratitude.

But just as unwanted tares and persistent burs often grow among the harvest, so these unlearned and stupid people unfortunately and stubbornly usurp even the preacher's office with their penitential whips. Concerning religious and clerical matters and the sacraments of the church, they do not think or speak wisely, they spit back any

---

*The term used here, *oblata,* which can be translated as oblations, also signifies the offerings made by parishioners every Sunday in church, which would imply an expectation of them by the flagellants.

reproof and correction, and they scorn and even despise attempts to persuade them otherwise. And when two friar preachers [Dominicans] met up with them in a field, they were so exasperated by their arguments that they wished to kill them, with the result that the more agile preacher escaped by running away, but the other was stoned to death, and they left his dead body covered under the stones on the outskirts of Meissen. And they did more such acts in many other places. If perchance someone were to say to them: "Why do you preach, when you are not sent [i.e., licensed by the bishop], saying with the Apostle [Paul], 'How shall they preach, unless they be sent?' [Romans 10:15]* and why do you teach what you do not understand and when you are illiterate?" they respond, as if they wish to beat back one nail with another [i.e., turn the opponent's argument against him]: "And who sent you, and how do you know that what you consecrate is the body of Christ, or that what you preach is the Gospel truth?" If it is answered them, as a certain friar preacher answered them, that we received these things from our Savior, who consecrated His body and ordered that it be consecrated by His disciples and their followers, thus instituting the form of consecration that has come down from them to us, and that we are sent by the Church to preach the Gospel, which teaches what is true and cannot err, since it is guided by the Holy Spirit, they say that they themselves are instructed and sent directly by the Lord and the spirit of God in accordance with what it says in Isaiah 48:[16]: "The Lord [God] hath sent me, and his spirit." . . .

Even the sentence of excommunication laid upon them by the bishops they either ignore or despise. They give no heed to the process of the pope against them.[†] Thus far, the princes and nobles and more powerful men of the cities have begun to keep their distance from them. The citizens of Osnabrück never let them in, even though their wives and other women called for them most impatiently. Nevertheless afterwards, almost as suddenly as they had come, they just as quickly disappeared, like the nocturnal phantoms and ghosts we laugh at. Horace[‡] around the end of his letters says: "Do you laugh at nocturnal ghosts and Thessalian portents?" And this is well said. Also there were among them some spectators, wise and honest men, and even bishops, such as the bishop of Utrecht and others, albeit they

---

*This passage from the New Testament was often invoked against heretics.

†This refers to Pope Clement VI's bull, *Inter Solicitudines,* of October 20, 1349, which ordered the suppression of the flagellants.

‡The Roman poet Horace (65–8 BCE) is famous for his poems celebrating the *pax Romana,* or Roman peace, of the emperor Augustus (27 BCE–14 CE).

were usually joined by common folk and even by lewd men. Also there were those who said that after performing their penance, all flagellants were defamed and could not stand trial because they had already undergone a public penance. But it was said that their penance was not inflicted on them, but they had freely subjected themselves to it. If it is said that the imposition of a penance does not make the infamy, but that the crime does, for which the penance, whether it is inflicted or not, is performed—not that it even matters whether someone performs it or does something similar—it is answered that not simply the crime, but also the punishment judicially bestows the status of criminal infamy. But that is not the case here.

32

FRITSCHE CLOSENER

Chronicle

1360–1362

The Chronicle *of Fritsche Closener, like that of Giovanni Villani, is an early example of municipal history entirely devoted to the author's native or adopted city—in this case, Strasbourg—that was to come into vogue toward the end of the fourteenth century. Closener was born into a noble family from Alsace, and his father is described as a bourgeois of Strasbourg. Ordained as a priest, he was appointed prebend of the chapel of St. Catherine in the cathedral of Strasbourg in 1340. He began writing his* Chronicle *in 1360 and, by his own account, completed it on July 8, 1362. Closener's history of the flagellants in Strasbourg is much more detailed than that of his contemporary, Mathias of Neuenburg, who also concerned himself with events related to Strasbourg.*

In 1349, fourteen days after midsummer [July 8], around mass time, about 200 flagellants came to Strasbourg,* who carried on in the man-

---

*Mathias of Neuenberg says that seventy flagellants came to Strasbourg from Swabia in the middle of June.

Die Chroniken der Deutschen Städte, 8 (1870): 105–20. Translated from the German by Thomas Huber.

ner I'm about to describe. First, they had the most precious flags of velvet cloth, rough and smooth, and the finest canopies, of which they had maybe ten or eight, and torches and many candles, which were carried ahead of them when they went into cities or villages. And all bells were rung in alarm then, and they followed their flags two by two in a row, and they were all wearing overcoats and hoods with red crosses. And two or four sang the beginning of a hymn, and the others joined in.... [The hymn begins: "Now the journey has become so grand/Christ Himself rides into Jerusalem."] And when they entered the churches, they knelt down and sang: "Jesus was fortified with gall/That's why we should be on the cross all." With these words they prostrated themselves in the form of a cross, so that it rang out. After they'd been thus for awhile, the lead singer began and sang: "Now we lift up our hands and pray/O God take the great death away!" Then they got up. They did this for three hours. When they had risen for the third time, the people invited the brothers—one invited twenty, another twelve or ten, each one as they could—and they led them to their homes and did them well.

Now this was their rule. Whoever wanted to join the brotherhood had to stay with it for thirty-three and a half days, and for that reason, he had to have so many pennies that he could offer four on every day while he was doing penance: This amounted to eleven shillings and four pence. This was why they did not ask or beg of any one, nor enter any house. When they came to a city or village, they were invited and taken in without their asking. After that, they might enter houses as long as they were in the city. They also were not allowed to speak to any woman.* If one broke this rule and spoke to a woman, he knelt in front of their master and confessed. Then the master set the penalty and whipped him with the scourge on his back and spoke: "Rise up from the cleansing pain/And stay away from sin from now on." They also had a rule that priests may be among them, but none of them should be a master nor belong to their secret council.

When they wanted to do penance, which was at least twice a day, in the morning and at night, they took their scourges and went outside the city limits. While one rang the bells, they gathered and went out in rows of two by two and sang their hymn as described earlier. And when they arrived at the place for whipping, they undressed to their

---

*This is contradicted by an anonymous chronicler from the monastery of St. Truiden in the Low Countries, who claims that a breakaway sect of the flagellants "was secretly lodged in the house of a woman across the Rhine." If this is true, it is surprising that Closener does not mention it, especially because it occurred in his vicinity.

underclothes and barefeet and wrapped little skirts or white cloths about them, which went from the belt to their feet. And when they were ready to begin their penance, they laid down in a wide circle, and whoever had sinned laid down anyway, but if there was a villain who had broken his oath, he laid down on one side and raised three fingers and his head, and if there was one who had broken his troth, he laid on his belly. This way, they laid down in many ways, according to the sins which everyone had committed. After they all had lain down, the master began where he saw fit and stepped over one of them and hit his back with the scourge and said: "Rise up from the cleansing pain/And stay away from sin from now on." Thus he walked about them all, and the ones he stepped over followed the master across those who were still down. Thus, when two of them had walked over the third, that one rose and walked with them to the fourth, and the fourth across the fifth one in front of him. They all followed what the master did with the scourge using the same words, until all of them had gotten up and walked over each other. And when they had risen into their circle, some of them, who were considered the best singers, began to sing a hymn. The brothers sang after them, in the same manner as one sings for a dance. All the time the brothers walked in the circle two by two and whipped themselves with the scourges, which had knots at the end into which thorns had been placed, and they whipped themselves across their backs so that many of them were bleeding a lot. . . .

The flagellants' sermon:* This is the message of our Lord Jesus Christ, who came down to the altar of the Good Lord St. Peter in Jerusalem, as written on a marble tablet from which a light issued forth, like lightning. God's angel set up this table. The congregation saw this and people fell on their faces and cried "Kyrie eleison," which means "Lord have mercy." The message of our Lord is this:

"You children of men, you have seen and heard what I've forbidden and you didn't heed it, so that you're sinful and unbelieving, and you didn't keep my holy Sunday. And you have not repented and improved, even though you heard in the gospel: 'Heaven and Earth shall perish, but my word stands forever.' I sent you enough grain, oil, and wine,† in

---

*Another version of this sermon, written in the form of an itemized letter that was said to have been delivered by the flagellants of Mechelen to the bishop of Kamerijk, is recorded in a contemporary French chronicle and printed in *Corpus Documentorum Inquisitionis Haereticae Pravitatis Neerlandicae,* ed. Paul Frédéricq, 3 vols. (Ghent: J. Vuylsteke, 1889–1906), 3:22–23.

†A reference to Joel 1:10. In this case, Israel's abundance was taken away by war.

good measure, and I took it all away in front of your eyes because of your wickedness and your sins and pride, because you didn't observe my holy Sunday and my holy Friday, with fasts and celebration. This is why I ordered the Saracens and other heathens that they shed your blood and take many of you prisoners. In a few years, much misery happened: earthquakes, hunger, fever, locusts, rats, mice, vermin, pocks, frost, thunder, lightning, and much disorder. I sent you all this because you haven't observed my holy Sunday. . . .

"I swear to you upon My right hand, that is, by My godly might and by My power: If you don't keep My holy Sunday and My holy Friday, I shall spoil you totally so that no one will ever think of you ever on this earth. Verily, I say: If you reform from your sins, I shall send you My holy divine blessing so that the earth shall bear fruit full of mercy and all the world shall be full of my power. I shall have you partake in My great joy, so that you can sally forth anew and will forget My anger against you and shall fill all your houses with My divine blessing. And when you come before My judgment, I shall share My pity with you, the selected ones in My heavenly empire. Amen. . . ."

Then the people saw the tablet on which was the message light up the domed church just like lightning. At that, the people took fright, so much so that they fell on their face and when they came to, what did they do? They separated and took counsel among themselves as to what they could do to better praise God so that He would overlook His anger. They deliberated and went to the king of Sicily* and asked him for his advice as to what they could do to make God amend His anger against them. He told them that they should fall on their knees and pray to Almighty God that He tell them what they should do and how to come to terms with Him so that He would forget His anger against all the poor of Christendom. The people did as they were told and fell on their knees and prayed from the bottom of their hearts. Then the angel said: "You know that God walked on earth for thirty-three and a half years† and never had a good day, not to mention the great torture He suffered from you on the cross, for which you never thanked Him and won't thank Him either. If you want to make your peace with God, you should go on a pilgrimage for thirty-three and a half days and should never have a good day nor night and spill your blood. Then He

*Assuming that this part of the letter is contemporary with the Black Death, this would be Louis the Great of Hungary (1342–1382), who in 1348 led a crusade to Naples and declared himself king of Sicily and Jerusalem.
†The age traditionally ascribed to Christ at his crucifixion.

will not want to have His blood lost upon you and He intends to forget His anger against poor Christendom." . . . [The pilgrimage started by the king of Sicily spread to Poland, Hungary, the German towns and eventually to the Rhineland and Alsace.]

Thus ended the letter. When it had been read, they returned to the city, two by two, following their flags and candles, and sang the first hymn: "Now is the first pilgrimage." And they rang the big bells for them, and when they came to the main church, they fell down in the shape of a cross and three stood as has been written. When they rose again, they went to their shelters or wherever they wanted to go. . . .

You should know that whenever the flagellants whipped themselves, there were large crowds and the greatest pious weeping that one should ever see. When they read the letter, there rose great lamentation from the people, because they all believed it was true. And when the priests said, how one should recognize that their whipping pilgrimage was the right one, they answered and spoke: "Who wrote the gospels?" Thus they make the people believe the flagellants' word more than those of the priests. And the people spoke to the priests: "What can you say? These are people who know the truth and tell it." And wherever they came, many people of the cities also became flagellants, both laymen and priests, but no learned priest joined them.* Many well-meaning men joined this whipping pilgrimage; in their simple-minded way, they could not see the falsehood which resided therein. But also, many a proved scoundrel joined these well-meaning people, who then turned nasty, or nastier than before. Some of them who remained were also well-meaning, but there were not many of them. Some loved the brotherhood very much; after they had done it twice, they started again. For this reason, it happened that when they were on the road, they were idle and didn't work. And wherever they came, as many as they were, people invited them all and gave them everything, and there were many people who liked to invite them, as many of them as they could, they were that highly esteemed.

The burghers in the cities gave them money from the city coffers so that they could buy flags and candles. The [flagellant] brothers also assumed great holiness and said that great things were happening by

---

*According to Mathias of Neuenberg, 1,000 people in Strasbourg joined the flagellants. Nonetheless, he goes on to say that the citizens and burgermeisters, or city councillors, of the city were "divided in opinion about the flagellants, one faction against them, another for them."

their will. First, they said, a well-meaning man gave them drink from a barrel of wine, and no matter how many of them drank from it, it was full. They also said that a martyr's image in Offenburg had sweated, and that a statue of Our Lady also had been sweating. Thus they said many things, which were all lies. They also said that cattle in Ersthein had been talking. It came about thus: There was someone in Ersthein whose name was Rinder [German word for cattle] who was very ill and couldn't speak. It came to pass that the flagellants were there so that the man got better and talked. One said to the other, "Rinder is talking." So the flagellants spoke as if the cattle in the stables had been talking. This shows how simple-minded the country was and the people in it. They also took it upon themselves to exorcize the mad people. . . . They also dragged a dead child about in a meadow around their ring as they whipped themselves and wanted to make it live again, but that didn't happen.

These whipping pilgrimages lasted for more than a quarter of a year, so that every week there was another band of flagellants. Then also women took off and wandered through the land and whipped themselves. Then also young boys and children took up the flagellants' pilgrimage. After that, the people did not want to ring bells for them anymore, and they didn't want to give them any more contributions for candles and flags. One also got tired of them, so that one didn't invite them into homes as one had done before. Thus they became a nuisance and one paid but little attention to them. Then the priests attacked the falsehoods and lies they were spreading around, and they said that the letter was a lie they were preaching. At first, the flagellants had brought the people to their side so much that no one dared speak out against them anymore. Any priest who spoke against them could hardly save himself from the people. But then their pilgrimages didn't go so well, and the priests spoke against them all over again. . . . It was forbidden them to form a brotherhood and whip themselves in public. If one wanted to whip himself, he had to do it secretly in his house. Bishop Berthold of Bucheck also forbade them in his bishopric [of Strasbourg] upon holy orders from the pope, who instructed the bishops that the seemingly spiritual beliefs they held, especially that one layman could confess to another, should be abandoned.

This I have described as it happened, and it was the same in towns all along the Rhine and in Swabia, Franconia, in the West and in many German lands. Thus, the flagellants' pilgrimages ended in half a year, but as they had said, it should have lasted thirty-three and a half years.

33

GILLES LI MUISIS

Chronicle

1350

Gilles li Muisis was abbot of the Benedictine monastery of St. Giles in Tournai. At that time part of the county of Flanders, technically a vassal state of the French crown, Tournai and other wealthy, cloth-producing towns of the Low Countries nevertheless enjoyed a large degree of political independence. Like most towns in the area, Tournai was ruled by a group of aldermen, who set public policy. The following selection from Muisis's Chronicle *depicting the flagellants of Flanders was written in early 1350.*

It happened that in the aforesaid year [1349] on the day of the Assumption of the glorious Virgin [August 15], there came [to Tournai] from the town of Bruges around lunchtime about two hundred men.* They gathered themselves in the square, and immediately word of them spread through the whole town, so that all came running. People came in crowds to the aforesaid place, because they had heard rumors about this, and therefore they aspired to see the real thing. Meanwhile those flagellants from Bruges prepared themselves, and they began to perform their ritual, which they called penance. People of both sexes, who had never seen such a thing, began to take pity on the performers and empathize with their sufferings and thank God for their great penance, which they judged to be most severe. And the said flagellants from Bruges remained in the city for all that day and night. And on the morrow, which was a Sunday, they assembled at the monastery of St. Martin [in Tournai] and there began to perform their penance, and after lunch they returned to the town square. And on those two days [August 15 and 16], the whole community felt pity for

---

*In the previous sentence, Muisis informs us that "some people in certain parishes began to die and succumb [to the plague] in the beginning of August or thereabouts."

Recueil des chroniques de Flandre, ed. Joseph-Jean de Smet, 4 vols. (Brussels, 1837–65), 2:341–42, 348–49, 361.

the said penitents, and there were various opinions about them: be-cause some people of sound mind did not praise them, and others greatly approved of what they were doing. . . . [Brother Gerard de Muro, a Franciscan friar, preached a sermon at St. Martin on August 18. Because Muro failed to offer up a prayer for the flagellants at the end of his sermon, "the majority of the audience was indignant, and people murmured against him in various ways through the whole of that week."]

Also on Saturday, the feast-day of the beheading of St. John the Baptist [August 29], there came [to Tournai] a fraternity of around 180 flagellants from Liège, and with them came a brother of the order of friar preachers of St. Dominic, and on that day and on the morrow, which was a Sunday, they stayed performing their penance, like the others. And the said friar preacher obtained a license from the dean and chapter to preach the word of God in the place where Brother Gerard [de Muro]* had preached, that is, at the monastery of St. Martin of Tournai. And word of this spread through the whole town. And assembled there was a crowd of men and women greater than can be seen anywhere in Tournai, because the courtyard of the monastery could barely accommodate all the people. Then the aforesaid friar began to preach, saying: "Unless a grain of wheat shall fall into the ground and die, etc." [John 12:24].† And after having preached on many things, almost in the middle of his sermon, he stooped to the subject concerning those with whom he had come—the penitents—calling them a fraternity of red knights, and calling the friars of the mendicant order [the Franciscans] scorpions and the Antichrist, he accused them of preaching against the religious devotion shown by a freely-assumed penance and of persuading many to stop performing it. He also, as many understood his words, compared the blood of those whom he called the red knights to the blood of our Lord, Jesus Christ. He also said that, aside from the shedding of the blood of our Savior, there was no nobler shedding of blood as that which came from those who whipped themselves [the flagellants]. And he preached many

---

*The Dominican's sermon preached just a week and a half later was obviously designed as a riposte to Muro's efforts.

†Jesus here speaks to his disciples just after his triumphant entry into Jerusalem, on what was to become known as Palm Sunday. On the one hand, he foresees his coming passion and suffering on the cross, which the flagellants believed they were reenacting, but, on the other, he also foretells his triumph over death through resurrection. St. Paul, in 1 Corinthians 15:36–38, uses the same seed imagery to explain the resurrection.

other things that bordered on error, and some men present who were assisting him wrote his words down. And when the preaching was finished, he pleased the community beyond measure, and nearly everyone began murmuring against the mendicant order and even against the whole clergy. . . .

On account of the above events and other arguments which reason dictates, clergymen and monks and men who, by dint of the catholic faith they believe and hold are of sound and expert mind, did not approve of their deeds because the Church had not consented to them and canon law forbade them. But the people, both men and women, noble and non-noble, all ignorant of scripture, approved their deeds beyond measure, especially in the regions mentioned above [i.e., "Flanders, Hainault, Brabant, and other adjoining areas to the west"]. And thus there was an extraordinary and profitless dissension, and this was chiefly that the whole populace accused mainly the mendicant order of completely blocking the penitents. And some may doubt that this is a new rite, because people do penance in churches, monasteries, and other ecclesiastical places where, by all rights, the violent shedding of blood ought not to take place in any way. But the penitents had no consideration and did not cease to perform their rite even when the divine office and private masses were being said in churches. And the majority of the common people, reckoning such penance to be acceptable, approved of it even more than of the divine office; because so much evil was changed to good when the penitents arrived, as is expressed above, the people very often derided ecclesiastical men who held the opposite opinion. And the common people held such a good opinion of the penitents that in many places, miracles were affirmed to have been performed by their penance. . . .

Let it be known that I have learned from certain superiors elected by the penitents that novices, along with their followers, promise to do and uphold, in so far as they are able throughout their whole lives, the following items, which are read out to them, otherwise they will not be received:

First, those entering promise and recite: "We pledge ourselves to avoid every opportunity of doing evil in so far as we are able, and to repent and make a general confession of all our sins in so far as we can remember them.

"Item, to dispose by will or testament of our legal acquisitions, to pay or satisfy our debts, and to make restitution of unlawful possessions.

"Item, we will live in peace, amend our lives and show forgiveness to others.

"Item, we will risk our bodies and our possessions in order to defend, uphold, and preserve the rights, honor and liberty, faith, doctrine, and laws of holy Church.

"Item, we must call one another brother, and not simply his friend, in recognition of the fact that we are all made from one substance, redeemed at one price [Jesus Christ], endowed with one talent [repentance]."

Item, the novice must ask for a license to receive the cross from his priest and request permission from his legitimate spouse; he must place himself in obedience to another and scourge himself for thirty-three and a half days; he must not sit upon cushions and must lie down without linen bedsheets or clothes* and without pillows; he must observe silence, unless given permission to speak; he may receive alms but not ask for them; he may enter a home only by invitation from the host and on his entry and exit from the home is to say five paternosters [Our Fathers] and five ave Marias [Hail Marys]. . . .

Item, no one, whether healthy or sick, may leave the fraternity without permission, nor sit at table without permission.

Item, no one may scourge himself to such an extent that he falls ill or dies.

Item, you must give alms to the poor in so far as you are able.

Item, no one, no matter how rich or exalted in status, ought to refuse alms that are offered for the love of God.

Item, you must, with head, heart, and mouth, persevere in your penance and your praiseworthy deeds and pray for all of Christendom, that God may cause this mortality to cease and forgive us our sins. . . .

The penitents would come to town when they had joined together into fraternities, now two hundred members, now three hundred, now more, now less. For their habit they wore a tunic, which we commonly call a *cloche* [cloak], over their ordinary clothes. On the front of this tunic they wore a red cross over the breast and another behind on the back, and the tunic was cut away in one place and there hung their whips, which we commonly call *scorgies* [scourges], each having three knots. And in each knot there were four piercing points or needles of iron [i.e., two pieces of iron sharpened at each end passing through the knot]. And carrying their penitential sticks in their

---

*Most medieval people slept on straw, so this would have been extremely irritating to the skin.

hands,* they wore their hoods over their heads, upon each of which was sewn a red cross before and behind. And upon entering the city, they carried before them a crucifix, banners, and spiraled candles in as great a quantity as they were able, sometimes more, sometimes less. And they marched and sang in their own language, the Flemish in Flemish, those from Brabant in German, and the French in French. And once they arrived at the cathedral church before the image of the Blessed Mary,† they finished their song. Afterwards, they congregated in the town square or in the courtyard of the monastery of St. Martin, and then turning aside into some alley or private place, they stripped themselves there of their clothes and shoes, entrusting these to custodians who returned them later. But then they arrived at the site with their heads covered up by their hoods or caps, with their feet and bodies naked, wearing only a garment made from cloth in the likeness of what butchers wear when performing their work.‡ Holding their whips in their hands, they wore this garment, which was completely round-edged on the top and bottom and encircled the waist round about the navel above the thigh, and in length hung down nearly to the ground.

And when they were in an open space that suited their purpose, their procedure was as follows: Those carrying the crucifixes, banners, and candles led the way, followed by the others in a certain order, as their numbers and the limits of the space dictated. And they began to form a circle and the assigned singers began a religious song arranged in their native language, with the others singing responsively with one voice. And thus singing and responding, they formed a circle, with both the singers and respondents whipping themselves, and the song was sung in such a way that they had to prostrate themselves on the ground three times. And when they came to the first passage of the song, in a moment everyone fell with his whole body flat on his chest, and they formed a cross out of their arms and body. And getting up on their knees, they performed various bodily torments, to such an extent that those watching were amazed and wept and had compassion on their sufferings. And the penitents performed this rite a second

---

*In other words, the penitents carried the handles of their whips in front of them, and the leather thongs with metal spikes embedded in knots on the ends hung down over their exposed backs.

†This was presumably sculpted on the facade near the main entrance of the cathedral.

‡Most likely this was a kind of apron, which for butchers was made of leather, but here fashioned out of lighter material, hanging down in front and tied in the back, so that the front and rear end were covered, leaving the back exposed for scourging.

and a third time, with the singers singing in the middle of the circle in which were also their leaders, namely priests or mendicant friars of various orders.* But when the circling and torments, in which they prostrated and whipped themselves, were completed, and the song ended, all got down on their knees and one of the friars said some invocations and prayers, as might be said in church, at funerals, and at the end of sermons, and they stayed on their knees until he had finished his invocations and prayers, and they performed so many prostrations and torments that it was most pious and horrible for the onlookers to see. This done, they got up and, singing a song about the Blessed Virgin in their own language, they went back to put on their clothes. And many, before putting on their clothes in front of an image of the Blessed Virgin, finished their song in some private place. . . .

In the same year [1350], in the first week of Lent [February 14– 21], public proclamation was made in the town square by the aldermen of the city [of Tournai] that everyone should cease from this voluntarily assumed public penance, otherwise all those who did not comply would be banished for all the days of their lives. There also was a proclamation from the king [of France] that all should likewise cease from this, because the king called them a sect in his letter, and this was to be under pain of losing body and goods.† There was also agreement on the part of the bishop of Tournai, the dean and chapter [of St. Martin's] and the aldermen of the city that in the second week of Lent, on the night of St. Peter's Throne [February 22] in the church of Notre Dame of Tournai, the word of God should be expounded. And the priest of St. Piatus parish gave a sermon, and an immense crowd gathered. And the pope's mandate concerning the penitents was read out there,‡ but the bull was not shown to them, on account of which there was a great murmuring among the people. But in the said sermon the priest announced a general [plenary] indulgence agreed upon by the pope and the college [of cardinals to those who go] to Rome and its churches and the tombs of the Blessed Apostles Peter and Paul. Moreover, from this day forward the aforesaid penitents ceased being invited [into the city] by popular demand.

---

*Technically, monks could not join the flagellants because they were cloistered, whereas friars, whose vocation allowed mobility, were ideally suited to the flagellants' wandering lifestyle.

†The text of this proclamation is provided in Document 34.

‡Pope Clement VI's bull, *Inter Solicitudines,* which ordered the suppression of the flagellants, was issued on October 20, 1349.

34

KING PHILIP VI OF FRANCE

Mandate to Suppress the Flagellants

February 15, 1350

King Philip VI of France issued an edict to suppress the flagellants on February 15, 1350, a little less than four months after Pope Clement VI had condemned the movement. This surviving copy was addressed to the municipal officials of Tournai in Flanders.

We have understood that a sect of people, under the color of devotion and a false penance, who call themselves flagellants and penitents, has arisen and multiplied in the said town [of Tournai] and is growing from day to day in violation of the good condition and observance of the Christian faith and of the salvation of the Christian people. Through their feints, simulations, and deceptions, several simple people, ignorant of holy scripture and of the true path of their salvation, have been deceived into following the said sect, to the great scandal of Christian people and to great peril to their salvation. And for this reason, our holy father the pope and all the holy college [of cardinals] of the Church of Rome condemns and rebukes the said sect as conceived in detriment of the Christian faith, against the commandments of our savior, Jesus Christ, and as a great peril to the souls of the said people; they have ordered that anyone adhering to the said flagellants and penitents break entirely from the said sect. But in order that they not increase and multiply by the least bit each day, which could become a great scandal and peril to the whole Christian faith, it is not amiss that we remedy the situation.

Therefore we, wishing to always obey our holy mother, the Church of Rome, and to provide, as much as is in our power, for the welfare of the Christian faith and to prevent anything to its disadvantage, order you to meet with the vicars of our beloved and loyal chancellor, and with the bishop of Tournai and the dean and chapter [of St. Martin] of

---

Corpus Documentorum Inquisitionis Haereticae Pravitatis Neerlandicae, ed. Paul Frédéricq, 3 vols. (Ghent: J. Vuylsteke, 1889–1906), 2:116–17.

Tournai, and that in this matter you hold good counsel and delibera-
tion among yourselves and provide for such a remedy that this sect,
condemned and rebuked by the said Church of Rome, cease to exist
entirely in the said city and wherever it holds sway. And henceforth no
one is to presume to enter or follow it, and those who continue to follow it must be constrained to cease and desist by the imposition of
temporal punishments, by bans, interdictions, and other means and
remedies such as seem to you to be expedient. And the said sect must
cease to exist altogether, in such a way that henceforth its error not
multiply in our realm, even if holy Church needs to invoke the aid of
the secular arm and a mailed fist to do it.

JEWISH POGROMS

Beginning in the spring of 1348, pogroms against Jewish communities
coincided with the arrival of the plague in Languedoc in southern
France and Catalonia in northeastern Spain. It is not clear what precip-
itated these attacks, but we have already seen how medical authorities
in these regions, like Alfonso de Córdoba (Document 10) and Jacme
d'Agramont, fueled the belief that enemies of Christianity could be
responsible for the disease through poisoning of air, water or food.[13]

A letter dated April 17, 1348, from the municipal officials of Nar-
bonne in Languedoc to their counterparts in Girona in Catalonia communicated the fact that poor men and beggars had confessed under
torture to spreading the plague through poison, for which they were
executed. Although the letter did not directly implicate Jews, it stated
ominously that others, vaguely identified as "enemies of the kingdom
of France," had paid the culprits to do the deed.[14] Yet there is no
record of any accusation of well poisoning made against the Jews in
these regions in 1348. According to a *takkanoth,* or accord, drafted at
Barcelona in December 1354 by representatives of Jewish communities throughout Catalonia and Valencia, Christian mobs attacked Jews
in time of plague out of a vague desire to avenge "the sins of Jacob,"
which may or may not include the crime of poisoning (Document 36).
The first accusation of well poisoning leveled against Jews came into
the open in the autumn of 1348, when several Jews were tried for the
offense at Chillon and Châtel in present-day Switzerland (Document
37). By February 1351, such accusations and executions had been
repeated in as many as one hundred towns and cities, mostly in Germany, encompassing thousands of victims (see Figure 3).[15]

Figure 3. The burning of Jews in an early printed woodcut. Jews were a common scapegoat for the Black Death in medieval Germany.
© Christel Gerstenberg/CORBIS.

Even though these alleged offenses seem to have been treated as secular crimes, the preferred method of execution—burning at the stake—suggests the antiheretical procedures of the Inquisition. Technically, Jews were exempt from the Inquisition, although relapsing Jewish converts were subject to it from the latter half of the thirteenth century. Moreover, the death penalty, invariably imposed upon Jews once they confessed to well poisoning, would have been a grave violation in a trial for heresy; burning at the stake was reserved only for obstinate or relapsed heretics. This leads one to ponder: If Jews had no hope of saving themselves, why did they confess? Fear of torture, hope of saving family and friends, and psychological coercion are all possible explanations. Yet it is unquestionable that there was no truth to any of the accusations. Even a few medieval observers saw through the absurdity of the charges (Documents 39 and 40). Nevertheless, some, perhaps most, people at the time were thoroughly convinced that such a crime was possible and that the Jews were capable of committing it.

Medieval Christians did not always demand the death of Jews for well poisoning or other blood libels, but sometimes offered them escape through baptism. Furthermore, several prominent individuals and communities spoke up in defense of the Jews. Pope Clement VI, following the precedent of a long line of predecessors, issued bulls for their protection in September and October 1348 (Document 40), and city officials in Cologne, in a letter of January 12, 1349, addressed to their counterparts in Strasbourg, similarly urged protection of the Jews, largely on the grounds that persecution would only fan the flames of popular revolt.[16] Even so, much of this altruism toward the Jews was economically motivated, as were the attacks against them. This created a tense dynamic between city rulers, anxious to preserve Jews as potential sources of tax revenue, and the populace, equally anxious to be rid of the debts they owed them (Document 38). Pope Clement left open the door for further persecutions, provided they were legal, and Cologne eventually massacred its Jews, when the Jewish quarter was swelled by refugees from other towns, according to the chronicler Gilles li Muisis.[17]

A major question remains as to whether to view the pogroms during the Black Death as a watershed in Christian-Jewish relations. According to one recent scholar of Jewish history, "for the medieval Ashkenazic world, the material, cultural, and psychological consequences of the dramatic events of 1348 were truly a point of no return."[18] Other scholars, however, question this view. Much of the debate has focused on Spain, where large Jewish communities, known as *aljamas,* persisted after 1348 but where persecutions also continued to occur. One historian of minority persecutions during the Middle Ages sees the pogroms of Spain—including those of 1321, 1348, and 1391—as isolated incidents punctuated by long periods of harmonious relations, to the point that Jews could participate in mid-fifteenth-century Christian processions to ward off the plague. He therefore rejects the view of 1348 as "a paradigm shift," or an irrevocable transformation of medieval Christians' "ritualized violence" against the Jews, in which hatred led "with ever greater ease to extermination."[19] But much work on late medieval persecutions of the Jews remains to be done before we can fully answer this and other questions.

NOTES

[13]Jacme d'Agramont, "Regiment de preservacio a epidimia o pestilencia e mortaldats," trans. M. L. Duran-Reynals and C. -E. A. Winslow, *Bulletin of the History of Medicine,* 23

(1949): 65. See also Séraphine Guerchberg, "The Controversy over the Alleged Sowers of the Black Death in the Contemporary Treatises on Plague," in *Change in Medieval Society,* ed. Sylvia L. Thrupp (New York: Meredith Publishing, 1964), 208–24.

[14] See *The Black Death,* ed. Rosemary Horrox (Manchester: Manchester University Press, 1994), 222–23.

[15] Frantisek Graus, *Pest, Geissler, Judenmorde: Das 14 Jahrhundert als Krisenzeit* (Göttingen: Vandenhoek and Ruprecht, 1987), 159–67.

[16] *The Black Death,* ed. Horrox, 219–20.

[17] *Recueil des chroniques de Flandre,* ed. Joseph-Jean de Smet, 4 vols. (Brussels, 1837–65), 2:343–44.

[18] Anna Foa, *The Jews of Europe after the Black Death,* trans. Andrea Grover (Berkeley and Los Angeles: University of California Press, 2000), 16.

[19] David Nirenberg, *Communities of Violence: Persecution of Minorities in the Middle Ages* (Princeton, N.J.: Princeton University Press, 1996), 246, 249.

35

KING PEDRO IV OF ARAGON

Response to Jewish Pogrom of Tárrega

December 23, 1349

The arrival of the Black Death in Catalonia in May of 1348 coincided with assaults upon Jewish communities in several towns in the region. The bloodiest pogroms took place at Barcelona, Cervera, and Tárrega; in the last town, three hundred Jews are alleged to have died. This description of the attack upon the Jews of Tárrega comes from an order dated December 23, 1349, and issued by King Pedro IV of Aragon (1336–1387) to his notaries and scribes to help reconstruct the financial records of the Jews that had been destroyed in the attack.

A complaint on behalf of the Jewish *aljame* [quarter] of the village of Tárrega and of each of the Jews there has been laid before us in a serious accusation. In the year just elapsed [1348], several men of the village, after whipping up the populace to a fever pitch, cast aside their fear of God and of our correction, and did not shrink from offending

Amada Lopez de Meneses, "Una consecuencia de la Peste Negra en Cataluña: el pogrom de 1348," *Sefarad,* 19 (1959): 336–38.

our majesty. Spurred on by a diabolic spirit, with arms in their hand and a determined mind, they were bent on malice and acted on a rash impulse. They marched on the street of the *aljame* in a war-like manner, and with bold daring, they violently broke down and destroyed the gates of the street, in spite of the fact that these were secured and defended by all kinds of armed men. And all at once they entered the street and shouted loudly with raucous voices, "Muyren los traydors!" ["Kill the traitors!"].* And not content with this, but going from bad to worse, they wickedly broke into the houses of the Jews with lances, stones, and bows and arrows, and then entered them. Like hypocritical robbers, they carried off all their goods and possessions, and they tore up and also burned many debt instruments and records that had been contracted with various Jews. And they foolishly killed many Jews of the *aljame,* and they cruelly beat and even wounded some others. And they committed and inflicted many other grave and immense damages, injuries, offenses, robberies, molestations, and violent acts against the Jews, concerning which we are most displeased.

Indeed, on the above occasion the Jews lost all their goods and as a result they do not have the instruments with which they can bind their debtors—some of these instruments being burnt, some torn up, and others lost—and they lack Jewish witnesses who can clearly and legitimately prove their debts in the absence of their instruments and records. Some of these witnesses have died during the subsequent mortality, so that they have humbly beseeched us that we see fit to reconstruct their instruments which were taken away from them for the reasons above and to enforce the observance of those destroyed and torn up instruments. We grant their request and feel for the Jews' misery and loss, and we give heed to the immense hardships and damages that they have truly sustained and suffered. Therefore, in order that their wives and families may be able to survive in the future, we expressly instruct and command each and every one of you, in a manner consistent with the violence noted above, to reconstruct, or cause to be reconstructed, whatever instruments were robbed from the Jews at that time, or which their heirs swear on the ten commandments were lost in all the above upheaval and were taken away by the perpetrators of the aforesaid excesses. This is provided that the instruments were contracted within five years of the acts wickedly committed and perpetrated, as above.

---

*This cry was a generic one and was used in assaults against Christians, as well as Jews.

36

Takkanoth (Accord) *of Barcelona*
September 1354

Partly in response to the pogroms described in Document 35, three Jew-ish leaders, Mossé (Moses) Natan, Cresques Salomó (Solomon), and Jafudà Alatzar (Judah Eleazar), assembled in Barcelona. With the ap-parent endorsement of the king of Aragon, Pedro IV (1336–1387), they drew up the following takkanoth, *or accord, in Hebrew on behalf of the communities of Catalonia and Valencia, with the intention of obtaining a bull of protection from Pope Innocent VI. The accord was notarized on the first and twenty-fifth of September 1354, and the bull duly granted on January 21, 1356. Only the opening paragraphs, which specifically ad-dress the behavior of Christians toward Jews in time of plague, are in-cluded here.*

We [the Jewish communities] have resolved to remain united as one man touching the accords that are written in this book, no matter if their method be positive or negative, until the end of five years time, [and we are] to part from the moment that our most excellent king and lord [Pedro IV] enforces and puts into effect the below-mentioned things on our behalf. We have also resolved to appoint from among us responsible men for these tasks and arrangements. Here is what they are to endeavor to accomplish:

First, to embrace the throne of our king, extolled and exalted may it be, because he, as much as his fathers and ancestors, have been at all times benevolent kings, under whose protection we have lived among the gentiles; it is this kindness that has protected our fathers and us, it has protected us from the day that we became exiled in a strange land and hung up our lyres. Also, now we should prostrate ourselves and kneel before him [the king] so that by his great love he treats us like the shepherd who gathers in the scattered sheep and guides the truly lame and the suckling infants, [and] for this reason he will bring us to our refuge.

Eduard Feliu, "Els acords de Barcelona de 1354," *Calls,* 2 (1987): 153.

And finally with fair and courteous words may he [Pedro IV] intercede in our favor with the king of nations, the Pope [Innocent VI], exalted may he be, by means of suitable letters or numerous and notable messengers dispatched there, who may negotiate in order to receive from him [a bull] that may put a stop to the bad behavior of the common people, who on the day when any plague or famine has occurred, make the earth tremble with their cry: "All this is happening because of the sins of Jacob [Israel]; let us destroy this nation, let's kill them!" And during this disaster, instead of behaving well and with love and doing good for the poor, they take the foolhardy path of attacking the hapless Jews. Likewise, God in the heavens above was disposed to judge these men unfavorably—if only He wouldn't do so!—and to punish them, [since] He commands them to not add to their transgressions the sin of being rebels to His will, but that they strive to follow His example, which is to protect us like the apple of one's eye, for we live [only] through their [the Christians'] faith.

37

Interrogation of the Jews of Savoy
September–October 1348

In September and October 1348, ten Jews—nine males and one female— from several towns in the county of Savoy were interrogated and tortured into confessing that they poisoned drinking wells to spread the plague to Christians. The interrogations were carried out in the castles of Chillon and Châtel under the direction of Count Amedeo VI (1343–1383). Then, probably in November or December 1348, the castellan (local official) of Chillon sent a copy of the record to Strasbourg, whose town council had requested information from neighboring regions about such accusations, evidently because the town was divided about what to do with its Jews. Of the eleven replies that Strasbourg received, this is by far the most lengthy and detailed. It also seems to be the first recorded instance of Jews executed during the Black Death because of these accusations. Only the trials held at Chillon are included here.

Urkunden und Akten der Stadt Strassburg, ed. Wilhelm Wiegand et al., 15 vols. (Strasbourg: K. J. Trübner, 1879–1933), 5:167–71.

The castellan of Chillon, acting on behalf of the bailiff of Chablis with all dispatch due to the honor and the office, to the noble and discreet men, the official, councillors, and community of the city of Strasbourg. Since I understand that you desire to know the confessions of the Jews and the proofs found against them, you should be aware that the people of Bern* have made a copy of the interrogations and confessions of the Jews newly residing in their parts, who were accused of putting poison into wells and many other places, and that what is contained in this copy is absolutely true. And many Jews, because they confessed after being put to the question [i.e., tortured], and some confessed without torture, were put on trial and sentenced to be burnt. Also some Christians, to whom some Jews had entrusted their poison in order to kill Christians, were placed on the wheel† and tortured. For the burning of the Jews and the torture of the said Christians has been done in many places in the county of Savoy. May the Almighty preserve you.

Here follows the confession of the Jews of Villeneuve made on September 15 in the year of our Lord 1348 in the castle of Chillon, where they were detained, who were accused of putting poison into wells, cisterns, and other places, as well as into food, in order to kill and destroy the entire Christian religion.

Balavigny, a Jewish surgeon living at Thonon, was nonetheless imprisoned at Chillon because he was apprehended within the castellan's jurisdiction. He was briefly put to the question, and when he was released from the torture, he confessed after a long interval of time that around ten weeks ago, Rabbi Jacob, who had come from Toledo [in Spain] and was staying at Chambéry since Easter [April 20], sent to him at Thonon through a certain Jewish serving boy a heap of poison about the size of an egg, which was in the form of a powder enclosed in a sack of fine, sewn leather, together with a certain letter, in which he ordered him under pain of excommunication and out of obedience to his religion to put the said poison into the greatest and most public well of the town, which was used the most often, in order to poison the people who would use the water of this well. And he was not to reveal this to anyone at all under the aforesaid penalty. It also was stated in the said letter that similar things were ordered in other

*Bern sent its letter to Strasbourg in November 1348. Its brief contents describe, in turn, the fate of the Jews of Sölden. It ends ominously with the words: "Know that all the Jews in all the lands know about the poisoning."

†This type of torture consisted of tying the victim to a horizontal wheel and then beating him or her with a rod or club. The person often died of internal bleeding.

mandates sent out by the Jewish rabbis of his religion to diverse and various places.

And he confessed that late one evening he put the said quantity of poison or powder under a stone in the spring by the lake-shore of Thonon. He also confessed that the said serving boy showed him many letters commanding the said deed of poisoning which were addressed to many other Jews: Some were directed in particular to Mossoiet, Banditon, and Samolet at Villeneuve; some to Musseo, Abraham, and Aquetus of Montreux, Jews at La Tour de Vevey; some to Beneton of St. Maurice and to his son; and some directed to Vivian, Jacob, Aquetus, and Sonetus, Jews at Évian les Bains; also some to Hebrea and Musset, Jews at Monthey. And the said serving boy told him that he carried many other letters to various and remote places, but he does not know to whom they were addressed. Also he confessed that after he put the said poison in the spring of Thonon he expressly forbade his wife and children from using that spring but refused to tell them why. In the presence of very many trustworthy witnesses he confessed by the faith in his religion and in all that is contained in the five books of Moses [Pentateuch] that the aforementioned things were absolutely true.

Also, on the following day Balavigny, of his own free will and without being put to the question, confirmed that his said confession was true, repeating it word for word, in the presence of very many trustworthy witnesses. What is more, he freely confessed that on the day when he came back from La Tour de Vevey, he threw into a spring below Montreux, namely the spring *de la Conereyde,* a quantity of poison the size of a nut, wrapped in a rag, which had been given to him by Aquetus of Montreux who lived in La Tour. The location of this poison he told and revealed to Manssionnus, a Jew living in Villenueve, and to Delosatz, son of Musselotus, so that they would not drink from that spring. Also he described the said poison as being red and black in color.

Also, on September 19 Balavigny confessed, without being tortured, that three weeks after Pentecost [i.e., three weeks from June 8], Mussus, a Jew of Villenueve, told him that he had put poison in the *Bornellorum* fountain of Villenueve, located namely in *la douane* [customs house], and he told him that afterwards he did not drink from that water but from the lake. He also confesses that Mussus the Jew told him that he had likewise put poison in the *Bornellorum* fountain of Chillon, located namely in *la douane,* under some stones. The fountain was then investigated and the said poison was found, which was then given to a certain Jew, who died thereafter, proving that it was poison. He also says that the rabbis of his religion had commanded him and other Jews to abstain from drinking the water for nine straight days from the day of its being poisoned, and he says that as soon as he put the poison in its receptacle, as he related above, he warned other Jews.

He also confesses that a good two months ago he was at Évian, and he spoke with Jacob the Jew concerning this matter, and among other things he asked Jacob if he had a letter and poison like the others. Jacob answered that yes, he did. Afterwards he asked him if he did what he was commanded, to which Jacob answered that he had not planted the poison himself, but had given it to Savetus the Jew, who put it in the spring *de Morer* at Évian. He urged Balavigny to obey orders and carry through this business just as well as he did.

He confesses that Aquetus of Montreux told him that he had put poison in the spring above La Tour, which he uses from time to time when he is at La Tour. He confesses that Samolet told him that he had put poison which he had received into a certain spring, but would not describe to him the spring.

Also, Balavigny says that, speaking as a surgeon, when someone gets sick from the poison and someone else touches him when he is sweating from his illness, that someone else will quickly feel worse from that touch. Also, one can be infected by the breath of the sick. And he believes these things to be true, because he has heard them explained by expert physicians. And it is certain that other Jews cannot acquit themselves of this charge, since they are well aware and are guilty of the aforesaid practices.

Balavigny was taken in a boat across the lake from Chillon to Clarens in order to look for and identify the spring in which he had put the poison, as he confessed. When, coming up from below, he arrived at the place and saw the spring where he had put the poison, he said: "Here is the spring where I put the poison." The spring was searched in his presence and a linen rag or cloth, in which the poison had been enclosed,* was found at the outlet of a stream that issues from the spring by the public notary, Henry Girard, with many persons present, and it was shown to the Jew. He confessed and confirmed that it was the linen rag or cloth in which he had wrapped the poison and which he had put in the public spring, adding that the

---

*Note that no one found the actual poison, only the rag that allegedly had contained the poison.

poison has the appearance of two colors, black and red. The linen rag or cloth was taken away and is in safe keeping.

Also, Balavigny confesses that all and several of the above things are true, adding that he believes the poison to come from the basilisk,* because the aforementioned poison cannot act except with the basilisk's intervention, as he has heard tell, and he is certain this is the case. . . .

[On September 15, Banditon, a Jew of Villenueve, confessed after torture that he poisoned the springs of Carutet and *Cerclitus de Roch* on the orders of Rabbi Jacob of Toledo, who sent through his Jewish serving boy "many other letters addressed to Jews." He named Samolet, a Jew of Villeneuve, and Massoletus the Jew as accomplices.]

On September 15 Mamson, a Jew of Villeneuve, after being put to the question, confessed nothing, saying that he was completely ignorant about the aforesaid matters. But on the following day, in the presence of many witnesses, he confessed of his own free will and without being tortured in any way that one day, on the quindene of Pentecost last [June 22], he was traveling from Monthey with a Jew called Provenzal, and along the way Provenzal said to him: "You must put the poison I'm going to give you into that spring, or it'll go badly for you." And this was the spring of *Chabloz Cruyez* between Vevey and Muraz. Mamson took the said quantity of poison, about the size of a nut, and put it in the spring. And he believes that the Jews of the regions round Évian held and took counsel among themselves before Pentecost [June 8] concerning this matter of the poisoning. And he says that Balavigny confided to him that one day he put poison in the spring *de la Conery* [*Conreyde*] below Montreux. Also, he says that none of the Jews can acquit themselves of the aforesaid charges, because all alike are aware and guilty of the above. When Mamson was brought before the commissioners on October 3, he changed nothing in his statement, except that he did not put poison in the said spring [of *Chabloz Cruyez*].

Indeed, before their execution, the aforementioned Jews confirmed by the faith of their religion that these things were true, adding that all Jews from the age of seven on could not acquit themselves of this charge, since they all alike knew and were guilty of the said matter. . . .

[On October 8 Belieta, wife of Aquetus the Jew, confessed through torture that Provenzal the Jew had given her, on June 24 in front of his

---

basilisk: A mythical creature that was believed to be able to turn men into stone.

house, some poison to put into springs, which she then gave to Mamson and his wife to do for her. Later, on October 18, again under torture, Belieta changed her testimony and said that she herself had done the deed. She named Geney the Jewess and Jocet of La Tour as her accomplices.]

Aquetus, son of Belieta the Jewess, was put to the question for a moderate time, and when he was released from the torture, he accused Aquetus, son of Banditon, an inhabitant of Villeneuve: The accuser explains that through a window of their house he overheard Aquetus tell his father, Banditon, that twelve weeks ago the Jew Provenzal, whom the accuser does not know, had handed him poison in a paper cornet [cone] and had told him to put the poison in some well-used spring. And the accuser heard the father command his son to put the poison in the first spring he found. And afterwards the accuser overheard Aquetus tell his father that he had sprinkled the poison into the spring of *Cerclitus de Roch.*

Aquetus, the man accused, was brought before two commissioners and in the face of Aquetus, his accuser, denied that the above was true. The accuser responded that this is what he heard and that he does not lie. And in the same instant the accused confessed that the aforesaid things were true, as is written above, and that he had sprinkled poison in the said spring so that people drinking water from that spring would die, and that he confided this to his father. When asked if his father and other Jews of Villeneuve know about this matter of the poisoning, he says that he well believes that they do, because the leading Jews always take counsel among themselves outside the upper gate of Villeneuve, and the less important Jews likewise keep counsel among themselves. And he confessed these things without torture, adding that the said poison was green and black. And he confessed this by the faith in his religion and by all that is contained in the books of Moses, adding that, by his soul, the Jews well deserved death and that he had no wish to escape being put to death immediately, because he well deserved death.

38

MATHIAS OF NEUENBURG

Chronicle

ca. 1349–1350

A clerk in the service of Berthold of Bücheck, bishop of Strasbourg (1328–1353), Mathias of Neuenburg was probably an eyewitness to the events that led to the Jewish pogrom at Strasbourg, the largest such atrocity to take place during the Black Death. Neuenburg's account of the pogroms is more coherent and has a broader scope than Fritsche Closener's although it lacks some of the latter's detail. Strasbourg at this time was ruled by a city council headed by three burghermeisters, among whom was the Lord Mayor, Peter Swarber, who spearheaded efforts to defend the Jews until he was overwhelmed by the popular will, as represented by the guilds. The later account of Jacob of Königshofen, often quoted in textbooks, is actually based on those by Neuenburg and Closener. Neuenburg's contributions end in 1350, after which other authors continued his Chronicle *up to 1378.*

And the Jews were accused of having created or amplified this pestilence by throwing poison down springs and wells. And they were burnt from the Mediterranean Sea to Germany, except for Avignon, where Pope Clement VI protected them. Since then, some Jews were tortured in Bern, in the county of Froburg, and elsewhere, and poison was discovered in Zofingen. And the Jews were destroyed in many places, and they wrote of this affair to the councillors of the cities of Basel, Freiburg, and Strasbourg. And the aldermen and even some nobles in Basel strove to protect the Jews from a long-term banishment. For behold, the people, armed with banners, mobbed the councillors' palace. The councillors were terrified, and the burghermeister asked them, "What do you want?" They responded, "We won't go away until you change your mind about banishing the Jews!" Their demand

Fontes Rerum Germanicarum: Geschichtsquellen Deutschlands, ed. Johann Friedrich Boehmer and Alfons Huber, 4 vols. (Stuttgart: J. G. Cotta'scher Verlag, 1843–68), 4:261–65, 301.

was swiftly communicated to the councillors, who did not dare leave
the palace until they came to a decision. The people cried out again,
"We don't want the Jews to stay here anymore!" And the councillors
and the people swore an oath that the Jews would not reside there
for two hundred years. And a meeting was convened of many of the
highest-ranking representatives from these three cities, which still
wanted to keep their Jews but feared the people's outcry. Nonetheless,
the Jews were arrested everywhere in those places.

The appointed meeting-place was Benfeld, Alsace, where assembled
the bishop [of Strasbourg, Berthold of Bücheck], and the lords,
barons, and representatives of the cities. Then the representatives from
Strasbourg spoke up, "We know nothing evil about our Jews," upon
which they were asked, "Then why are the buckets of your wells hidden?" For the whole populace was crying out against the Jews. Then
the bishop, the lords of Alsace and the citizens of the [Holy Roman]
empire met in order to decide how to get rid of the Jews.* And so in
this way they were burnt, first in one place, then in another. Moreover,
in some places they were expelled; when the common people got their
hands on them, they burnt one group, killed some, and impaled others.
But Lord Mayor Peter Swarber and some other citizens of Strasbourg
still strove to protect the Jews, saying to the people: "If the bishop and
the barons prevail in this matter, they will not rest until they prevail in
other things too." But it was of no use in the face of the clamor of the
mob. Therefore on the Friday after the feast of St. Hilary [January 16]
in the year of our Lord 1349, in a house newly built for this purpose on
an island in the Rhine, all the Jews of Basel were burnt without a judicial sentence in accordance with popular demand. And on the following
Friday [January 23], the citizens of Freiburg put twelve of their richest
Jews in safe custody, so that those who owed money to them would
still be contractually bound to pay their debts.

But the Jews of Speyer and Worms gathered together in a house
and burnt themselves. And all the Jews were found to have committed
some kind of evil, even in Spain, where an assembly [córtes] was convened not long ago concerning these poisonings and also concerning
the slaughter of many boys, counterfeit letters and money, theft and

*It should be noted that this was not the first time that Neuenburg's patron, the
bishop of Strasbourg, had persecuted Jews on a blood libel charge. In Neuenburg's
biography of the bishop, he recounts how in 1330, Berthold of Bücheck, needing to pay
the dowries of his three nieces and in debt to his Jews for the sum of 300 marks,
extorted 6,000 marks from Jews arrested on a charge of "having despoiled his [Chris-
tian] populace" and a further 2,000 marks from "some rich Jews" who had confessed
under torture of having killed an eleven-year-old boy at Mutzig, after the body was
found under a millwheel "bearing infinite wounds on one side."

many other matters which were an offense to his most high majesty [King Pedro IV of Aragon].*

But in order to appease an agitated public, some Jews in Strasbourg were put on the wheel and then immediately executed, so that the living couldn't say anything against the accused.[†] For this reason, the aldermen began to be greatly distrusted. In addition, an extreme hatred was conceived by both nobles and commoners against the aforesaid mayor of Strasbourg, Peter [Swarber], on account of his over-mighty influence. And debate turned bitter among the aldermen, who desired to have four burghermeisters, each in office for part of the year, as was the practice from ancient times. . . .

Then on the Sunday before Valentine's Day [February 8] in the year of our Lord 1349, the bishop and lords of Strasbourg held a conference on this business of the Jews, and on the morrow, some butchers came to the house of the aforesaid Peter and asked that some of the Jews' money be given to the workmen. And he became alarmed and wished to contain some of the crowd in his courtyard, except that on one occasion they ran through the streets shouting: "To arms!" And then the workmen came with banners to the cathedral, and the nobles also were armed as were their accomplices. And when the mayor came accompanied by his retinue carrying many banners, he, although terrified, ordered that they all go back to their homes. But when he warned and threatened the butchers with banishment, the skinners in the front of the crowd stood by them. Furthermore, when this was told to the other commoners who had gone away, they straightaway turned back to assist the butchers and remain there with them. Also, when the guildmasters were ordered to go away, they had to be persuaded to do so at sword-point. Then Peter went back to his house, while two other officials went to a public platform near the monastery, where by popular demand they resigned their office.[‡] And likewise they came to the house of Peter, where they renounced their oath of office, and they asked that he also resign his office and give them the keys to the city gates and to the bell tower, his seal of office, and all other such paraphernalia. After this was fearfully done and he

---

*Compare this account to that of Document 35.

[†]According to Fritsche Closener, these sacrificial victims were first tortured with thumbscrews and then broken on the wheel, yet never confessed to the poisoning. Meanwhile, the Jewish quarter was sealed off and an armed guard posted to prevent lynching by the mob.

[‡]According to Closener, these officials were the two other burghermeisters who sat on the city council alongside Peter Swarber as Lord Mayor. Claus Lappe, speaking on behalf of the guilds, called for their resignation, after a conference of guildmen, knights, and burghers.

was stripped of his office, four burghermeisters and a master of the butchers' guild serving one year terms were created, and new councillors were appointed. And many articles of accusation were read out and brought against Peter.*

And so, on the following Saturday [February 14], the Jews, who had been brought by the new burghermeisters to the Stoltzenecke so that they could be led away from there, were conducted to their cemetery to be burnt in a specially prepared house. And two hundred of them were completely stripped of their clothes by the mob, who found a lot of money in them. But the few who chose baptism were spared, and many beautiful women were persuaded to accept baptism, and many children were baptized after they were snatched from mothers who refused this invitation. All the rest were burnt, and many were killed as they leaped out of the fire.[†]

But the duke of Austria [Albert II of Hapsburg] and the duke of Moravia [Emperor Charles IV] protected their Jews, who were said to have poisoned many baptized Jews and Christians. And afterwards many of these Jews, having confessed their crimes, were burnt. And many Christians confessed under torture that they had taken money and received instructions from the Jews, in which they promised to willingly kill all Christians by poisoning them, which approaches severe madness. Therefore, one after another, all the Jews who had been baptized were burnt, because they confessed that they were all guilty.

Moreover, the citizens of Alsace resented all those who were protecting the Jews. In this regard, a minister of the duke of Austria was barely able to prevail upon him to send a messenger in his place to Enisheim, Austria, where all his Jews were being held, so that he not be attacked. But Ulrich of Heisenberg, in a characteristic breach of faith, burnt the Jews he was protecting. After this, toward the end of July, all the Jews were killed at Oppenheim. Also they were attacked in Frankfurt after the departure of the emperor [Charles IV], and they all burnt themselves in their houses and neighborhoods. What is more, toward the end of August, there came many flagellants from Moravia, who spread a rumor against the Jews through cutpurses [i.e., pickpockets] and the people's gullibility. And behold, all the people rushed to attack the Jews, and when the Jews saw that they could not escape

*According to Closener, Swarber was accused of forcing guild members to take secret oaths that they would oppose the public will concerning the Jews. Apparently, he fled the mayor's residence in fear of his life and died in exile at Benfeld a few years later.

[†]According to Closener, a total of 2,000 Jews were sentenced to death. He adds that "whatever was owed to the Jews was considered paid up, and all pledges and notes which they held were returned to the people who owed them."

after having killed so many Christians, they burnt their houses and themselves, along with their goods.

39

KONRAD OF MEGENBERG

Concerning the Mortality in Germany

ca. 1350

Perhaps the most balanced and rational medieval author to comment on the pogroms against the Jews was the scientific writer Konrad of Megenberg. In the following selection from his De Mortalitate in Alamannia *(Concerning the Mortality in Germany), he debates both sides of the question as to whether the Jews caused the plague through the poisoning of wells. Megenberg seems to have written this treatise in 1350.*

Therefore it is commonly believed in Germany that certain men called the Jews, who declare themselves to be bound by the Mosaic law and practice circumcision and who deny the crucified Christ and the true God made flesh from a pure virgin for the sins of human kind, poisoned the water of wells used for drinking and other human uses with a very potent poison; and that they did so throughout the various regions of the world where Christians and men of other faiths live with them, chiefly in order that, once the people of the Christian religion are dead, the kingdom of the Jewish race and their status as the Lord's anointed may be restored, which was taken away from them by the word of God, that is, by the only begotten flesh of God, as is written: "The scepter shall not be taken away," and again it says in Scripture: "until the Lord of Hosts shall come, etc."* And this belief is

---

*The full passage from Genesis 49:10 reads: "The scepter shall not be taken away from Juda, nor a ruler from his thigh, till he come that is to be sent, and he shall be the expectation of nations."

Sabine Krüger, "Krise der Zeit als Ursache der Pest? Der Traktat De mortalitate in Alamannia des Konrad von Megenberg," in *Festschrift für Hermann Heimpel zum 70. Geburtstag am 19. September 1971* (Göttingen: Vandenhoeck and Ruprecht, 1971), 866–68.

confirmed by the fact that in many wells and streams of Germany, little sacks have been found, which, so they say, are full of decay and brimming with the most deadly poison. This poison, so they affirm, was tested on brute animals, such as pigs, dogs, and chickens and other animals, by mixing it with something edible, namely bread or meat, so that in this way they would taste some of the vile poison. Immediately the animals succumbed to a most swift death and their life was snuffed out as in a moment.*

And again, [they cite the fact] that very many men, commonly called "sack-bearers" or "sack-porters" [i.e., vagabonds], have been apprehended, who, when put to various kinds of tortures, confessed to this crime and did not deny it, namely that they brought this deadly matter to the crowded places of the world in order to kill all Christian men throughout the land. And what is surprising is how many of these "sack-porters" or poisoners were Christians, who, while in the midst of an all-consuming fire, swore with their last breath that they were bribed by the Jews with money to commit this most wicked crime, that they were seduced into this evil by everything delectable in this world, nor could they restrain themselves in any way from their hearts' desire for these delights.

Therefore the Christian people throughout nearly the whole of Germany, moved by these reasons, rushed upon the Jewish race with fire and with a most violent fury stained their hands with their blood. And their nation perished, namely Hebrews of both sexes, at the hands of the Christians, so that neither the nursing infant nor the child enclosed in its mother's womb was spared. Oh, how much weeping and wailing and what fear of heart and hissing between teeth was to be seen among a forsaken people! You would have seen maidens and wives with an unforgettable look upon their angelic faces being slaughtered by stupid rustic men with axes and nailed clubs and other instruments of war without mercy, as if they were slaughtering pigs or strangling chickens that were destined for the kitchen. Also, sometimes in some places they [the Jews] shut themselves up in a house with the doors barred and, after setting the house on fire, they died by their own hands by slitting the throats of their children, along with their own.†

---

*In principle, Megenberg was not opposed to the concept of poison spreading the plague, as he employs it when discussing whether earthquakes caused the Black Death.

†Except for setting the house on fire, this was how the Jews of Mainz committed *kiddush ha-Shem* during the First Crusade in May 1096, according to the chronicle of Solomon Bar Simson. Having the throat cut with a knife recalled Abraham's attempted sacrifice of Isaac.

Oh, what a wicked and detestable crime by the parents, which is thus visited upon their children, so that justly "they say to the mountains: 'Come, cover us' and 'Blessed are the barren who have not given birth,'" concerning which He [Christ] spoke the truth to mothers when he was led miserably to be crucified for our sins: "Daughters of Jerusalem, weep not over me, but weep for yourselves and for your children."* For He knew what was to happen to them now and in times past.

But although the Jewish people are justly detested by us Christians in accordance with the fundamentals of the Catholic faith, which are proven not only by the words of the prophets, but are also confirmed by the most manifest miracles of God, which they [the Jews] stubbornly deny, nevertheless it does not seem to me that the said opinion concerning the cause of so general a mortality throughout the whole world, with all due respect to whomever is expressing it, can be totally and sufficiently maintained. My reasoning is as follows: It is well known that in most places where the Hebrew people had remained, they themselves had died in droves from the same exact cause of this common mortality, as in the city of Vienna in Austria and in the city of Ratisbon in Bavaria, as well as in castles and fortresses where they were concealed by certain Christian noblemen. But it is not likely that the same people who ardently desire to multiply themselves upon the land should with malice aforethought destroy themselves and others of the same faith. And again: After the wells and cisterns full of stagnant water have been purified, and even when the original source and complete origin of the gushing and flow has been secured and finally blocked off, the people, who never used other springs, died in great numbers. To which one also can add that if there had been such poison that could infect brute animals, as our adversaries say they have tested on them, then without doubt horses, cows, and sheep and livestock that drink the water ought to have been infected and died in great number like humans, which has not been seen. Nor is it probable, as is claimed, that livestock get their water more often from rivers, so that thus they cannot be infected from such things as wells and trickling streams, since the whole populace of Bavaria in the cities bordering on the Danube and other navigable rivers only use the

*This is a rather garbled version of Luke 23:28–30: "But Jesus turning to them, said: 'Daughters of Jerusalem, weep not over me; but weep for yourselves, and for your children. For behold, the days shall come, wherein they will say: Blessed are the barren, and the wombs that have not borne, and the paps that have not given suck. Then shall they begin to say to the mountains: Fall upon us; and to the hills: Cover us.'"

water of these same rivers and most scrupulously avoid well water, and nevertheless they have died.

Moreover, even after all the Jews in many places have been killed and completely driven out for nearly two years prior, the Death now first strikes these same places with a strong hand and powerfully conquers the men who remain there, as in the city of Nuremberg in Swabia and in the countryside roundabout. For this and similar reasons it does not seem to me that the pitiful Jewish race is the cause of this general mortality which has spread throughout almost the whole world.

40

POPE CLEMENT VI

Sicut Judeis (Mandate to Protect the Jews)
October 1, 1348

The papacy had a standard bull, Sicut Judeis, *which it periodically reissued beginning in the twelfth century to declare the Church's protection of the Jews. Pope Clement VI accordingly reissued it on July 5, 1348, but on September 26 he ordered his clergy to take measures to stop the Jewish pogroms. His reissue of the order on October 1, which is the one included here, adds an important clause about economic motivations for the pogroms. It is possible that Clement personally identified with the Jews as scapegoats. According to Konrad of Megenberg, people blamed the pope for the plague after he removed himself from the people, apparently on the advice of his physician, Gui de Chauliac.*

Even though we justly detest the perfidy of the Jews, who, persisting in their stubbornness, refuse to interpret correctly the sayings of the prophets and the secret words of their own writings and take notice of Christian faith and salvation, we nevertheless are mindful of our duty to shelter the Jews, by reason of the fact that our Savior, when he

The Apostolic See and the Jews, ed. Shlomo Simonsohn, 8 vols. (Toronto: Pontifical Institute of Medieval Studies, 1988–91), 1:396–99.

assumed mortal flesh for the salvation of the human race, deemed it worthy to be born of Jewish stock, and for the sake of humanity in that the Jews have called upon the assistance of our protection and the clemency of Christian piety. . . . Recently, however, it has come to our attention by public fame, or rather infamy, that some Christians out of rashness have impiously slain several of the Jews, without respect to age or sex, after falsely blaming the pestilence on poisonings by Jews, said to be in league with the devil, when in fact it is the result of an angry God striking at the Christian people for their sins. And it is the assertion of many that some of these Christians are chasing after their own profit and are blinded by greed in getting rid of the Jews, because they owe great sums of money to them. And we have heard that although the Jews are prepared to submit to judgment before a competent judge concerning this preposterous crime, nevertheless this is not enough to stem Christian violence, but rather their fury rages even more. As long as their error is not corrected, it seems to be approved. And although we would wish that the Jews be suitably and severely punished should perchance they be guilty of or accessories to such an outrageous crime, for which any penalty that could be devised would barely be sufficient, nevertheless it does not seem credible that the Jews on this occasion are responsible for the crime nor that they caused it, because this nearly universal pestilence, in accordance with God's hidden judgment, has afflicted and continues to afflict the Jews themselves, as well as many other races who had never been known to live alongside them, throughout the various regions of the world.

We order all of you by apostolic writing, and each of you in particular who will be asked to do so, to warn your subjects, both the clergy and the people, during the service of the mass in your churches, and to expressly enjoin them on pain of excommunication, which you may then inflict on those who transgress, that they are not to presume to seize, strike, wound, or kill Jews, no matter what the occasion or by what authority (more likely their own rashness), or to demand of them forced labor. But we do not by these presents deprive anyone of the power to proceed justly against the Jews, which they may do concerning this or any other excesses committed by them, provided that they have grounds for proceeding against them, either in this or any other business, and that they do so before competent judges and follow judicial procedure.

7

The Artistic Response

There are many ways to measure the artistic impact of the Black Death. One approach is to examine the art produced by the generation immediately following the plague of 1348 to 1350, even if its themes make no literal reference to disease or death.[1] The limitations of this approach stem from the difficulties in dating medieval works precisely—and thus establishing the Black Death as a definitive break in a genre—and by the subjective nature of interpretation.[2] In one view, the Black Death brought the Renaissance spirit of innovation to a grinding halt through the deaths of its leading artists, which inaugurated a more conservative and rigid school.[3] But in another view, the plague was a positive force, either by reinforcing faith through a refocused depiction of traditional plague saints, or by providing a major impetus to the Renaissance theme of individualism, represented by the fact that so many patrons felt impelled to commission portraits to be remembered in the face of mass death (Document 27).[4]

The approach of this chapter is to study art and literature whose themes are intimately connected with, and highly revealing of, late medieval attitudes toward death. We focus on artistic and poetic depictions of a desiccated and decaying corpse, a type of representation known as the "macabre," or *memento mori* (remembrance of death). Of all artistic representations, this genre, although in its origins predating the Black Death, is most closely associated with the plague.

THE DANCE OF DEATH

It is quite possible that a dance associated with the figure of Death first arose in conjunction with the Black Death of 1348. The *Great Chronicle of France* (Document 41) testifies to a dance performed in that year to ward off the plague. Other chronicles report that in 1374 a dancing mania seized hundreds of people in German and Flemish towns. The people periodically interrupted their dance to fall to the ground and allow onlookers to trample on them in the belief that this would cure them of their "extreme oppression," although it is nowhere stated that this was the disease.[5] These people may have been exhibiting or masking through dance one of the neurological symptoms of the bubonic plague, called chorea or St. Vitus's Dance, which produces involuntary muscle contractions.

The first artistic production of the dance is open to some debate. A German scholar claims that the Dominican convent of Würzburg was the first to produce a poem on the Dance of Death in 1350, but others believe that the French poet Jean le Févre wrote the first one in 1376.[6] By the end of the fourteenth century, the dance was being performed as a kind of morality play in parish churches, and later as secular entertainment.[7]

The first known painting of the Dance of Death is the fresco that once adorned the southern cloister of the cemetery of Les Innocents in Paris, which was painted by 1425.[8] Accompanied by a text, the images depicted thirty-one partners—from pope and emperor to infant and hermit—dancing a reel with death. During the 1430s—when the English occupied the French capital and plague and famine occurred on both sides of the Channel—the English poet John Lydgate made a loose transcription and translation of the poem (Document 42), to which he added, at least according to one version of his poem, six other characters, including several females. By 1440, pictures to accompany Lydgate's version of the poem were painted on the north cloister of Pardon Churchyard at St. Paul's Cathedral in London. Neither the frescoes at St. Paul's nor those at Les Innocents have survived.

The Dance of Death lends itself artistically to the experience of the Black Death for a number of reasons. As the great leveler, Death comes for all regardless of their position in the social hierarchy, just as plague made no distinctions in its onslaught on Europe's population.[9] In some versions of the dance, Death is a chess player (Document 43), which seems to express the arbitrary and unpredictable nature of the plague's geographical behavior. The chronicler Heinrich of Herford noticed this behavior, comparing the plague's movements to "a game of chess."[10] In addition, a dancing Death, though frightening, is more approachable and familiar than the awesome figure of the Fourth Rider of the Apocalypse (depicted on the cover of this volume). Here, at least, a mortal can communicate with Death before being taken away. An elaboration on this theme is the late medieval English morality play *Everyman* (ca. 1485), in which Death appears at the beginning of the play to claim Everyman and lead him to his "reckoning." A long dialogue then ensues in which Death remains unmoved by Everyman's pleas for a delay of execution, until finally Death allows Everyman a brief respite to prepare his soul for the after-life. As in Lydgate's poem of the Dance of Death, the afterlife in *Everyman* is described as a "pilgrimage" and Death comes regardless of rank or riches, setting nought "by pope, emperor, king, duke, nor princes."[11] But there is a revealing commentary at the end of the play in a monologue by Doctor, who points to the coming resurrection at the Last Judgment, when "we may live body and soul together."[12] The implied message that even a body rent by plague boils and other deformities will be fully restored at the end of time, finds a parallel in the translator's introduction at the beginning of Lydgate's poem (Document 42).

The Dance of Death and other art forms representing death or mortality often have been invoked to symbolize the "waning" of late medieval society and culture which had become "obsessed" with death. Scholars either dismiss late medieval *memento mori* art as "the too much accentuated and too vivid representation of Death hideous and threatening,"[13] or characterize the art and literature of the period as "pervaded by a profound pessimism and sometimes a renunciation of life."[14] There is, however, an alternative interpretation of *memento mori,* one that sees it as a positive, even uplifting, response to the morbid atmosphere created by the Black Death. This interpretation is closely related to medieval beliefs concerning the apocalypse, the final destruction of the world and the salvation of the righteous as prophesied in the book of Revelation in the New Testament.[15] Yes, medieval minds imagined the end of the world as a time of great suffering, terror, and death. But at the same time, the end of the world also holds out the promise of rebirth, renewal, and resurrection. Although it does not deny the terrible evils that plague could bring in its wake, this outlook could provide great comfort and reassurance in the face of mass death.

NOTES

[1]Millard Meiss, *Painting in Florence and Siena after the Black Death: The Arts, Religion and Society in the Mid-Fourteenth Century* (Princeton, N.J.: Princeton University Press, 1951).

[2]H. W. Van Os, "The Black Death and Sienese Painting: A Problem of Interpretation," *Art History*, 4 (1981): 237–49; Joseph Polzer, "Aspects of the Fourteenth-Century Iconography of Death and the Plague," in *The Black Death: The Impact of the Fourteenth-Century Plague*, ed. Daniel Williman (Binghamton, N.Y.: Center for Medieval and Early Renaissance Studies, 1982), 107–30.

[3]Meiss, *Painting in Florence and Siena after the Black Death*, 64–73.

[4]Louise Marshall, "Manipulating the Sacred: Image and Plague in Renaissance Italy," *Renaissance Quarterly*, 3 (1994): 485–532; Samuel K. Cohn Jr., *The Cult of Remembrance and the Black Death: Six Renaissance Cities in Central Italy* (Baltimore: The Johns Hopkins University Press, 1992); idem, "The Place of the Dead in Flanders and Tuscany: Towards a Comparative History of the Black Death," in *The Place of the Dead: Death and Remembrance in Late Medieval and Early Modern Europe*, ed. B. Gordon and P. Marshall (Cambridge: Cambridge University Press, 2000), 17–43.

[5]Justus Friedrich Carl Hecker, *The Epidemics of the Middle Ages*, trans. Benjamin Guy Babington (London: G. Woodfall and Son, 1844), 80–84; Johannes Nohl, *The Black Death: A Chronicle of the Plague*, trans. C. H. Clarke (New York: Harper and Row, 1969), 250–52.

[6]Helmut Rosenfeld, *Der Mittelalterliche Totentanz; Entstehung, Entwicklung, Bedeutung* (Münster: Bönlau, 1954), 56–66. See also Leonard Paul Kurtz, *The Dance of Death and the Macabre Spirit in European Literature* (New York: Columbia University Press, 1934), 21; James Midgley Clark, *The Dance of Death in the Middle Ages and the Renaissance* (Glasgow: Jackson, 1950), 91; and Joel Saugnieux, *Les Danses Macabres de France et d'Espagne et leurs prolongements littéraires* (Paris: Belles Lettres, 1972), 16.

[7]John Aberth, *From the Brink of the Apocalypse: Confronting Famine, War, Plague, and Death in the Later Middle Ages* (New York: Routledge, 2000), 205; Paul Binski, *Medieval Death: Ritual and Representation* (Ithaca, N.Y.: Cornell University Press, 1996), 156–57.

[8]Valentin Dufour, *Recherches sur la Danse Macabre peinte en 1425 au cimetière des Innocents de Paris* (Paris: Bibliophile Français, 1873); *La Danse Macabre des charniers des Saints Innocents à Paris*, ed. Edward F. Chaney (Manchester: Manchester University Press, 1945); P. Vaillant, "La Danse Macabre de 1485 et les fresques du charnier des Innocents," in *La mort au Moyen Âge* (Publications de la Société Savante d'Alsace et des Regions de l'Est, 25, 1975); I. le Masne de Chermont, "La Danse Macabre du cimetière des Innocents," in *Les Saints-Innocents*, ed. M. Fleury and G. -M. Leproux (Paris: Délégation à l'Action Artistique de la Ville de Paris, Commission du Vieux Paris, 1990).

[9]J. Brossollet, "L'influence de la peste du Moyen Âge sur le theme de la Danse Macabre," *Pagine di storia della medicina*, 13 (1969): 38–46; J. Batany, "Les 'Danses Macabres': une image en negatif du fonctionnalisme social," in *Dies Illa: Death in the Middle Ages*, ed. J. H. M. Taylor (Liverpool: F. Cairns, 1984).

[10]Henricus de Hervordia, *Liber de Rebus Memorabilioribus sive Chronicon*, ed. Augustus Potthast (Göttingen: Dieterich, 1859), 280.

[11]*Everyman*, ll. 126, 146.

[12]*Everyman*, l. 919.

[13]Johan Huizinga, *The Waning of the Middle Ages: A Study of the Forms of Life, Thought and Art in France and the Netherlands in the Dawn of the Renaissance*, trans. Frederik Jan Hopman (London: E. Arnold and Co., 1924), 151.

[14]Meiss, *Painting in Florence and Siena after the Black Death*, 74.

[15]Robert E. Lerner, "The Black Death and Western European Eschatological Mentalities," in *The Black Death*, ed. Williman, 77–105.

41

The Great Chronicle of France
ca. 1348

The Great Chronicle *is a record of events of national importance kept by the monks of the abbey of Saint-Denis, where the kings of France were traditionally buried. According to the chronicle's editor, Jules Viard, this particular selection, which tells of people dancing to ward off the plague in 1348, was probably written by an eyewitness who actually participated in the events described.*

In the year of grace 1348, the aforesaid mortality began in the kingdom of France and lasted for about a year and a half, more or less, and it was such that in Paris there died daily 800 persons. . . . And even though they died in such numbers, everyone received confession and their other sacraments. It happened that during the mortality, two monks from Saint-Denis rode into a town and were passing through it on a visitation at the command of their abbot. Thus they saw that the men and women of this town were dancing to the music of drums and bagpipes, and having a great celebration. So the monks asked them why they were making so merry, to which they replied: "We have seen our neighbors die and are seeing them die day after day, but since the mortality has in no way entered our town, we are not without hope that our festive mood will not allow it to come here, and this is the reason for why we are dancing." Then the monks left in order to go finish what had been entrusted to them. When they had accomplished their commission, they set out on the return journey and came back through the aforesaid town, but they found there very few people, and they had on very sad faces. The monks then asked them: "Where are the men and women who not long ago were holding such a great celebration in this town?" And they answered: "Alas! Good sirs, the wrath of God has descended upon us in the form of hail, for a

Les grandes chroniques de France, ed. Jules Marie Édouard Viard, 10 vols. (Paris: Société de l'histoire de France, 1920–53), 9:314–16.

great hailstorm fell upon us from the sky and came to this town and all around, and it came so unexpectedly that some were killed by it, and others died of fright, for they did not know where they should go or which way to turn."

42

JOHN LYDGATE

The Dance of Death

ca. 1430

A monk from Bury St. Edmunds in England, John Lydgate transcribed and translated the verses of the French poem of the Dance of Death at Les Innocents, apparently with the help of some native clerks, on a visit to Paris in the early 1430s, when the city was in English control. However, Lydgate introduced some variations that do not appear in the original French version, including references to the pestilence that appear in the stanzas printed in this selection. The first three stanzas are from the translator's introduction, a section that has no parallel in the French original. The last two are stanzas 53 and 54 from one widely accepted text of Lydgate's poem, in which Death dances with the Physician.

O yee folkes, harde herted as a stone
Which to the world have al your advertence [attention]
Like as hit sholde laste evere in oone [forever and anon]
Where ys youre witte, where ys youre providence
To see a-forne [in advance] the sodeyne vyolence
Of cruel dethe, that ben so wyse and sage
Whiche sleeth [slays] allas by stroke of pestilence
Bothe yonge and olde, of low and hie parage [station]. . . .

John Lydgate, *The Dance of Death,* ed. F. Warren and B. White (Early English Text Society, 181, 1931), 2–6, 52–54.

By exaumple that thei yn her ententis
Amende her life in everi maner age
The whiche daunce at seint Innocentis
Portreied is with al the surpluage [superfluities]
To schewe this world is but a pilgrimage
Geven unto us owre lyves to correcte
And to declare the fyne [end] of owre passage
Ryght anoon my stile [pen] I wille directe.

O creatures ye that ben resonable
The life desiringe whiche is eternal
Ye mai sene here doctryne ful notable
Yowre life to lede whiche that ys mortal
Ther be to lerne in [e]special
How ye schulle trace the daunce of machabre
To man and woman yliche [each is] natural
For dethe ne spareth hye ne lowe degre. . . .

Dethe to the Phisician:
Maister of phisik [medicine] whiche [o]n yowre uryne
So loke and gase and stare agenne the sunne*
For al yowre crafte and studie of medicyne
Al the practik and science that ye cunne [know]
Yowre lyves cours so ferforthe [far along] ys I-runne
Ageyne my myght yowre crafte mai not endure
For al the golde that ye therbi have wonne
Good leche [physician] is he that can hym self recure.

The Phecissian answereth:
Ful longe a-gon that I unto phesike
Sette my witte and my diligence
In speculatif [theory] and also in practike
To gete a name thurgh myn excellence
To fynde oute agens pestilence
Preservatifes to staunche hit and to fyne [cure it]
But I dar saie, shortli in sentence
Agens dethe is worth no medicyne.

---

*Examination of a patient's urine by color, smell, and even taste was a common diagnostic technique of medieval physicians.

43

Death as Chess Player,
St. Andrew's Church, Norwich

ca. 1500

Medieval chroniclers of the Black Death of 1348, like Heinrich of Herford, often used chess imagery to describe the spread of plague mortality. In Lydgate's poem, both the Empress and the Amorous Gentlewoman describe themselves as "checke-mate" by Death. The stained-glass panel on page 168, from the church of St. Andrew in Norwich, England, dating to the late fifteenth or early sixteenth century, is the only one to survive from an original set of forty-four that depicted the Dance of Death.

Death as Chess Player, Stained-Glass Panel, ca. 1500.
© Crown copyright.EH

TRANSI TOMBS

The transi tomb (from the Latin word *transire,* meaning to pass away), provided a variation on tomb monuments by substituting or contrasting a skeletal and rotting cadaver to the idealized life-like portrait of the patron. The earliest transis seem to date from the 1390s, with the tombs of physician Guillaume de Harcigny at Lyon, France, and of François de la Sarra at La Sarraz, Switzerland (Document 44). Such tombs had their heyday in the fifteenth century, but persisted on into the seventeenth century. Nearly two hundred examples survive from northern Europe, particularly in France and England.[16] Transi tombs never seem to have been adopted in Mediterranean countries, perhaps because there custom decreed that the real corpse be on display during funerary ceremonies instead of being discreetly hidden away in a shroud or coffin.[17]

Interpretations of transi tombs have generally seen them as evidence of the "waning" of the Middle Ages. The most comprehensive study views them as the product of "a strong sense of anxiety about the fate of the soul [combined] with an intense preoccupation with death," to which the Black Death was undoubtedly a major contributing factor.[18] In this view, the function of the transi tomb is to reconcile "the conflict between the growing worldly interests of the period and the traditional religious demand for humility," a thesis that ties in remarkably well with the hypothesis that a guilt culture—in which people were overly concerned with their fate in the afterlife—pervaded Europe during the late Middle Ages.[19] Accordingly, it was not until the sixteenth century that the transi tomb came to symbolize a "new spirit" of the "triumph of worldly glory," despite the fact that the iconography remains essentially the same.[20]

Other interpretations have opted for a more esoteric approach, perhaps because these tombs seem so frankly bizarre. One historian sees the English "double-decker" versions of the transi tomb, in which a lifelike effigy of the patron above contrasts with a naked cadaver image below, as reflecting rival Lancastrian and Yorkist allegiances during the War of the Roses,[21] a civil war in England that lasted from 1455 to 1485. Another claims that the transi is a sophisticated anti-tomb, displaying a revolting corpse that previously had been discreetly hidden from view.[22] Some patrons, like Henry Chichele, archbishop of Canterbury (Document 45) and Thomas Beckington, bishop of Bath and Wells, constructed cadaver tombs during their lifetimes. Thus they could view themselves as dead well before their own deaths. In these cases, the transi tomb served to subvert the normal function of tomb monuments and burial, which St. Thomas Aquinas asserted was "for the sake of the living, lest their eyes be revolted by the disfigurement of the corpse."[23] Yet none of these interpretations really explains why patrons should have spent so much to have such unflattering representations of themselves erected for all eternity.

A common feature of the transi tomb examples included here is a reference to worms. As a sign of corruption and decay, worms were closely associated with the Black Death. An anonymous chronicler from the monastery of Neuberg in Austria describes a rain of "pestilential worms" as heralding the plague.[24] The physicians Gentile da Foligno and Jacme d'Agramont (Documents 11 and 12) both believed that a "generation of worms" inside the body could cause plague deaths, and Agramont devoted a whole chapter to dietary and other preservatives against worms.[25] The use of worms to signify a spontaneous decomposition of the body was quite old: From the time of Pliny the Younger (61–113 CE), popular folklore made reference to a human's spinal marrow being transformed into a snake upon death.[26] There also was a long tradition of associating frogs and worms, like those depicted on the cadaver tomb of François de la Sarra (Document 44), with sin and evil, especially in early fourteenth-century German depictions of Frau Welt, or the Lady of the World, whose vain, beautiful body is secretly eaten from behind by these creatures.[27] St. Thomas Aquinas declared in the thirteenth century that one must interpret the gnawing of worms in a figurative sense as symbolizing "the pangs of conscience."[28]

Yet the worms may have an altogether different meaning, one that points to the resurrection and restoration of the body out of its mortal corruption and decay. In the Old Testament, worms signify the resurrection when Job says: "For I know that my redeemer liveth, and that He shall stand at the latter day upon the earth; and though after my skin worms destroy this body, yet in my flesh shall I see God." [Job 19:25–27] In fact, it is possible to see the worms on the tomb of François de la Sarra as issuing *out* of the body, rather than crawling into it, symbolizing that the body is being restored to its original purity.[29] This theme could equally well apply to the frogs, according to Revelation 16:13: "And I saw three unclean spirits like frogs come out of the mouth of the dragon, and out of the mouth of the beast and out of the mouth of the false prophet." The presence of two scallop shells on François's pillow, one on either side of his head, strengthens such an interpretation. The scallop shell was an ancient symbol of rebirth, going back to the Greek myth of the birth of Aphrodite. (Although the scallop shell also symbolized pilgrimage to the shrine of St. James at Santiago de Compostella in Spain, François never made a journey to this site.[30]) Similarly, one can variously interpret the double-decker transi tomb of Archbishop Henry Chichele (Document 45), whose epitaph makes a couple of references to worms. Usually, modern observers "read" downwards on this tomb, seeing the cadaver as the gruesome end product of decay of the resplendent effigy from above. But reading upwards, one would see the upper effigy as rising in resurrected glory accompanied by a host of heavenly angels out of the ashes of the corpse below.

Perhaps the strongest affirmation of this latter interpretation comes from a mid-fifteenth century English poem, *A Disputacioun betwyx the Body and Wormes* (Document 46),[31] a kind of contemporary explication of the transi tomb. The *Disputacioun* is a dream vision by the poet, who in the opening lines establishes the setting for his poem: "In the ceson of huge mortalite / Of sondre disseses with the pestilence." The debate envisioned in the poem between the female patron of the tomb and the worms that crawl through her dead body ends only with the body's realization that at the resurrection, it will finally triumph over death, corruption, and the worms.[32]

NOTES

[16]A list of surviving transi tombs is included in Kathleen Cohen, *Metamorphosis of a Death Symbol: The Transi Tomb in the Late Middle Ages and the Renaissance* (Berkeley and Los Angeles: University of California Press, 1973), 189–94. Note that Cohen does not include transi tombs in Ireland, which are discussed in H. M. Roe, "Cadaver Effigial Monuments in Ireland," *Journal of the Royal Society of Antiquaries of Ireland*, 99 (1969): 1–19.

[17]Philippe Ariès, *The Hour of Our Death*, trans. Helen Weaver (New York: Oxford University Press, 1991), 114.

[18]Cohen, *Metamorphosis of a Death Symbol*, 48.

[19]Ibid.; Jean Delumeau, *Sin and Fear: The Emergence of a Western Guilt Culture, 13th–18th Centuries*, trans. Eric Nicholson (New York: St. Martin's Press, 1990), 35–114.

[20]Cohen, *Metamorphosis of a Death Symbol*, 120–81.

[21]Pamela M. King, "The English Cadaver Tomb in the Late Fifteenth Century: Some Indications of a Lancastrian Connection," in *Dies Illa: Death in the Middle Ages*, ed. J. H. M. Taylor (Liverpool: F. Cairns, 1984); idem, "The Cadaver Tomb in England: Novel Manifestation of an Old Idea," *Church Monuments: Journal of the Church Monuments Society*, 5 (1990): 26–38.

[22]Paul Binski, *Medieval Death: Ritual and Representation* (Ithaca, N.Y.: Cornell University Press, 1996), 149.

[23]St. Thomas Aquinas, *Summa Theologiae*, supplement to third part, question 71, article 11.

[24] *The Black Death,* ed. Rosemary Horrox (Manchester: Manchester University Press, 1994), 59.

[25] Jacme d'Agramont, "Regiment de preservacio a epidimia o pestilencia e mortaldats," trans. M. L. Duran-Reynals and C. -E. A. Winslow, *Bulletin of the History of Medicine,* 23 (1949): 85–87.

[26] Pliny the Younger, *Natural History,* book 10, chapter 66.

[27] Cohen, *Metamorphosis of a Death Symbol,* 81; Binski, *Medieval Death,* 139–40.

[28] St. Thomas Aquinas, *Summa Theologiae,* supplement to third part, question 97, article 2.

[29] Raoul Nicolas, "Les monuments funéraires de Neuchâtel et de la Sarraz," *Musée Neuchâtelois,* new ser., 10 (1923): 160.

[30] See Cohen, *Metamorphosis of a Death Symbol,* 83, n. 120, and references cited there.

[31] British Library, London, Additional MS 37049, fols. 32v.–35r. For an extensive discussion of the poem, see M. M. Malvern, "An Earnest 'Monyscyon' and '[Th]inge Delectabyll' Realized Verbally and Visually in 'A Disputacion betwyx [th]e Body and Wormes,' a Middle English Poem Inspired by Tomb Art and Northern Spirituality," *Viator,* 13 (1982): 415–43.

[32] John Aberth, *From the Brink of the Apocalypse: Confronting Famine, War, Plague, and Death in the Later Middle Ages* (New York: Routledge, 2000), 223–27, 242–45.

44

FRANÇOIS DE LA SARRA

Tomb at La Sarraz, Switzerland

ca. 1390

A leading nobleman from the Vaud region in present-day Switzerland, François de la Sarra served in various posts for his lord, Count Amedeo VI of Savoy, during the mid-fourteenth century. He died around 1363 and was buried in a chapel he founded with his wife, Marie, in his hometown of La Sarraz. On the basis of artistic influences, however, scholars favor dating the tomb to the 1390s, when it would have been erected by François's grandsons, rather than to the decade immediately after his death. The most prominent features of François's nude transi figure are the worms that crawl in or out of his arms and legs, and the frogs or toads that cover his eyes, lips, and genitalia. Two scallop shells were carved on the body's chest and two on the pillow on either side of his head, of which only one survives.

Erwin Panofsky, *Tomb Sculpture: Four Lectures on Its Changing Aspects from Ancient Egypt to Bernini* (New York: Harry N. Abrams, Inc., 1956), figure 258.

François de la Sarra, Tomb at La Sarraz, Switzerland, ca. 1390.
Reproduced courtesy of Harry N. Abrams, Inc.

45

ARCHBISHOP HENRY CHICHELE

Tomb at Canterbury Cathedral

ca. 1425

One of the most important churchmen and political figures in England during the first half of the fifteenth century, Henry Chichele was closely linked to his patron, King Henry V. In 1414, Chichele became archbishop of Canterbury, the most powerful churchman in the country. By 1425, less than three years after the untimely demise of Henry V in 1422 and nearly twenty years before his own death in 1443, Chichele had completed his transi tomb. The first such monument built in England, it started the trend of double-decker tombs. Chichele may have been inspired to make this kind of monument from the double image of effigy and coffin that was paraded at state funerals, including that of Henry V, or from witnessing the elaborate monument of Cardinal Jean de la Grange at Avignon (1402), a town Chichele no doubt visited in his capacity as an ambassador to France. Although no worms are depicted on Chichele's transi, worms feature prominently in the inscription of Latin rhyming couplets that runs around the lower border of the tomb surrounding the transi.

I was a pauper born, then to this primate [archbishopric] raised.
Now I am lain in the ground, ready to be food for worms.
Behold my tomb: 1442 [1443].
Whoever you be who will pass by, I ask you to remember,
You will be like me after you die,
For all [to see]: horrible, dust, worms, vile flesh.
May the assembly of saints unanimously intercede for him
    [Chichele],
So that God may be appeased by their merits on his behalf.

Kathleen Cohen, "The Changing Meaning of the Transi Tomb in Fifteenth- and Sixteenth-Century Europe" (Ph.D. diss., University of California, 1973), 652–53.

Archbishop
Henry Chichele,
Tomb at Canter-
bury Cathedral,
ca. 1425.

© Angelo Hornak

46

A Disputacioun betwyx the Body and Wormes
ca. 1450

A variation on the debate poems between the body and soul popular during the Middle Ages, A Disputacioun betwyx the Body and Wormes *is unique in that it is illustrated by marginal watercolor drawings, the first of which shows the tomb of a great lady, while underneath, her shrouded body is riddled with what look like worms, frogs, and salamanders. The ten-line caption below the tomb illustration reads:*

Take hede un to my fygure here abowne [above]
And se how sumtyme I was fresche and gay
Now turned to wormes mete and corrupcoun
Bot fowle erth and stynkyng slyme and clay
Attende therfore to this disputacioun written here
And writte it wisely in thi hert fre
At that sum wisdom thou may lere [learn]
To se what thou art and here aftyr sal be
When thou leste wenes [expect]: *venit mors te superare*
  ["death comes to conquer you"]
When thi grafe greves [grave awaits]: *bonum est mortis meditari*
  ["it is good to think on death"]

In the style of other debate poems, the Disputacioun then proceeds with a dream vision by the poet, who in this case has fallen asleep next to a lady's tomb in a church along his pilgrimage route. Significantly, the pilgrim-poet informs us that he was moved to make his pilgrimage "In the ceson of huge mortalite/Of sondre disses with the pestilence." What follows is a rather bizarre debate between the lady's corpse and the worms that crawl through it, complete with marginal illustrations of a skeleton in female headdress conversing with the wriggling creatures below. The corpse must accept that the worms will continue to devour her formerly beautiful body, as worms have conquered all the great men and women of the past. However, by the end of the poem, the body reconciles with the worms on the grounds that at the Resurrection its flesh will be restored and remade whole out of its present corruption.

A Disputacioun betwyx the Body and Wormes, ca. 1450.
© The British Library Board, MS Add. 37049.

This that I hafe complened and sayd
In no displesyng take it yow unto.
Lat us be frendes at this sodayn brayde [outburst],
Neghbours and luf as before we gan do.
Let us kys and dwell to gedyr evermore,
To that God wil that I sal agayn upryse
At the day of dome [Last Judgment] before the Hye Justyse,
With the body glorified to be.
And of that nowmbyr that I may be one
To cum to that blis of heven in fee [by right]
Thorow the mene [intervention] and the mediacione
Of our blissed Lord our verry patrone.
Thar in abilite [good condition] to be for His hye plesaunce.
Amen, amen pour charite at this instaunce.

A Chronology of the Black Death
(1347–1363)

1347   Plague comes to the Black Sea region, Constantinople, Asia Minor, Sicily, Marseille on the southeastern coast of France, and perhaps the Greek archipelago and Egypt.

1348   Plague comes to all of Italy, most of France, the eastern half of Spain, southern England, Switzerland, Austria, the Balkans and Greece, Egypt and North Africa, Palestine and Syria, and perhaps Denmark.

The flagellant movement begins in Austria or Hungary.

Jewish pogroms occur in Languedoc and Catalonia, and the first trials of Jews accused of well poisoning take place in Savoy.

1349   Plague comes to western Spain and Portugal, central and northern England, Wales, Ireland, southern Scotland, the Low Countries (Belgium and Holland), western and southern Germany, Hungary, Denmark, and Norway.

The flagellants progress through Germany and Flanders before they are suppressed by order of Pope Clement VI.

Burning of Jews on charges of well poisoning occurs in many German-speaking towns, including Strasbourg, Stuttgart, Constance, Basel, Zurich, Cologne, Mainz, and Speyer; in response, Pope Clement issues a bull to protect Jews.

Some city-states in Italy and the king's council in England pass labor legislation to control wages and ensure a supply of agricultural workers in the wake of plague mortality.

1350   Plague comes to eastern Germany and Prussia, northern Scotland, and all of Scandinavia (Denmark, Norway, Sweden).

King Philip VI of France orders the suppression of the flagellants in Flanders.

The córtes, or representative assembly, of Aragon passes labor legislation.

1351–
1352 Plague comes to Russia, Lithuania, and perhaps Poland.

The córtes of Castile, the parliament of England, and King John II of France pass labor legislation, but the córtes of Aragon revokes it.

1354 King John II of France passes labor legislation.

The Jews of Catalonia and Valencia draw up a *takkanoth,* or accord, with King Pedro IV of Aragon in order to obtain a bull of protection from Pope Innocent VI.

1358 Rise of the Jacquerie, a peasants' revolt, in France.

1361–
1363 Plague breaks out again in Europe.

Questions for Consideration

1. Where did the Black Death originate? How was it first communicated to Europeans?
2. If you were a doctor making a diagnosis, how would you characterize the symptoms of the Black Death, based on the chroniclers' accounts? Is it possible to detect the true presence of bubonic or pneumonic plague?
3. What advice given by medieval physicians to ward off or cure the Black Death seems to you to have been most beneficial? What was least effective, or even harmful?
4. To what extent did doctors rely on empirical observation in response to the challenges posed by the Black Death? To what extent did they rely on tradition or authority?
5. Which aspects of the social or psychological response to the Black Death seem similar to our own response to modern "plagues," such as the AIDS epidemic? Which aspects are different?
6. Compare the supposedly eyewitness testimony of Giovanni Boccaccio (Document 16) with the later, fifteenth-century reflections of al-Maqrīzī (Document 19). Which is a more accurate reflection of the new social and economic realities created by the plague? What are the advantages and disadvantages of each kind of source?
7. Who, precisely, enacted the economic legislation of various European countries in response to the Black Death, and why? How else might landlords have responded to the economic challenges posed by the plague? Based on the evidence from England (Document 22), how did laborers respond to this legislation, and how effective was it?
8. Chroniclers commenting on the social and religious context of the Black Death report that the disease was both caused by and resulted in a moral decline in society. Which, if any, is true, and why?
9. Did medieval people lose their faith in God as a result of the Black Death? Defend your answer. Did their religious response have any practical effect? How well did the Church and its priesthood respond to this crisis (Documents 25 and 26)?

10. What was uppermost in the mind of Libertus of Monte Feche (Document 27) as he lay dying from the plague?

11. Compare the Christian and Muslim responses to the Black Death (Documents 23, 24, 28, 29, and 30). How were they similar and different? What tensions did each community experience during the plague? Would they respond in the same way to an apocalyptic crisis today?

12. What kind of emotion vis-à-vis the Black Death did the flagellants inspire in onlookers and in themselves? Was it elation, relief, fear, terror? Based on the chroniclers' accounts, why did Pope Clement VI suppress the flagellants on October 20, 1349?

13. Why were Jews targeted as scapegoats during the Black Death? How did medieval Jews and some Christians refute the accusation of well poisoning (Documents 36, 39, and 40)? How closely, if at all, do the pogroms of 1348–51 resemble the Holocaust of the 1940s?

14. Compare Documents 35 and 38 with respect to the Jewish pogroms in Spain. What does this tell us about how historians should approach original sources? Consider the origins, credentials, and general reliability of each document and of its respective author.

15. Why is the Dance of Death considered such a suitable artistic expression of the Black Death? What connection do you think the Dance of Death has to the actual epidemic of the plague?

16. Look at the pictures of the tombs of François de la Sarra and of Archbishop Henry Chichele (Documents 44 and 45). Are the worms entering or leaving François's corpse? Should one "read" downwards or upwards on Chichele's double-decker monument? Why do you think Chichele had his cadaver image made and erected in a public place nearly twenty years before his death (in 1443)? How does the poem *A Disputacioun betwyx the Body and Wormes* (Document 46), act as a commentary on Chichele's tomb?

17. Consider the totality of Europeans' response to the Black Death, including medical, social, economic, religious, and artistic responses. Was it characteristic of a "medieval" or "Renaissance" outlook? Should it be taken as evidence of a decline or rebirth of culture and society?

Selected Bibliography

GENERAL WORKS

Aberth, John. *From the Brink of the Apocalypse: Confronting Famine, War, Plague, and Death in the Later Middle Ages.* New York: Routledge, 2000.

Biraben, Jean Noël. *Les hommes et la Peste en France et dans les pays européens et méditerranéens.* 2 vols. Paris: Mouton, 1975–1976.

Bowsky, William M., ed. *The Black Death: A Turning Point in History?* New York: Holt, Rinehart and Winston, 1971.

Cantor, Norman F. *In the Wake of the Plague: The Black Death and the World It Made.* New York: Free Press, 2001.

Cohn Jr., Samuel K. "The Black Death: End of a Paradigm." *The American Historical Review,* 107 (2002): 703–38.

———. *The Black Death Transformed: Disease and Culture in Early Renaissance Europe.* London and New York: Arnold and Oxford University Press, 2002.

Dols, Michael W. *The Black Death in the Middle East.* Princeton, N.J.: Princeton University Press, 1977.

Gottfried, Robert S. *The Black Death: Natural and Human Disaster in Medieval Europe.* New York: Free Press, 1983.

Herlihy, David. *The Black Death and the Transformation of the West.* Edited by Samuel K. Cohn Jr. Cambridge, Mass.: Harvard University Press, 1997.

McNeill, William H. *Plagues and Peoples.* Garden City, N.Y.: Anchor Press/ Doubleday, 1976.

Ormrod, W. Mark, and Phillip G. Lindley, eds. *The Black Death in England.* Stamford, Lincolnshire.: Watkins, 1996.

Platt, Colin. *King Death: The Black Death and Its Aftermath in Late-Medieval England.* Toronto: University of Toronto Press, 1996.

Williman, Daniel, ed. *The Black Death: The Impact of the Fourteenth-Century Plague.* Binghamton, N.Y.: Center for Medieval and Early Renaissance Studies, 1982.

Ziegler, Philip. *The Black Death.* New York: Harper and Row, 1969.

PLAGUE DEMOGRAPHY AND GEOGRAPHY

Aberth, John. "The Black Death in the Diocese of Ely: The Evidence of the Bishop's Register." *Journal of Medieval History,* 21 (1995): 275–87.

Carpentier, Élisabeth. "Autour de la Peste Noire: famines et épidémies dans l'histoire du XIVe siècle." *Annales: economies, sociétés, civilisation,* 17 (1962): 1062–92.

Davies, Richmond A. "The Effect of the Black Death on the Parish Priests of the Medieval Diocese of Coventry and Lichfield." *Bulletin of the Institute of Historical Research,* 62 (1989): 85–90.

Derbes, Vincent. "De Mussis and the Great Plague of 1348: A Forgotten Episode of Bacteriological Warfare." *Journal of the American Medical Association,* 196 (1966): 59–62.

Emery, R. W. "The Black Death of 1348 in Perpignan." *Speculum,* 42 (1967): 611–23.

Gottfried, Robert S. *Epidemic Disease in Fifteenth-Century England: The Medical Response and the Demographic Consequences.* New Brunswick, N.J.: Rutgers University Press, 1978.

Gyug, Richard. "The Effects and Extent of the Black Death of 1348: New Evidence for Clerical Mortality in Barcelona." *Mediaeval Studies,* 45 (1983): 385–98.

Hatcher, John. "Mortality in the Fifteenth Century: Some New Evidence." *Economic History Review,* 2nd ser., 39 (1986): 19–38.

Herlihy, David. "Population, Plague, and Social Change in Rural Pistoia, 1201–1430." *Economic History Review,* 2nd ser., 18 (1965): 225–44.

Norris, John. "East or West? The Geographic Origin of the Black Death." *Bulletin of the History of Medicine,* 51 (1977): 1–24. With replies by Michael Dols and John Norris in idem, 52 (1978): 112–20.

BIOLOGICAL AND MEDICAL ASPECTS

Arrizabalaga, Jon. "Facing the Black Death: Perceptions and Reactions of University Medical Practitioners." In *Practical Medicine from Salerno to the Black Death.* Edited by L. García-Ballester, R. French, J. Arrizabalaga, and A. Cunningham. Cambridge: Cambridge University Press, 1994.

Benedictow, Ole J. *Plague in the Late Medieval Nordic Countries: Epidemiological Studies.* Oslo: Middelalderforlaget, 1992.

Campbell, Anna Montgomery. *The Black Death and Men of Learning.* New York: Columbia University Press, 1931.

Carmichael, Ann G. *Plague and the Poor in Renaissance Florence.* Cambridge: Cambridge University Press, 1986.

———. "Bubonic Plague: The Black Death." In *Plague, Pox, and Pestilence.* Edited by Kenneth F. Kiple. London: Weidenfeld and Nicolson, 1997.

Conrad, Lawrence I., Michael Neue, Vivian Nutton, Roy Porter, and Andrew Wear. *The Western Medical Tradition, 800 B.C. to A.D. 1800.* Cambridge: Cambridge University Press, 1995.

Crisciani, Chiara, and Michela Pereira. "Black Death and Golden Remedies: Some Remarks on Alchemy and the Plague." In *The Regulation of Evil: Social and Cultural Attitudes to Epidemics in the Late Middle Ages.* Edited by Agostino Paravicini Bagliani and Francesco Santi. Sismel: Edizioni del Galluzzo, 1998.

Drancourt, Michel, Gérard Aboudharam, Michel Signoli, Olivier Dutour, and Didier Raoult. "Detection of 400-Year-Old *Yersinia pestis* DNA in Human Dental Pulp: An Approach to the Diagnosis of Ancient Septicemia." *Proceedings of the National Academy of Science,* 95 (1998): 12637–40.

———. "Molecular Identification of 'Suicide PCR' of *Yersinia pestis* as the Agent of the Medieval Black Death." *Proceedings of the National Academy of Science,* 97 (2000): 12800–803.

Ell, Stephen R. "Interhuman Transmission of Medieval Plague." *Bulletin of the History of Medicine,* 54 (1980): 497–510.

Grmek, Mirko D., ed. *Western Medical Thought from Antiquity to the Middle Ages.* Cambridge, Mass.: Harvard University Press, 1998.

Henderson, John. "The Black Death in Florence: Medical and Communal Responses." In *Death in Towns: Urban Responses to the Dying and the Dead, 100–1600.* Edited by Steven Bassett. London and New York: Leicester University Press, 1992.

Hirst, L. Fabian. *The Conquest of Plague: A Study of the Evolution of Epidemiology.* Oxford: Clarendon Press, 1953.

Lenski, Richard E. "Evolution of Plague Virulence." *Nature,* 334 (1988): 473–74. See also the companion article by R. Rosqvist, M. Skurnik, and H. Wolf-Watz, "Increased Virulence of *Yersinia Pseudotuberculosis,*" idem: 522–25.

Scott, Susan, and Christopher J. Duncan. *Biology of Plagues: Evidence from Historical Populations.* Cambridge: Cambridge University Press, 2001.

Shrewsbury, J. F. D. *A History of Bubonic Plague in the British Isles.* Cambridge: Cambridge University Press, 1970.

Siraisi, Nancy G. *Medieval and Early Renaissance Medicine: An Introduction to Knowledge and Practice.* Chicago: University of Chicago Press, 1990.

Twigg, Graham. *The Black Death: A Biological Reappraisal.* New York: Schocken Books, 1984.

SOCIAL AND ECONOMIC ASPECTS

Bean, J. M. W. "The Black Death: The Crisis and its Social and Economic Consequences." In *The Black Death: The Impact of the Fourteenth-Century Plague.* Edited by Daniel Williman. Binghamton, N.Y.: Center for Medieval and Early Renaissance Studies, 1982.

Blockmans, W. P. "The Social and Economic Effects of Plague in the Low Countries, 1349–1500." *Revue Belge de philologie et d'histoire,* 58 (1980): 833–63.

Bolton, Jim. "'The World Upside Down': Plague as an Agent of Economic and Social Change." In *The Black Death in England.* Edited by W. M. Ormrod and Phillip G. Lindley. Stamford, Lincolnshire: Watkins, 1996.

Bowsky, William. "The Impact of the Black Death upon Sienese Government and Society." *Speculum,* 39 (1964): 1–34.

Campbell, Bruce M. S. *Before the Black Death: Studies in the 'Crisis' of the Early Fourteenth Century.* Manchester: Manchester University Press, 1991.

Fryde, E. B. *Peasants and Landlords in Later Medieval England.* New York: St. Martin's Press, 1996.

Goldberg, P. J. P. *Women, Work, and Life Cycle in a Medieval Economy: Women in York and Yorkshire, c. 1300–1520.* Oxford: Oxford University Press, 1992.

Hatcher, John. *Plague, Population and the English Economy, 1348–1530.* London: Macmillan, 1977.

———. "England in the Aftermath of the Black Death." *Past and Present,* 144 (1994): 3–35.

Herlihy, David. "Deaths, Marriages, Births, and the Tuscan Economy (ca. 1300–1550)." In *Population Patterns in the Past.* Edited by Ronald Demos Lee. New York: Academic Press, 1977.

Herlihy, David, and Christiane Klapisch-Zuber. *Tuscans and Their Families: A Study of the Florentine Catasto of 1427.* New Haven, Conn.: Yale University Press, 1985.

Kircher, Timothy. "Anxiety and Freedom in Boccaccio's History of the Plague of 1348." *Letteratura Italiana antica,* 3 (2002): 319–57.

Klapisch-Zuber, Christiane. "Plague and Family Life." In *The New Cambridge Medieval History. Volume 6: c. 1300–c. 1415.* Edited by Michael Jones. Cambridge: Cambridge University Press, 2000.

Mate, Mavis E. *Daughters, Wives, and Widows after the Black Death: Women in Sussex, 1350–1535.* Woodbridge, Suffolk: Boydell and Brewer, 1998.

Penn, S. A. C., and Christopher Dyer. "Wages and Earnings in Late Medieval England: Evidence from the Enforcement of the Labour Laws." *Economic History Review,* 2nd ser., 43 (1990): 356–76.

Putnam, Bertha Haven. *The Enforcement of the Statutes of Labourers during the First Decade after the Black Death, 1349–1359.* New York: Columbia University Press, 1908.

Thompson, James Westfall. "The Aftermath of the Black Death and the Aftermath of the Great War." *American Journal of Sociology,* 26 (1920–21): 565–72.

RELIGIOUS MENTALITIES

Cohn Jr., Samuel K. *The Cult of Remembrance and the Black Death: Six Renaissance Cities in Central Italy.* Baltimore: The Johns Hopkins University Press, 1992.

————. "The Place of the Dead in Flanders and Tuscany: Towards a Comparative History of the Black Death." In *The Place of the Dead: Death and Remembrance in Late Medieval and Early Modern Europe.* Edited by Bruce Gordon and Peter Marshall. Cambridge: Cambridge University Press, 2000.

Delumeau, Jean. *Sin and Fear: The Emergence of a Western Guilt Culture, 13th–18th Centuries.* Translated by E. Nicholson. New York: St. Martin's Press, 1990.

Dohar, William J. *The Black Death and Pastoral Leadership: The Diocese of Hereford in the Fourteenth Century.* Philadelphia: University of Pennsylvania Press, 1995.

Dols, Michael W. "The Comparative Communal Responses to the Black Death in Muslim and Christian Societies." *Viator,* 5 (1974): 269–87.

Harper-Bill, Christopher. "The English Church and English Religion after the Black Death." In *The Black Death in England.* Edited by W. Mark Ormrod and Phillip G. Lindley. Stamford, Lincolnshire: Watkins, 1996.

Lerner, Robert E. "The Black Death and Western European Eschatological Mentalities." In *The Black Death: The Impact of the Fourteenth-Century Plague.* Edited by Daniel Williman. Binghamton, N.Y.: Center for Medieval and Early Renaissance Studies, 1982.

Smoller, Laura A. "Plague and the Investigation of the Apocalypse." In *Last Things: Death and the Apocalypse in the Middle Ages.* Edited by Caroline Walker Bynum and Paul Freedman. Philadelphia: University of Pennsylvania Press, 2000.

FLAGELLANTS

Colville, A. "Documents sur les Flagellants." *Histoire litteraire de la France,* 37 (1938): 390–411.

Dickson, Gary. "The Flagellants of 1260 and the Crusades." *Journal of Medieval History,* 15 (189): 227–67.

Graus, Frantisek. *Pest, Geissler, Judenmorde: Das 14 Jahrhundert als Krisenzeit.* Göttingen: Vandenhoek and Ruprecht, 1987.

Henderson, John. "The Flagellant Movement and Flagellant Confraternities in Central Italy, 1260–1400." In *Religious Motivation: Biographical and Sociological Problems for the Church Historian.* Edited by Derek Baker. Oxford: Basil Blackwell, 1978.

Kieckhefer, Richard. "Radical Tendencies in the Flagellant Movement of the Mid-Fourteenth Century." *Journal of Medieval and Renaissance Studies,* 4 (1974): 157–76.

JEWISH POGROMS

Breuer, M. "The 'Black Death' and Antisemitism." In *Antisemitism through the Ages.* Edited by S. Almog and translated by N. H. Reisner. Oxford and New York: Pergamon Press, 1988.

Chazan, Robert. *Medieval Stereotypes and Modern Antisemitism*. Berkeley and Los Angeles: University of California Press, 1997.

Cohen, J. *The Friars and the Jews: The Evolution of Medieval Anti-Judaism*. Ithaca, N.Y.: Cornell University Press, 1982.

Crémieux, A. "Les Juifs de Toulon au Moyen Age et le massacre du 13 Avril 1348." *Revue des études juives*, 89–90 (1930–31): 33–72, 43–64.

Foa, Anna. *The Jews of Europe after the Black Death*. Translated by Andrea Grover. Berkeley and Los Angeles: University of California Press, 2000.

Graus, Frantisek. *Pest, Geissler, Judenmorde: Das 14 Jahrhundert als Krisenzeit*. Göttingen: Vandenhoek and Ruprecht, 1987.

Guerchberg, Séraphine. "The Controversy over the Alleged Sowers of the Black Death in the Contemporary Treatises on Plague." In *Change in Medieval Society*. Edited by Sylvia L. Thrupp. New York: Meredith Publishing, 1964.

Katz, Stephen T. *The Holocaust in Historical Context. Volume 1: The Holocaust and Mass Death before the Modern Age*. New York: Oxford University Press, 1994.

Langmuir, Gavin I. *Toward a Definition of Antisemitism*. Berkeley and Los Angeles: University of California Press, 1990.

———. *History, Religion, and Antisemitism*. Berkeley and Los Angeles: University of California Press, 1990.

López de Meneses, Amada. "Una consecuencia de la Peste Negra en Cataluña: el pogrom de 1348." *Sefarad*, 19 (1959): 92–131, 321–64.

Nirenberg, David. *Communities of Violence: Persecution of Minorities in the Middle Ages*. Princeton, N.J.: Princeton University Press, 1996.

Stow, Kenneth R. *Alienated Minority: The Jews of Medieval Latin Europe*. Cambridge, Mass.: Harvard University Press, 1992.

ARTISTIC ASPECTS

Ariès, Philippe. *The Hour of Our Death*. Translated by Helen Weaver. New York: Oxford University Press, 1991.

Batany, J. "Les 'Danses Macabres': une image en negatif du fonctionnalisme social." In *Dies Illa: Death in the Middle Ages*. Edited by J. H. M. Taylor. Liverpool: F. Cairns, 1984.

Binski, Paul. *Medieval Death: Ritual and Representation*. Ithaca, N.Y.: Cornell University Press, 1996.

Boeckl, Christine M. *Images of Plague and Pestilence: Iconography and Iconology*. Kirksville, Mo.: Truman State University Press, 2000.

Brossollet, J. "L'influence de la peste du Moyen-Age sur le theme de la Danse Macabre." *Pagine di storia della medicina*, 13 (1969): 38–46.

Clark, James Midgley. *The Dance of Death in the Middle Ages and the Renaissance*. Glasgow: Jackson, 1950.

Cohen, Kathleen. *Metamorphosis of a Death Symbol: The Transi Tomb in the Later Middle Ages and the Renaissance*. Berkeley and Los Angeles: University of California Press, 1973.

Huizinga, Johan. *The Waning of the Middle Ages: A Study of the Forms of Life, Thought and Art in France and the Netherlands in the Dawn of the Renaissance.* Translated by Frederik Jan Hopman. London: E. Arnold and Co., 1924.

King, Pamela M. "The English Cadaver Tomb in the Late Fifteenth Century: Some Indications of a Lancastrian Connection." In *Dies Illa: Death in the Middle Ages.* Edited by J. H. M. Taylor. Liverpool: F. Cairns, 1984.

————. "The Cadaver Tomb in England: Novel Manifestations of an Old Idea." *Church Monuments: Journal of the Church Monuments Society,* 5 (1990): 26–38.

Kurtz, Leonard Paul. *The Dance of Death and the Macabre Spirit in European Literature.* New York: Columbia University Press, 1934.

Marshall, Louise. "Manipulating the Sacred: Image and Plague in Renaissance Italy," *Renaissance Quarterly,* 3 (1994): 485–532.

Meiss, Millard. *Painting in Florence and Siena after the Black Death: The Arts, Religion, and Society in the Mid-Fourteenth Century.* Princeton, N.J.: Princeton University Press, 1951.

Panofsky, Erwin. *Tomb Sculpture: Four Lectures on its Changing Aspects from Ancient Egypt to Bernini.* New York: Harry N. Abrams, 1956.

Polzer, Joseph. "Aspects of the Fourteenth-Century Iconography of Death and the Plague." In *The Black Death: The Impact of the Fourteenth-Century Plague.* Edited by Daniel Williman. Binghamton, N.Y.: Center for Medieval and Early Renaissance Studies, 1982.

Rosenfeld, Helmut. *Der Mittelalterliche Totentanz: Entstehung, Entwicklung, Bedeutung.* Münster: Böhlau, 1954.

Saugnieux, J. *Les Danses Macabres de France et d'Espagne et leurs prolongements littérraires.* Paris: Belles Lettres, 1972.

Tristram, Philippa. *Figures of Life and Death in Medieval English Literature.* New York: New York University Press, 1976.

Van Os, H. W. "The Black Death and Sienese Painting: A Problem of Interpretation." *Art History,* 4 (1981): 237–49.

Acknowledgments

Acknowledgments continued from page iv.

Document 1. Nicephorus Gregoras, *Byzantine History,* 1347–1349. In Christos S. Bartsocas, "Two Fourteenth Century Greek Descriptions of the 'Black Death,'" *Journal of the History of Medicine and Allied Sciences* 21 (1966): 4, p. 395. Reprinted by permission of Oxford University Press.

Document 2. Abū Hafs ʿUmar Ibn al-Wardī, *Essay on the Report of the Pestilence,* ca. 1348. Reprinted by permission of the American University of Beirut.

Document 6. Giovanni Boccaccio, Introduction to *The Decameron,* 1348. From *The Decameron* by Boccaccio, translated by G. H. McWilliam (Penguin Classics, 1972, Second Edition, 1995). © G. H. McWilliam, 1972, 1995. Reprinted by permission of Penguin Books Ltd.

Document 8. John VI Kantakouzenos, *History,* 1347–1348. In Christos S. Bartsocas, "Two Fourteenth Century Greek Descriptions of the 'Black Death,'" *Journal of the History of Medicine and Allied Sciences* 21 (1966): 4, p. 396. Reprinted by permission of Oxford University Press.

Document 12. D'Agramont, Jacme. M. L. Duran-Reynals and C.-E. A. Winslow, trans. "Regiment de Preservacio a Epidimia o Pestilencia e Mortaldats." Bulletin of the History of Medicine 23:1 (1949), 75, 78–85. © 1949 The Johns Hopkins Press. Reprinted with permission of Johns Hopkins University Press.

Document 16. Giovanni Boccaccio, Introduction to *The Decameron,* 1348. From *The Decameron* by Boccaccio, translated by G. H. McWilliam (Penguin Classics, 1972, Second Edition, 1995). © G. H. McWilliam, 1972, 1995. Reprinted by permission of Penguin Books Ltd.

Document 29. Abū Hafs ʿUmar Ibn al-Wardī, *Essay on the Report of the Pestilence,* ca. 1348. Reprinted by permission of the American University of Beirut.

Document 42. *The Dance of Death,* edited by Warren (1931), 42 lines from pp. 2–6, 52–54. Used by permission of Oxford University Press and the Council of the Early English Text Society.

Index